PARISIAN FIELDS

Critical Views

In the same series

The New Museology
edited by Peter Vergo

Renaissance Bodies
edited by Lucy Gent and
Nigel Llewellyn

Modernism in Design
edited by Paul Greenhalgh

Interpreting Contemporary Art
edited by Stephen Bann and
William Allen

The Portrait in Photography
edited by Graham Clarke

Utopias and the Millennium
edited by Krishan Kumar and
Stephen Bann

The Cultures of Collecting
edited by John Elsner and
Roger Cardinal

Boundaries in China
edited by John Hay

*Frankenstein,
Creation and Monstrosity*
edited by Stephen Bann

A New Philosophy of History
edited by Frank Ankersmit
and Hans Kellner

PARISIAN
FIELDS

Edited by
Michael Sheringham

REAKTION BOOKS

Published by Reaktion Books Ltd
11 Rathbone Place
London W1P 1DE, UK

First published 1996

Designed by Humphrey Stone
Jacket and cover designed by Ron Costley
Photoset by Wilmaset, Wirral, Merseyside
Printed and bound in Great Britain by
The Alden Press, Oxford.

British Library Cataloguing in Publication Data:

Parisian fields. – (Critical views)
1. Literature – History and criticism 2. French literature
History and criticism
I. Series II. Sheringham, Michael
809

ISBN 0948462841
ISBN 094846285X (pbk)

This volume was published with the aid of a subsidy
from the Centre for Modern Cultural Studies,
University of Kent at Canterbury.
The Centre was established by the Faculty
of Humanities in 1990.

Contents

Photographic Acknowledgements   vi

Notes on the Editor and Contributors   vii

Introduction   *Michael Sheringham*   1

1   Threading the Maze: Nineteenth-century Guides for British Travellers to Paris   *Roger Clark*   8

2   Shifting Cultural Centres in Twentieth-century Paris *Nicholas Hewitt*   30

3   *Vénus noire*: Josephine Baker and the Parisian Music-hall *Jon Kear*   46

4   'Le Cinéaste de la vie moderne': Paris as Map in Film, 1924–34   *Tom Conley*   71

5   City Space, Mental Space, Poetic Space: Paris in Breton, Benjamin and Réda   *Michael Sheringham*   85

6   The City and the Female Autograph   *Alex Hughes*   115

7   The Poetics of Space Rewritten: From Renaud Camus to the Gay City Guide *Adrian Rifkin*   133

8   'Mirages de Paris': Paris in Francophone Writing *Belinda Jack*   150

9   Electronic Paris: From Place of Election to Place of Ejection *Verena Andermatt Conley*   162

10   Paris and the Ethnography of the Contemporary World *Marc Augé*   175

References   180

Bibliography   194

Index   197

Photographic Acknowledgements

The editor and publishers wish to express their thanks to the following for supplying photographic material and/or permission to reproduce it: The Estate of Paul Colin/DACS (© ADAGP, Paris, and DACS, London, 1996): pp. 51, 66; The Yale Collection of American Literature (James Weldon Johnson Collection), Beinecke Rare Book and Manuscript Library, Yale University, New Haven: pp. 63, 69) The Bibliothèque Nationale Archives, Paris, p. 52; The Folies-Bergère, Paris: pp. 47, 60, 61.

Notes on the Editor and Contributors

MICHAEL SHERINGHAM is Professor of French at Royal Holloway, University of London. He has written widely on André Breton and Surrealism, on modern and contemporary French poetry, and on autobiography and related genres; he has written essays on Beckett, Duras, Genet, Sartre and many other writers. He is General Editor of Cambridge Studies in French. His most recent book is *French Autobiography: Devices and Desires. Rousseau to Perec* (Oxford, 1993).

ROGER CLARK is Senior Lecturer in French and Comparative Literary Studies at the University of Kent at Canterbury. He has written extensively on French nineteenth-century fiction and drama, and is preparing studies of Balzac's *Le Pére Goriot* and Zola's *Nana*. His essay in the present volume touches upon some of the ground to be covered in a planned work on attitudes of nineteenth-century British visitors to Paris.

NICHOLAS HEWITT is Professor of French and Director of the Institute for Modern Cultural Studies at the University of Nottingham. He has worked extensively on the literary and cultural history of France in the interwar years and the Fourth Republic, and his major publications include *Henri Troyat* (1986), *The Golden Age of Louis-Ferdinand Céline* (1987), *Les Maladies du siècle* (1988), *The Culture of Reconstruction* (1989), *France and the Mass Media* (1991), *Popular Culture and Mass Communication in Twentieth Century France* (1993), *Controlling Broadcasting: Access Policy and Practice in North America and Europe* (1993); *The Culture of the Liberation* (1995), and *Literature and the Right in France* (forthcoming).

JON KEAR is a Lecturer in the History and Theory of Art at the University of Kent at Canterbury. He has recently published articles dealing with late nineteenth-century French painting, montage and early twentieth-century Modernism. He is working on books on the late works of Cézanne and the avant-garde film-maker Chris Marker and is currently researching the representation of history in the mid-nineteenth century.

TOM CONLEY is Professor in the Department of Romance Languages and Literature, Harvard University, and the author of *Film Hieroglyphs (1991)*, *The Graphic Unconscious in Early Modern French Writing* (1992), and *The Self*

Made Map: Cartographical Writing in Early Modern France (forthcoming, 1996). He is currently working on the relations between space and event in film and literature. He has translated works by Michel de Certeau, Gilles Deleuze and others.

ALEX HUGHES is Lecturer in the Department of French Studies at the University of Birmingham, has published books and articles on Simone de Beauvoir, Serge Doubrovsky, Violette Leduc, French feminist theory and French women's erotic writing, and is currently co-editing an encyclopaedia of French culture with Keith Reader.

ADRIAN RIFKIN is Professor of Fine Art at the University of Leeds, and is the author of *Street Noises: Parisian Pleasure 1900–1940*. He writes on classical aesthetics and art criticism as well as modern cultural studies, and is currently completing two books, *Staging the Artist: Ingres between Then and Now*, and *Gay Poetics*.

BELINDA JACK is Lecturer in French at Christ Church, University of Oxford, and also British Academy Post-doctoral Research Fellow at the European Humanities Research Centre, Oxford. Her work on Black Francophone Literatures and Criticism is to be published shortly in the United States. She has contributed several articles on African and Indian Ocean writing in French for the recent *Oxford Companion to Literature in French*, and writes for a number of journals.

VERENA ANDERMATT CONLEY is interested in the relations between feminism, ecology and technology. The editor of *Rethinking Technologies* (1993), her study of ecology in contemporary French thought, *Eco-subjects* will be published in 1996.

MARC AUGÉ is Director of Studies at the Ecole des Hautes Etudes en Sciences Sociales, Paris. A leading French ethnologist, his many books include *Le Rivage alladian* (1969), *Symbole, Fonction, Histoire* (1979) and *Génie du paganisme*. *La Traversée du Luxembourg* (1985) was his first contribution to an 'ethno-analysis' of contemporary French culture. Other works in this vein include *Un Ethnologue dans le métro* (1986), *Domaines et Châteaux* (1989) and *Non-lieux: Introduction à une anthropologie de la surmodernité* (1992), of which an English version, titled *Non-Places: Introduction to an Anthropology of Supermodernity*, appeared in 1995.

Introduction

MICHAEL SHERINGHAM

From the start, in its very name, Jean-Luc Godard's film about Paris, *Deux ou trois choses que je sais d'elle* (Two or three things I know about her), strongly resists totalization.[1] The use of the feminine ('Her: the Paris area' reads a subtitle early on in the film) wryly cites the trope of Paris-as-mysterious-woman, but here the Parisian body resists penetration and allows only partial recognitions (two or three). Yet the film continually emphasizes the question of knowledge. The *sotto voce* soundtrack (Godard's 'own' whispering voice) seems at once to summon up and to interrogate the sequence of images. The rather attenuated narrative foregrounds a female protagonist (played by Marina Vlady) whose recourse to part-time prostitution in order to pay the bills (a sociological angle on the city deriving in the first instance from a survey reported in the *Nouvel Observateur* magazine) spawns bouts of epistemological curiosity or ecstasy on the woman's part, reflecting a desire to understand her position in a *grand ensemble* of rather wider significance than the suburban high-rises this expression euphemistically designates. Neo-Brechtian alienation effects – Vlady stepping in and out of her role, vox-pop declarations to camera, stagey set-piece dialogues laden with contemporary references (Vietnam) – and extensive use of visual and verbal quotation deny the viewer any stable position. Above all, perhaps, the film's radiant images confound the varieties of verbal discourse that seek to pin them down. Or rather, the inadequacy of these verbal encapsulations raises the image to a higher power, conferring on it the ability to speak to something inexhaustibly but inaccessibly present in the densely woven fabric of urban reality.

There can be few more suggestive pointers to at least some of the meanings enfolded in Walter Benjamin's concept of the 'dialectical image' – so central to his work on Paris – than the brilliant sequence Godard set in a filling-station, and particularly the shot of wind-tossed leaves reflected in the gleaming roof of a red mini that has just emerged from a car-wash. Here indeed, in Benjamin's words, 'thought comes to a standstill in a constellation saturated with tensions'.[2] The dialectical imagery of *Deux ou trois choses que je sais d'elle* does not seek to resolve the tensions involved in the project of 'knowing' Paris; rather, it produces a space where these tensions can be displayed in different ways. Central to Godard's film is the pull between Paris as some kind of unity and *la région parisienne* (the Paris area) as an amalgam of irretrievably heterogeneous zones, made up of the many different ways of living that are conditioned by social, economic, political and cultural pressures which, as they work on each individual, produce widely disparate modes of human reality and exchange.

To see Paris as a set of fields — the starting-point for this collection of essays — is to put aside any attempt to pin down an elusive essence. The point is to dispel the illusion of an imaginary unity that threatens to immobilize perceptions of the city and instead to open less familiar sightlines, looking for example at how Paris is constructed in tourist guides (Roger Clark), in the migrations of intellectual groups across its *quartiers* (Nicholas Hewitt), in the tradition of urban wandering inherited and transmitted by the Surrealists (Michael Sheringham) or in the remappings of its topography effected by film-makers in the 1920s and '30s (Tom Conley). Viewed through the prisms of gender and sexuality, as a site for female inscriptions (Alex Hughes) or gay transgressions (Adrian Rifkin), or approached from the perspective of ethnicity, through the figure of Josephine Baker (Jon Kear), or from the imaginings of those for whom the French capital is the colonial powerhouse (Belinda Jack), Paris becomes not myth but a complex, ever-evolving reality whose present and future potential is at the centre of speculative work on the future of cities (Verena Conley) and of ethnographic enquiry (Marc Augé). But like the dialectical images of Benjamin and Godard, each of these fields — gender, sexuality, textuality, ethnicity, cultural geography, film, technology, entertainment — embodies tensions that are symptomatic of the larger ensemble to which they belong. The physical fabric of Paris was conditioned, in the nineteenth century, by strict demarcation and homogenization, and in the mid-twentieth century by accelerated expansion outwards (the new suburbs), accompanied by the relative depopulation of a centre increasingly dominated by tourism, business and traffic. The cultural space of the city — the way it exists in the minds of its inhabitants and visitors, in the varied media that shape their responses, and in the 'practices of everyday life' (Michel de Certeau) that flow from the manner in which it is perceived and constructed – is likewise always involved in a process of transformation without established boundaries or categorical restrictions.

The notion of the field befits this reality. Force field, magnetic field, field of vision, field of battle, field of play: at the centre of this semantic network is the idea of a space whose coordinates are determined by the movement of agents or agencies to which it plays host. The field is at once purely notional and highly situated, constrained and constraining. But if, in terms of this metaphor, Paris may be seen as a field, why opt for the plural? Why Parisian *fields*? The point is not only to ward off the spectres of unity and totality, but in doing so to underline plurality. To see Paris as a single field would certainly have the merit of addressing a feature that is undoubtedly of great importance. Compared with London, say, Paris is physically and culturally homogeneous to a marked degree. Despite a tradition examplified by the *Physiologies* of the 1820s and '30s, Paris is not an assemblage of disparate quarters.[3] The undeniable specificity of each *quartier* is largely defined by nuances and differences within a general harmony determined by a common reservoir of memories and styles. In his recent book, *La Ville à l'oeuvre* (1992), Jean-Christophe Bailly stresses the way Paris is a city that has been woven together: 'If there are historically constituted ensembles that form wholly distinct *quartiers*, possessing a specific architectural code – the Marais for instance, which is no doubt the most compact of such *quartiers* [. . .] – Paris nonetheless never offers itself to be read or experienced as a patchwork or as a composite of disparate elements.'[4][†] Rather than bland uniformity, what is involved here is a propensity to incorporate the individual into the city's rhythm, to make the passer-by a participant in the theatricality that, as Benjamin observed, is so much a part of Parisian reality. Yet the existence of Paris as an overall field or texture in fact helps explain why it makes sense to identify a plurality of separate yet interlocking fields at the level of cultural representations and lived experiences. Wherever one starts from – in representations, or ways of living and seeing, inflected by aesthetic or political programmes, by perspectives of space, gender, leisure or work – one is likely to encounter not separate worlds, which make sense only as autonomous enclaves, but ways of incorporating the whole field of Parisian reality and thus of

---

[†]*S'il y a bien des ensembles constitués historiquement formant des quartiers à part entière, dotés d'un code architectural spécifique – ainsi le Marais, qui est sans doute le plus compact de ces quartiers [. . .] Paris pourtant ne se donne jamais à lire, ni à vivre, comme un patchwork ou comme une composition d'unités disparates.*

creating fields within it that are more restricted. Indeed, it is the superimposition and interchange between these fields, the overlap and crisscrossing of networks spread widely across the capital's expanse and incorporating its inherent complexities of formation, that make up the cultural space of Paris, its overall field as a site and generator of meanings.

The essays commissioned for this book survey a necessarily selective but nevertheless extremely wide-ranging set of Parisian fields. If one of its main sources of stimulation is the work of Benjamin and its legacy in such recent productions as Christopher Prendergast's *Paris and the Nineteenth Century* (1992) and Adrian Rifkin's *Street Noises: Parisian Pleasures, 1900–1940* (1992), the focus here is not on 'Paris: Capital of the Nineteenth Century' but largely on the relatively less familiar territory of post-1900 representations and discourses. Like Prendergast, the contributors are conscious of the need to reassess Benjamin's enterprise in the light of more recent theoretical reflection on cities, whether inspired by political and social theory (Henri Lefebvre, David Harvey), history, philosophy and psychoanalysis (Michel de Certeau), cultural geography (Edward Soja), or ethnography (Marc Augé). Verena Conley addresses this issue directly by establishing an illuminating contrast between the optimistic vision of Certeau and the darker picture to be found in the work of another important theorist, Paul Virilio. At the close of this book the distinguished anthropologist Marc Augé provides a fascinating retrospect on the place of Paris in the intellectual itinerary that led to his pioneering *Un Ethnologue dans le métro* (An ethnologist in the Métro) and subsequent volumes such as *Non-lieux* (Non-places), which explores the concept of 'surmodernité' (super- or hyper-modernity).

If Benjamin's example still remains compelling and inspirational with regard to Paris's more recent metamorphoses, it is of course partly because of the multi-faceted nature of his approaches and methods, and more particularly because for Benjamin (who in this respect was strongly influenced by those arch-Parisians, the Surrealists) any phenomenon, however seemingly minor or insignificant, could offer a thread to guide us through the city's labyrinth. Benjamin used the rare word *Konvolut* for each of the dossiers into which he divided up the voluminous materials he assembled on such topics as Prostitution, Gambling, Forms of Lighting, Methods of Display, Dolls and Automata, and so forth. The German word *Konvolut* comes from the Latin verb *convolvere*, which means to roll together, and this suggests that each of the dossiers, largely made up of quotations from literary, journalistic and historical material, is a simple bundle, but also something that is convoluted, in other words meshed or woven together into a unity that preserves the diverse and heterogeneous character of its constituent parts. In one of the most substantial of the *Konvoluten*, Benjamin stockpiled reflections on the theoretical underpinning of his project, and particularly its epistemology. Seeking to pin down the kinds of knowledge he was aiming at, he offered a searching critique of the assumption that history necessarily implies progress and narrative. Asserting that 'History decomposes into images, not into narratives', he put forward the notion of the 'dialectical image', which he defined in this way:

Where thought comes to a standstill in a constellation saturated with tensions, there appears the dialectical image. It is the caesura in the movement of thought. Its positioning, of course, is in no way arbitrary. In a word, it is to be sought at the point where the tension between the dialectical oppositions is the greatest. The dialectical image [. . .] is identical to the historical object; it justifies blasting the latter out of the continuum of history's course.[5]

When an authentically productive field of tensions has been located amidst the vast array of materials offered by the city, a new configuration arises out of the disruption of habitual modes of thinking and seeing.

Given the eccentricity of Benjamin's genius, the often opaque and enigmatic character of his thought, and the unfinished, unresolved character of the *Passagen-Werk*, it would be foolhardy to suggest any direct comparison between his enterprise and the kinds of enquiry pursued in *Parisian Fields*. None the less, the reader may find it useful to think of the essays that follow this Introduction as explorations in the field of dialectical images opened up by Benjamin's work. Certainly, Jon Kear's multi-faceted investigation into the iconic figure of Josephine Baker makes the dancer's body the site of unstable, sometimes antithetical, meanings and swirling ideological currents that at once generate and subvert settled representations of 'Parisianness'. In more directly historical vein, Nicholas Hewitt's essay in Parisian cultural geography analyses the construction of Montmartre as a *lieu de plaisir*, and then explores the cultural and symbolic logic of subsequent splits and shifts as the cultural centre of gravity migrates across the capital. My own essay relocates the figure of the Benjaminian *flâneur* in the context of the poetic currents running, like another Métro line, from Baudelaire through Apollinaire, the Surrealists and Queneau to the brilliant and engaging work of Jacques Réda. Urban wandering is seen to accompany a form of meditation that generates fertile interactions between city, mind and text.

In many respects Benjamin's *magnum opus* is a monument to the extraordinary mythic power Paris had accumulated in the period running from the early nineteenth century to the 1930s. Clearly, to assemble an anthology of tributes to what Roger Caillois, in a seminal essay of 1937, called 'Paris, mythe moderne', would be entertaining, if largely predictable.[6] As Roger Clark's well documented study of English tourist-guides to Paris shows, indigenous mythologizing was amply supplemented by foreign implants, often xenophobic in spirit, but overall the record is one of steady change, as the tourist market and its mythmaking potential evolved rapidly under the pressure of economic and technological change. In the face of this mythologizing process, one of the aims of *Parisian Fields* is to demonstrate the powerful, and culturally very resonant and productive, revisionary currents at work in the twentieth century, interrogating, subverting and contesting, from many different angles, the established myths of Paris. Tom Conley's remarkable essay shows how in its early relations with Paris (for example in Clair's *Paris qui dort* and in Renoir's *Boudu sauvé des eaux*), cinematic language deployed a power to change and re-map the city, engendering representations matching new positionings of subjectivity in social and physical space. Like filmic representation, gender and sexuality, in their interaction with urban experience, are fields of considerable turbulence. Focusing on autobiographical texts, Alex Hughes contrasts the 'paternal' Paris of Simone de Beauvoir's *Mémoires*, where the city, as the site of masculine privilege, offers the lure of un-gendered self-realization, with the 'maternal' feminized city of Violette Leduc's *La Bâtarde*. Like film, gender remaps the city, in Leduc's case by endowing Paris with the power to erode the barriers between mother and daughter and to offer itself as a space of imaginary reconciliation. Gay writing on Paris has also recently shown that it has at least the potential to subvert established hierarchies and demarcations. Taking the fictions and diaries of Renaud Camus as his starting-point, Adrian Rifkin invites the reader on a tour of the 'gay spaces' of the contemporary city, and seeks to gauge them against antiquated but still powerful mythologies of low life and abjection, associated, in cultural terms, with figures such as Genet and Green, but also perpetuated in the recent films of Collard and Téchiné. If, for the gay writer, Paris can be perceived as the mirror of his alienation or as a utopian site where individual difference is absorbed in the play of differences that make up urban reality, Belinda Jack's essay shows how, for the African, Caribbean or French-Canadian who writes in French, the capital can also be seen in antithetical ways. As the monopolistic, fixed colonial centre, Paris is often represented as a place of exile in Francophone writing, locus of a compulsory rite of passage into the power relations of colonialism. But as the *linguistic* capital of Francophonia, Paris can be revalorized, as in some of Edouard Glissant's writings, becoming a place of freedom, a mobile source of new energies and potentialities as beneficent to the francophone writer as to his metropolitan colleagues.

Once again the issue here could be formulated in the elegant antithesis contained in Verena Andermatt Conley's title: place of election or place of ejection? Conley's own essay focuses initially on the loss of aura (in Benjamin's terms) undergone by Paris in the age of electronic communication, mass media, international conglomerates and so forth, and then seeks to assess possible terms for the survival of an 'art of the eco' (Félix Guattari). If for Michel de Certeau the everyday practices of mobile, individual citizens maintain habitability, the analyses of Paul Virilio suggest that the city street is no longer the locus of power and wonder, and that citizens cut off from the networks engendered by advanced technology may be as immobile as sitting ducks. The survival of Paris as a habitable city will depend on creative mental reflexes rather than on tactical responses. Marc Augé confronts the same issues from the perspective of a professional ethnographer, with many years of African fieldwork to his name, who is also a diehard Parisian. If the anthropological function of place (to secure memory and identity) was transformed but still preserved by modernity (Baudelaire, Proust, Certeau), the *non-lieux* (non-spaces) of what Augé calls *surmodernité* (super- or hyper-modernity) – shopping malls, airport lounges, Formule 1 hotels – pose a formidable challenge. In pointing to the resources that may enable Paris, and Parisians, to meet this challenge, Augé considers the future of Paris as well as its past, and touches on issues that are central to *Parisian Fields*: the city's capacity for re-invention in the minds of its users, the astonishingly diverse constituents out of which its unity is made, the extraordinary resilience of some of the discourses Paris has inspired and by which it is known. In the twentieth century as in the nineteenth, Paris has been not only a source of inspiration but a creative partner in the elaboration of new ways of thinking about a rapidly changing world. In highlighting some of the newer areas encompassed by the city, *Parisian Fields*, in its turn, pays tribute not only to Paris as a 'magasin d'images' (storehouse of images), in Baudelaire's phrase, but to its potential as an exemplary city of the future.

I

Threading the Maze: Nineteenth-century Guides for British Travellers to Paris

ROGER CLARK

I want by way of preamble (in the etymological sense of the word) to look briefly at two fictional visitors to Paris, at the protagonists of two of the most claustrophobically Parisian of French nineteenth-century novels. The difficulties these characters have to deal with, their uncertainties when confronted by the complex realities of the modern city, are not dissimilar to the perplexities that will be experienced by their contemporaries, the real-life travellers to Paris. And in turn, the guidance and advice that both fictional and actual visitors receive, albeit from very different sources, may be seen as having certain similarities.

I am sure the allusion that supplies the title of my essay is immediately recognizable. The young law student Eugène de Rastignac has recently arrived in the French capital from his native Angoulême; in Paris he takes lodgings at Mme Vauquer's squalid *pension* on the southern fringe of the Latin quarter. One of the first things Balzac's young provincial does is to pay a visit to his cousin, the elegant, wealthy and thoroughly worldly-wise Claire de Beauséant, one of the leading luminaries of the faubourg Saint-Germain and thus of the Parisian establishment. It is she who supplies Rastignac with his first guidance into the intricacies of life in Paris as she volunteers to help him blaze a path through the mysterious city that confronts him: her name will be the 'Ariadne's thread' (p. 73) that will allow this modern Theseus to thread his way through the moral and physical maze that is Paris in the early years of the nineteenth century.[1] It is she also, in the course of her unforgettable final appearance at the farewell ball that she offers to Parisian high society, who presents her glove-box to Rastignac; he, by now more conversant with the detours of the Parisian labyrinth, accepts the gift as a permanent reminder of his Ariadne ('There is a lot of me in there, a whole Madame de Beauséant who has ceased to exist', p. 236),[†] but also as a talisman that will continue to guide him through the explorations he will make in the capital after the close of *Le Père Goriot*. Mme de Beauséant, Athena to this Parisian Telemachus in quest of a father figure, is of course not the only mentor Rastignac receives guidance from during his brief residence at the *pension* Vauquer. The arch-criminal (and future head of police) Jacques Collin, better known as Trompe-la-Mort and still better known as Vautrin, also puts his Parisian expertise at the young student's disposal. Mephistopheles to Mme de Beauséant's Ariadne, Vautrin sees Paris in different terms but with similar intricacies:

Paris, you see is like some forest in the New World, where a score of savage tribes run about like Illinois or Huron Indians, living off the spoils of their hunt in different social circles. You are hunting for millions. To catch them you use traps, bird-limes, decoys. (pp. 100–01)[‡]

We have here two characters that are social and moral antitheses, whose discourses could scarcely be more different, yet whose guidance goes in much the same direction: their words and respective departures from the world of *Le Père Goriot* will contribute to Rastignac's enlightenment as he begins to decipher the mysteries of Paris and confronts the difficulty of living in the modern city. It is of course undeniable that much of the advice that Mme de Beauséant and Vautrin have to offer is moral and/or social in nature; yet practical or topographical recommendations, such as are to be found in more orthodox guidebooks, are not absent from their counselling. Rastignac's ignorance is not *just* in the moral and social ways of Paris; his itinerary is as much literal and spatial as it is moral and intellectual, even if the various Parisian movements that the novel charts serve to underline the spiritual development of the novel's pivotal character. Rastignac thus moves from Mme Vauquer (her name provides the novel's opening words) and her dingy house on the rue Neuve-Sainte-Geneviève to Mme de Nucingen (the final words of the novel) and her grandiose mansion on the rue Saint-Lazare; from a dank autumn morning and the foggy depths of the faubourg Saint-Marceau to a pellucid spring evening and the heights of the Père-Lachaise cemetery; from beneath the twin domes of the Val-de-Grâce and the Panthéon, with their sombre associations of sickness and death, to the twin peaks of the

---

†*Il y a beaucoup de moi là-dedans, il y a toute une madame de Beauséant qui n'est plus.*
‡*Paris, voyez-vous, est comme une forêt du Nouveau-Monde, où s'agitent vingt espèces de peuplades sauvages, les Illinois, les Hurons, qui vivent du produit que donnent les différentes chasses sociales; vous êtes un chasseur de millions. Pour les prendre, vous usez de pièges, de pipeaux, d'appeaux.*

Louis-Leopold Boilly, *Les Galeries des Palais Royal*, 1809. Musée Carnavelet.

Invalides and the Vendôme column with their connotations of military grandeur and national glory. No less important, however, are the niceties of Parisian etiquette that *Le Père Goriot* provides a practical introduction to: Rastignac learns of the filthy state of the Parisian streets in the days before Haussmann; of the importance of appearing in society with yellow gloves but not with muddy boots; of the consequent need to resort to some form of public transport when journeying across the city. Equally, in an enigmatic snatch of dialogue with a cab-driver, Rastignac is forced to confront his ignorance of some of the details of Parisian topography as he fails to distinguish between the rue de Grenelle and the rue Saint-Dominique (p. 58).

My second stranger in Paris is of different gender and social class, lives at a different historical moment and inhabits a very different part of the metropolis. Yet, like Rastignac, as she arrives from the provincial town of Plassans in the south-easternmost reaches of *la France profonde*, Gervaise Macquart is a first-time visitor to Paris; like her Balzacian predecessor, she has immense difficulty in making sense of what confronts her in the city and, like him too, she needs to seek the assistance of a number of guides in her attempts to come to terms with the city. But, unlike Rastignac, Gervaise is in the end defeated as she falls victim to the traps that are ever present in the urban labyrinth, constantly threatening to ensnare those who are ill equipped and unready. Paris for Gervaise, as it had been for Rastignac, is a maze – or rather, in her case, a vertiginous succession of mazes set within a global maze, that she is finally incapable of threading a path through. Her life story (at least in its Parisian part) is made up of a series of encounters with increasingly perplexing and anguishing labyrinths, each one of which stands as a metonymy for the tentacular metropolis as a whole. The opening scene of *L'Assommoir* thus offers a vista of Baudelaire's 'fourmillante cité' as dawn breaks over Paris, the workers flood into the city and Zola's heroine finds herself trapped between hospital and abattoir, surrounded by the *octroi* wall. The tenement house on the rue de la Goutte d'Or, with its interminable corridors and its Piranesi-like stairwells, offers a first microcosmic image of the labyrinthine city that will devour Gervaise:

She looked up, blinking her eyes, and saw the towering void of the stairwell, lit by three gaslights, one on every other floor; the last one, way up above, looked like a star flickering in a black sky, while the other two cast long, strangely-shaped shafts of light up and down the endless spiral of steps (p. 53).[2][†]

Much the same images will be exploited to similar effect by Zola in his evocation towards the end of *L'Assommoir* of another Parisian maze, the Sainte-Anne psychiatric hospital on the southern fringes of the city: it is here that the demented Coupeau has been interned, here that Gervaise visits him and witnesses the attacks of delirium tremens that will ultimately result in his death. But the most telling use of the Paris-as-maze metaphor comes in the celebrated episode recounting the visit Gervaise and her friends make to the Louvre and other monuments in the course of her wedding day. Lying at the very heart of the city, both spatially and spiritually, the Louvre is a 'must' for any self-respecting visitor, whether French or foreign. For Zola's characters, however, the gilded palace of establishment art is experienced as an impenetrable and incomprehensible labyrinth ('The place was very big, and you could get lost', p. 75) within the macrocosmic maze that lies outside. The wedding party stumbles into the Assyrian galleries, firmly placed under the cryptic sign of inscrutable sphinxes and unreadable Phoenician hieroglyphics ('No, it wasn't possible, nobody had ever read that scribbling', p. 76); it gallops with increasing desperation through the various picture galleries,

†*Elle leva les yeux, cligna les paupières, en apercevant la haute tour creuse de la cage de l'escalier, éclairée par trois becs de gaz, de deux étages en deux étages; le dernier, tout en haut, avait l'air d'une étoile tremblotante dans un ciel noir, tandis que les deux autres jetaient de longues clartés, étrangement découpées, le long de la spirale interminable des marches.*

through spaces whose discourse can for them only be decoded in purely personal terms (the *Mona Lisa* makes sense to them only in that the portrait reminds Coupeau of one of his aunts). Finally the wedding party loses itself ('Never would they get out again', p. 79) in an endless and meaningless succession of rooms containing an incoherent jumble of drawings ('just scrawled-on pieces of paper', p. 78), of oriental ceramics and (appropriately, given the importance of sea imagery in the novel) of maritime artefacts. It is only with the help of an official guide that Gervaise's guests manage to escape this cultural vortex. Once outside and before going off to a meal at the Moulin-d'Argent (a scene of *grande bouffe* that will be the high-point of their day), in an episode that has strong echoes with the ending of *Le Père Goriot* and also complements the parallel scene of Zola's own *La Curée*, the wedding guests ascend the Vendôme column from which they look down on Paris. But where Rastignac and Saccard, from the perspective of similar vantage points (respectively the Père-Lachaise and the butte Montmartre), are fully able to decode the maps of Paris that lie stretched out beneath them, Gervaise and her friends are confronted by a space that in the end they are incapable of reading. Their attempts to make sense of the Parisian map, like their attempts to read the signs in the Louvre, are reduced to a purely personal significance as the members of the wedding party end up squabbling between themselves over the precise location of familiar landmarks:

Then, it occurred to Madame Lorilleux to ask whether you could see the Moulin-d'Argent on the Boulevard de la Chapelle, where they were going to have their dinner. They spent ten minutes searching for it and squabbling as each of them picked out a different spot (p. 81).[†]

So it is that Gervaise's different guides prove to be either incompetent (Madinier) or feckless (Coupeau) or devious, parasitical and deliberately misleading (Lantier[3]). So it is, in a city whose emblems include a sailing-ship and whose motto warns the visitor against the possibility of drowning ('Fluctuat nec mergitur'), that Gervaise suffers the fate that had befallen the unfortunate passengers of the frigate *Méduse*. Géricault's painting, a metonomy within a metonomy, is one of the very few works of art to be identified by name during the wedding party's visit to the Louvre: *pace* Julian Barnes, rafts in French, as Flaubert (*Dictionnaire des*

[†]*Puis, madame Lorilleux eut l'idée de demander si l'on apercevait, sur le boulevard de la Chapelle, le marchand de vin où l'on allait manger, au* Moulin-d'Argent. *Alors, pendant dix minutes, on chercha, on se disputa même; chacun plaçait le marchand de vin à un endroit.*

A contemporary photograph of the rebuilding of Paris under Haussmann.
Garnier's opera house nears completion, with the avenue de l'Opéra
still under construction.

idées reçues) and Brassens (*Les Copains d'abord*) tell us, are after all
'toujours de la Méduse'.[4] Where Rastignac, with the assistance of his
great uncle's maritime past and the influence this allows, is able
successfully to navigate the shoals of the Parisian ocean, Zola's heroine
half a century later will be unable to chart her course, founders and is in
the end devoured by the cannibals who surround her. Her dilemma will
become insuperable and her fate sealed when, in the novel's final
chapters, the layout of the Parisian labyrinth is redrawn before her eyes as
the city undergoes the violent trauma of Haussmann's redevelopment:

The demolition of the octroi wall had long since widened the outer boulevards,
with pavements on the sides and a central strip for pedestrians, planted with four
rows of small plane trees. It was now a huge crossing leading to the distant
horizon, along interminable streets that swarmed with people; everywhere there
was chaos from the building operations. [. . .] Beneath the ever-increasing luxury
of Paris the dreadful poverty of the slums forced itself upon the eye, defiling these
sites where the new city was being so hastily erected (pp. 406–7).†

†*Depuis longtemps, la démolition du mur de l'octroi avait déjà élargi les boulevards
extérieurs, avec les chaussées latérales et le terre-plein au milieu pour les piétons, planté de
quatre rangées de petits platanes. C'était un carrefour immense débouchant au loin sur
l'horizon, par des voies sans fin, grouillantes de foule, se noyant [emphasis mine] dans le
chaos perdu des constructions. [. . .] Sous le luxe montant de Paris, la misère du faubourg
crevait et salissait ce chantier d'une ville nouvelle, si hâtivement bâtie.*

If French nineteenth-century visitors found it difficult to blaze their
trail through the city, foreign travellers for their part found Paris no less
perplexing and had an equal need for expert guidance if they were to
make sense of their experiences. I would want to stress from the outset
the extraordinary abundance of English-language travel literature (using
the word in its widest sense) relating to the British experience of Paris in
the nineteenth century: I am not aware of the existence of a similar
volume of material for the complementary French experience of London.
What seems equally unquestionable is that episodes from nineteenth-
century novels in English evoking British visitors to Paris outnumber by
some distance those in French fiction from the same period that tell of the
experiences of French visitors to London.

The English-language material can be broken down into a number of
categories. There is in the first instance a wide range of first-hand
accounts of experiences of living in Paris by British nineteenth-century
residents: innumerable *Twenty Years* [or some other period of time] *in
Paris*, quantities of *Parisian Notebooks* and *Englishmen in Paris*, a pot-
pourri of *British Chaplains* [or some other such worthy profession] *in
Paris*. More general impressionistic accounts of the Parisian experience
as seen from a British perspective are also very numerous, with titles such
as *A Wanderer in Paris*, *The Lure of Old Paris* or just simply *Old Paris*. A
third category would consist of impressionistic representations of specific
aspects of Paris: one can thus find – among many, many others – a *The
Dungeons of Old Paris*, a *Memorable Paris Houses* and several *Stories of
Paris Churches*. A further group is made up of specialist guides to specific
areas within the space of the city, with several books devoted notably
(and usually for fairly obvious cautionary reasons) to the Latin Quarter,
to the Palais Royal, to Montmartre and to the parks of Paris. A fifth and
final category consists of the several series of general English-language
visitors' guides to Paris that were published at regular intervals throughout the nineteenth century and that sought to provide the traveller with
information of an increasingly objective and reliably factual kind. Four
different series of these guides may be distinguished: those written by
Edward Planta and published in England during the early decades of the
century; those produced in Paris in the middle decades of the century by
the Galignani family (publisher also of an English-language newspaper,
the famous *Galignani's Messenger*, and whose English bookshop is still
going strong today); and the two rival series that dominate the second
half of the century, those produced in a very similar format with a
broadly similar corporate image and a quasi-identical red livery by the

firms founded respectively by John Murray and, of course, by the man
whose name has become virtually synonymous with travel guides, Karl
Baedeker. I will concentrate here on the earliest (Planta) and latest
(Baedeker) of these series: they are in any event the most interesting of the
four, presenting as they do very strikingly contrasting conceptions of the
purposes and function of travel as well as radically different images of
Paris and of the Parisian traveller.

Edward Planta's *Paris* (or to give it its complete and revealingly
ambitious title, *A New Picture of Paris or, The Stranger's Guide to the
French Metropolis Accurately Describing the Public Establishments,
Remarkable Edifices, Places of Amusement, and every other Object
Worthy of Attention*) was first published by Samuel Leigh in 1814; the
book was revised and reissued until 1831 when a sixteenth (and final)
edition appeared. This chunky little publication (it measures 14.5 × 9 ×
4.5 cm), the format of which clearly marks it out as a handbook rather
than a pocket-book, was manifestly intended for the new wave (deluge
might be a better term) of independent travellers who were (re)discover-
ing the Continent (and for us specifically Paris) in the aftermath of the
enforced intermission in travel that had been one of the most obvious
by-products of the Revolutionary and Napoleonic wars. That the treaty
of Paris marked a watershed in the sociology of travel and in its
function, that it signalled the emergence of a new breed of traveller, a
more independent, less aristocratic though still essentially well-off and
still primarily male traveller – all this may be demonstrated by an
abundance of anecdotal evidence as well as by a wealth of contemporary
texts, for example Coleridge's scathing *The Delinquent Travellers*, of
1824:

> But O, what scores are sick of home,
> Agog for Paris or for Rome!
> Nay! tho' contented to abide,
> You should prefer your own fireside;
> Yet since grim War has ceas'd its madding,
> And Peace has set John Bull agadding,
> 'Twould such a vulgar taste betray,
> For every shame you must away! . . .
> . . . .
> Keep moving! Steam, or Gas, or Stage,
> Hold, cabin, steerage, hencoop's cage –
> Tour, Journey, Voyage, Lounge, Ride, Walk,
> Skim, Sketch, Excursion, Travel-talk –
> For move you must! 'Tis now the rage,
> The law and fashion of the Age.

'John Bull and his Family at an Ice Café. The Occupation', from
The Reminiscences of Captain Gronow, John C. Nimmo, London, 1900.

'The occupation of Paris, 1814. English visitors in the Palais Royal', from
The Reminiscences of Captain Gronow, John C. Nimmo, London, 1900.

Another telling indication of the emergence of a new generation of British traveller and of the way he impinged on contemporary consciousnesses is to be located in the existence of a *physiologie* devoted entirely to the figure of the English visitor to Paris. Enormously popular in the 1820s, '30s and '40s, and frequently illustrated by caricaturists (Daumier, Monnier, and others now less famous), the *physiologies*, together with their companion sub-genres the *arts* (e.g., *L'Art de mettre sa cravate*) and *codes* (e.g., *Le Code de l'honnête homme*), in a discourse characterized by a strange juxtaposition of a taxonomic ambition with a markedly tongue-in-cheek tone, seek to identify and tabulate social phenomena and types that appear to have been seen as emblematic of post-Revolutionary France. They were thus intended to serve as ironic catalogues of, and guides to, the mechanisms that regulated the new France. The most famous are unquestionably Brillat-Savarin's *Physiologie du goût* (1825) and Balzac's *Physiologie du mariage* (1829). At random, among less worthy examples of these quasi-scientific and proto-Realist vignettes, one might cite a *Physiologie de l'homme de loi, du garde national*, (inevitably?) *de l'étudiant* and (equally inevitably?) *de la grisette*. Charles Marchal's *Physiologie de l'Anglais à Paris* (?1844) is one of the longest of the series: we clearly have here a phenomenon that was sufficiently noteworthy to justify an extended examination and one that has been brilliantly documented by the Musée Carnavalet and its recent exhibition devoted to the English in Paris in the nineteenth century. Besides peddling a fiercely anti-Romantic line and liberally rehashing many of the *idées reçues* that the French entertain(ed?) about the English (the Englishman 'suffers from migraine, from spleen, from suicide, from anger – and from an incalculable multitude of other infirmities'), about the ugliness of their women and their fondness for drink (two of the most prevalent French topoi where attitudes to the British are concerned),[5] Marchal's *Physiologie* has the merit of underlining the essential meaning of the Parisian experience for the new visitor ('For the Englishman, Paris then represents happiness, a story from *The Thousand and One Nights*, total freedom!'), a message that Planta and his followers would, in their different ways, be keen to expand on.

A reading of Planta's *Paris* leaves one in little doubt as to the social and intellectual status of the audience it was intended for.[6] The preface to his guide, in which the author addresses his public directly, thus speaks of 'readers of taste and literature, whose praise is alone valuable' (p. iv): we are here clearly dealing with the sons or grandsons of the eighteenth-century Grand Tourists (pronouns used are consistently masculine),

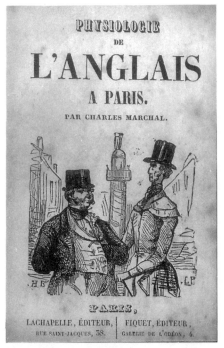

Title-page of Charles Marchal's *Physiologie
de l'Anglais à Paris*, Paris, (?)1844.

A Frenchman's representation of a typical English family
in Paris, from Charles Augustus Sala, *Paris Herself Again*,
Remington & Co., London, 1880.

independent travellers of a certain social and economic standing, who instead of travelling, as did their forebears in the company of a personal tutor/guide, are voyaging on their own but with the assistance of Planta's directory. The layout and structuring of the book are also highly instructive. The first 100 of its 500 pages are taken up by an introductory 'narrative' (*sic*) detailing different possible routes from London to Paris and the logistical and practical difficulties facing the traveller on his journey. These difficulties, in a period before the advent of the railway, appear horrendous by present-day standards: financial transactions were thus dependent on a complex system of letters of credit or of circular exchange notes (an early form of traveller's cheque) to be negotiated with certain Parisian banks; passports had to be obtained from the French embassy and shown at every fortified town the traveller passed through; customs formalities called for considerable expenditure of both time and money; Channel 'packets' (ferries) were frequent, though timetables were erratic and the crossing, at best uncomfortable, took a minimum of three hours (Planta adds ominously that 'it is sometimes prolonged to five or six': p. 25); the journey to Paris from the Channel port, either by private carriage or by public diligence, was time-consuming (36 hours), expensive and extremely uncomfortable.

This first section of Planta's guide is followed by a brief listing (30 pages) of Parisian hotels, coffee- and eating-houses, and by an equally brief survey of the 'History and present State of Paris' and of the 'Character and Manners of the Parisians'. The hotel most fulsomely recommended is Meurice's City of London Hotel on the rue Saint-Honoré. The reasons for the recommendation are noteworthy and rest on a reassuring avoidance of otherness. The visitor, when staying at this establishment, will thus find himself in an essentially non-French environment, in a comforting Parisian little England, a home away from home. At first sight surprising, Planta's recommendation makes perfect sense in the light of his generally unfavourable opinions of the French:

I recommend this hotel to Englishmen who know but little of French, for the following reasons: the master speaks the English language fluently, the waiters speak English, the accommodation is completely in the English style, and the visitors are usually from the British islands. The traveller will not here feel himself alone in a foreign land; but, amidst the constant and rapid influx of new guests, he will recognise some one whom he can claim as an acquaintance, or with whom he can associate as a friend: and when the emotions of novelty and surprise have subsided in his own bosom, it will afford him an inexhaustible fund of amusement to witness the various and often ludicrous ways in which every new-comer reveals the impression which the first sight of Paris has made on his mind. (pp. 101–2)

Planta's picture of the physical state of Paris presents a vivid image of the labyrinthine squalour that characterized the heart of the city in its pre-Haussmannian days, an image that is no less memorable than that to be found in the novels of Balzac or Eugène Sue and in the photographic *œuvre* of, for example, Charles Marville. This is very much the sort of environment familiar to readers of *Le Père Goriot* or of Sue's *Les Mystères de Paris*:

The pedestrian is not only exposed to continual danger from the carriages; but the air and sun being almost completely excluded by the height of the houses, and there being few subterranean drains, a stream of black mire constantly runs through many of the streets; and they are as wet and dirty in the middle of summer as the streets of the British metropolis are in the depth of winter.

This stream in the centre of the road often becomes a rapid torrent. It requires no inconsiderable agility to leap across it, and the driver of the cabriolet delights in plentifully splattering its black and disgusting contents on every unfortunate pedestrian. In dirty weather it is absolutely necessary for the stranger, and even for the native, to avail himself of a fiacre or cabriolet to traverse the more crowded and unpleasant streets. (pp. 129–30)

The remaining 340 pages of the book offer a descriptive enumeration of the 'Curiosities of Paris' based on a perceived order of importance or status, rather than on geographic criteria or on any rationally planned utilization of the visitor's time: we thus start with Palaces, make our way through Public Buildings, Religious Edifices, Courts of Justice and the like and end up with such evidently more trivial matters as Modes of Conveyance, Theatres, Promenades and Public Gardens. Planta's work turns out in this sense to be more of a dictionary or a compendium (a *Picture* as he terms it) than an actual *guide*: he proposes no tours or itineraries that the traveller might follow; no ordering or prioritizing of the foreigner's Parisian experiences is suggested. The visitor is left very much to his own devices, to thread his own way through the Parisian maze.

It will be clear from the above that Planta was writing primarily for the gentleman-traveller undertaking an independent visit to Paris: his book offers a menu of the 'Objects worthy of Attention' from which the visitor will make his own individual selection. It should also be clear that the style of his discourse is highly personal in tone and register: anything but objective, the *New Picture of Paris* is thus liberally sprinkled with the author's opinions and prejudices; it also contains a wealth of anecdotal material based on his own or his friends' experiences. Overall, Planta's attitude to the French appears distinctly critical and, in the frequent comparisons he makes between French and English institutions, he invariably comes down in favour of the latter. The appearance of Parisian shops is thus judged to be disappointing (p. 132), the Parisian 'has little idea of the comforts of his domestic fireside' (p. 138), the finery of the Parisians has 'much of the strange inconsistency of their character' (p. 142); relations between the sexes in Paris are characterized by an 'unnatural dominion' (p. 144) of women which, even though they may now use less rouge, a development for which they are given credit (p. 146), 'gives to the character of the most virtuous and accomplished woman a confidence and boldness not suited to the English taste, and not favourable to domestic felicity' (p. 145); as a result 'it is notorious that conjugal infidelity is too prevalent in every class of society' (p. 144). The 'negligence and rudeness' (p. 147) of French servants are deemed insufferable, whilst the French peasants are 'distinguished by an improvidence and disregard of futurity' (*sic*) that is 'scarcely conceivable' (ibid.). Parisian cafés are generally praised even if the promiscuity of behaviour that they are judged to encourage is viewed with suspicion (p. 107), but those in the Palais-Royal are put firmly out of bounds since they are 'the harbour of gamblers and prostitutes' by whom the traveller may be 'decoyed into hazardous play, and pillaged without mercy' (p. 109). French horse-racing is baldly dismissed as being 'much inferior to sports of this kind in England' (p. 432). The boulevards, of which a highly vivid description is given, are alone praised unreservedly (pp. 439–42), even if the word is given a somewhat fanciful etymological derivation. Planta thus ends up creating a mythical and personal Paris, a city from whose threatening differences the British visitor could insulate himself by staying at Meurice's reassuring City of London Hotel.

The first English-language Baedekers were published in the early 1860s, after the death in 1859 of Karl Baedeker, the founder of the firm. These first handbooks were produced in direct imitation (down to the use of the famous red covers) of John Murray's handbooks for travellers. *The Rhine* (1861) and *Switzerland* (1863), the first titles in English, were in fact little more than direct translations of the corresponding Murrays. Because of his apparent dislike of the French (one of the few characteristics he seems to have shared with Edward Planta), Karl Baedeker was at first reluctant to embark on a series of guides to France. In 1844 he thus wrote to Murray that 'I do not think that such a book [a guide to France] would find a rewarding market in Germany. My countrymen [. . .]

journey little in France, with perhaps the exception of Paris. In any case, I do not feel inclined to take on such an enterprise. I do not like France, I have not been to Paris myself, and do not feel moved to do so.' In the event the first edition in English of the Paris Baedeker was published in Leipzig in 1865, but *Northern France* did not appear until 1889 and *Southern France* not until 1891. *Paris* (later *Paris and Northern France* and later still *Paris and its Environs*, the book's definitive title) ran through twenty editions in its classic format between 1865 and 1937.

Paris and its Environs differs in just about every respect from Planta's *Picture of Paris*.[7] Taller and slimmer in format (16 × 11 × 3 cm), so that they might fit comfortably into the traveller's handbag or jacket pocket, the Baedeker volumes, with their elegant red covers, the gold-blocked lettering of their titles and their marbled edges, are the first genuinely modern travel guides: as such they have acquired an almost mythical status in any discussion of travel literature. Clearly laid out and attractively printed, they use all the resources of late nineteenth-century typography; with an abundance of highly legible maps and plans (these replacing, in the case of *Paris*, Planta's charmingly naïve vignettes), they aimed to provide the traveller with as much accurate, objective, practical and factual information as possible: this frequently takes the form of an extraordinary abundance of historical and statistical data. It is in this sense that they may be seen as contributing, in their own very specific register, to the vast current of encyclopaedic discourse that characterizes so much of the literary endeavour in the second half of the nineteenth century: accordingly, in his desire to provide guides that would encompass all the countries of the European continent (and indeed some beyond: a Baedeker *Round the World* – though in probably more than 80 days – was envisaged in 1904 but never appeared), Karl Baedeker deserves to stand alongside his fellow literary entrepreneurs and compilers – Pierre Larousse and Emile Littré with their encyclopaedias and dictionaries, Emile Zola and Jules Verne (author we now know of a novel-guide to Paris of 1860) with their respective novel cycles. All, with their different voices and following their own individual paths, seem to me to be motivated by a similar globalistic zeal, in quest of a similar cumulative and panoramic goal.

Travelling conditions between England and the Continent had improved dramatically by 1865, and even more so by 1894: with the inauguration of a regular and reliable steamboat service (not yet called ferries), the Channel crossing now took only two-and-a-half-hours, while the opening of the railway link between Paris and the Channel ports further reduced both the difficulty and the length of the journey, the fastest trains taking a mere four-and-a-quarter hours. (Interestingly, the 1894 Baedeker, when evoking Cap Gris Nez, touchingly refers to it on p. 364 as 'the proposed starting-point of the submarine tunnel between France and England'.) It is no accident that the development of this more modern transport network coincides both with the advent of Baedeker's guides and with the appearance of the group tours offered by Thomas Cook & Sons from the summer of 1861 onwards: all three phenomena should be seen as underpinning a new conception of travel and addressing a new species of visiting public. The layout of Baedeker's *Paris* clearly reflects these new attitudes and new customers. A somewhat cursory 80-page opening section provides a certain amount of practical 'Preliminary Information' that includes details of hotels, theatres and the like (though with none of Planta's picturesqueness: Baedeker has little that is the equivalent of the earlier guide's section on the 'Character and Manners of the Parisians'). There follow diaries giving a day by day (in fact almost hour by hour) schedule (what James Buzard aptly terms the 'arithmetical allotting of cultural time'[8]) for what sound like highly exhausting one-week, two-week and three-week programmes of visit. The remainder of the book's 430 pages are devoted to what is clearly central to Baedeker's preoccupations: the *catalogue raisonné*, done in exhaustive detail, of the cultural 'Sights of Paris' (today's 'tourist attractions') organized around a series of 26 punishing Parisian excursions. The tone of the discourse is earnestly pedagogic throughout, since 'it is taken for granted that they [the travellers] devote the entire day to sight-seeing' (p. 57): autonomous self-improvement is clearly the name of the Baedekerian game, given that the chief object of the handbooks is to 'render the traveller as nearly as possible independent of the services of guides, commissionnaires, and innkeepers' (p. v). No sight, whether ancient or modern, escapes Baedeker's meticulous attention, and his guides are in terms of value judgements admirably even-handed: Belgrand's new sewer network, Baltard's Halles Centrales and Eiffel's recently completed tower are as fully and sympathetically reviewed as Notre-Dame, the Invalides or Versailles.

Some notion of Baedeker's system of values may, however, be inferred from the fact that no fewer than 60 pages of the guide are devoted to the traveller's visit to the Louvre, 'the museum of Europe' (p. 88). Asterisks, the forerunner of Bibendum's crossed forks and red rocking-chairs from another *red* guide that was about to be born (first edition of the Michelin guide to France in 1900), are (for the first time in a travel-guide?) used as

A nineteenth-century Channel crossing, from Charles Augustus Sala,
Paris Herself Again, Remington & Co., London, 1880.

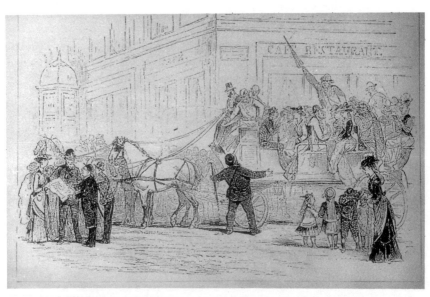

'A Party of Cook's Tourists', from Charles Augustus Sala,
Paris Herself Again, Remington & Co., London, 1880.

A contemporary lithograph of Belgrand's new sewers,
a required stop on the tourist's visit to Paris.

semiotic 'marks of commendation', though only up to a meagre maximum of two, to indicate items that the visitor should on no account miss. Mindful perhaps of the fate of Gervaise and her wedding party, Baedeker sternly enjoins his visitors to the Louvre 'to adhere closely to the following order of proceeding through the rooms, so as to avoid missing their way or losing time by going twice over the same ground' (p. 89). Comments explicitly comparing British and French institutions or customs, such as are to be found in abundance in Planta, are however almost totally absent, this due in part to the international nature of Baedeker's guides (the English *Paris* is after all to a large extent an adaptation of the French and German originals) but also to the more scientific and encyclopaedic nature of the enterprise. Objective facts not subjective opinions are clearly Baedeker's very straight-batted preserve, his judgement on Haussmannization being in this respect unusually fair. Despite his generally sympathetic attitude towards the Second Empire and its innovations and his reiterated condemnation of the 'Communist rebellion',[9] polemical issues are accordingly no sooner raised than dropped. Thus the following from the introductory section to the guide:

Persons well acquainted with the Paris of the earlier part of the present century sometimes declare that the former spirit of French society is well-nigh extinct; but whether it has really lost a degree of its characteristic sprightliness, or is merely superficially obscured by the ever-increasing anxieties of so populous a city, is a question which we need not here attempt to decide. (p. xxv)

Karl Baedeker and his descendants, it should now be clear, were writing for a new generation of travellers. Team efforts rather than the work of a single individual, their guides were produced for an economically and socially more catholic travelling public; for people travelling in groups and families; for female travellers and for middle-class travellers; for travellers who were perhaps less sure of themselves than had been their predecessors and who accordingly needed more specific guidance; for people who required the support of a text that could stand (and be displayed) as some sort of cultural authority and that would have a concomitant status and validity; for the first generations of mass travellers; in short for the first modern tourists. The dichotomy between traveller and tourist has of course been much elaborated on in some of the recent discussion around the sociology, anthropology and semiotics of travel.[10] It is a distinction that, it seems to me, underpins the differences that I have attempted to delineate between the travel books of Edward Planta and the tourist guides of the firm of Baedeker, between the conception of travel as a free and independent activity that emerges from the one and the much more directed and passive travelling (what in contemporary jargon could be termed 'packaged' touring) that appears to be the focus of the other: Baedeker's use of asterisks does after all literally star things that *ought* to be seen, to occasions that *must* be experienced, to memories that *have* to be stored and then traded in once back home as cultural capital or social kudos (yesteryear's lithographs or sketches, today's photographs or videos, brass Eiffel Towers and other such memorabilia).

And it is perhaps for this reason, because of their association with a modern conception of directed mass travel, with a more superficial sort of tourism, that the Baedeker guides have acquired some of the mythical status mentioned earlier (the trenchant hatchet-job that Roland Barthes has done on the rival *Guides bleus* series in *Mythologies* could have been directed with equal panache against Baedeker); and, at the same time, the very name Baedeker has not infrequently been endowed with a distinctly pejorative connotation. There were, of course, the infamous Baedeker raids of World War Two, but one might think in this context of, say, one of T. S. Eliot's eponymous visitors to Venice, the pretentious 'Burbank with a Baedeker'; of Aldous Huxley's virulent invective against 'Baron' [*sic*] Baedeker's system of asterisks in his essay 'Guide-Books' (to be found in Huxley's *Along the Road: Notes and Essays of a Tourist* alongside a charmingly tongue-in-cheek attack on travel in general – 'Why not Stay at Home?'); of Edmund Wilson's collection of travel sketches entitled *Europe without Baedeker* or of Beckett's identification, in his essay on Proust, of the superficial state of much modern perception as being worthy of Baedeker.

Why, then, should one read guidebooks? What, in particular, is the point of reading *old* and therefore out-of-date guidebooks? Why bother? I answer as follows. Besides their self-evident interest for the social historian, and specifically the historian of travel, the antiquarian fascination of these books also seems to me undeniable: witness the number of bibliophiles who specialize in the collection of travel books. Elegant and attractive as objects in their own right, these volumes, like many another kind of memento, exert considerable period charm while, at the same time, they have their own idiosyncratic appeal, one that I can only describe as palimpsestically spooky. They commonly bear ownership signatures or inscriptions (presumably because they were easily mislaid and habitually borrowed) so that one finds oneself wanting to know more about these original owners and about *their* Parisian experiences. And of course these are things that we are unlikely ever to find out about: we are then reduced to dreaming, to revisiting an imaginary Paris in the ghostly company of the original and now long-dead owners.

And it is perhaps here, in their oneiric charge, that the real charm of these nineteenth-century travel books is to be sought. Like any work of fiction, they promote an excursion (in the etymological sense of the word) of the reader's imaginative faculties – an excursion in both space (to a foreign location) and time (to a period long dead) but also an excursion in taste. In this last sense the books I have discussed provide a means of access to past and foreign *mentalités* and to the changes that these states of mind – those both of the visitor and of the visited – have undergone. Guidebooks tell us how a foreign culture is (or in my case *was*) presented to a local (in this case British) audience and how the latter perceives

(perceived) it. It can I think accordingly be argued that the representations the guidebooks offer – their re-presentations or repackagings –
inform us as much about the 'other' culture that is being represented as
they do about the culture to which that 'other' is being shown; and, at the
same time, they may be seen as offering some contribution to our
understanding of the relativist nature of the links between the two
cultures and the two times (past and present) that are being juxtaposed
(one suspects in this context that a study of the way in which the guides,
especially Baedeker, evolve diachronically from one edition to another
would prove particularly revealing).

Two final, and again complementary, fictional excursions that would
seem to merit one last detour at least will bring our journey full circle.
The youthful Lucy Honeychurch has travelled to Florence as a first-time
visitor: she is accordingly equipped with Baedeker's *Handbook to
Northern Italy*, the most important features of which she has committed
to memory. But, entrusting the book to one of her elderly lady-
companions, she finds herself obliged to be 'In Santa Croce with no
Baedeker'. As a result she successfully escapes the straitjacket of
Baedekerian confinement and liberates herself from what Forster neatly
terms 'the orthodox Baedeker-bestarred Italy'; and the novel (*A Room
with a View*) will tell in part of her encounter with a more authentically
'Italian Italy', of her discovery of 'the true Italy' (again Forster's
expressions) of which the guidebooks can only scratch the surface. And
Lucy's liberation will be more than just that from her persona as a tourist:
by losing her Baedeker and with it her ingenuousness as a foreign
traveller, Forster's heroine, as well as discovering a truer Italy, will also
discover herself.

Duke Jean Floressas des Esseintes is suffering from a bad attack of the
moody blues. Prompted by his reading of Dickens, he resolves to visit
England and, before leaving, stops at Galignani's to acquire his Baedeker.
While waiting for his train, des Esseintes takes dinner in an English tavern
on the rue d'Amsterdam; there, surrounded by a crowd of typical English
tourists and his imagination further fuelled by the contents of his
guidebook, by its 'laconic and precise details',[11] Huysmans's hero (*À
Rebours*) finds himself catapulted into a phantasmagorical journey of the
mind, a veritable *voyage imaginaire*, to an ideal and total London. By
comparison any actual journeying, any real London must inevitably
produce disappointment: for how could these ever compete with the
sharpness of the imagined journey and the vividness of the dream London
that des Esseintes experiences on that rainy (and very English) evening in

Paris? Why then bother? Why not stay at home? In the face of this realization, Huysmans's hero gleefully aborts his (real) journey:

After all, what was the good of moving, when a fellow could travel so magnificently sitting in a chair? Wasn't he already in London, whose smells, weather, citizens, food, and even cutlery, were all about him? What could he expect to find over there, save fresh disappointments such as he had suffered in Holland? (pp. 142–4)†

One might thus want to argue that the moral journeys of Lucy Honeychurch and Jean des Esseintes both have as one of their points of departure that archetypal tourist guide, the laconic handbooks of Karl Baedeker. And, in both cases again, the jettisoned tourist's vade-mecum (a case perhaps of 'Jette ce livre des Esseintes'?) will have provided the springboard for the soaring of the traveller's imagination through a movement similar to that evoked by Jacques Réda in the preamble to his *Premier livre des reconnaissances*: books 'allow our modest itinerary to communicate with their prodigious networks so that, following in their footsteps, we continue to travel down roads that project their light around us, as we sit beneath the illiterate and unhearing lamps of hotel bedrooms.'[12]

†*A quoi bon bouger, quand on peut voyager si magnifiquement sur une chaise? N'était-il pas à Londres dont les senteurs, dont l'atmosphère, dont les habitants, dont les pâtures, dont les ustensiles l'environnaient? Que pouvait-il donc espérer, sinon de nouvelles désillusions, comme en Hollande.*

2

Shifting Cultural Centres in Twentieth-century Paris

NICHOLAS HEWITT

It is possible to talk of a cultural geography in respect of all of the great European cities of the nineteenth and twentieth centuries, which enables us to identify those specific urban districts that became centres of cultural activity and production, and those institutions, particularly cafés, that served as regular meeting points for writers and artists. In the case of Paris, that cultural geography was initially heavily dependant on the institutions of cultural power, in particular the University and allied institutions of higher education, such as the *grandes écoles*, especially the Ecole des Beaux-Arts and the Ecole Normale Supérieure, and the publishing houses that flourished around the University. In other words, Parisian cultural geography is inextricably enmeshed, as Herbert Lottman reminds us,[1] in the history of the Quartier Latin in particular, and the Rive Gauche in general. What is interesting about Left Bank culture in the nineteenth century, however, is that it is composed of two distinct cultural traditions that will fragment in the early part of the twentieth century, only to reunite in the heyday of Existentialism in Saint-Germain-des-Prés in the immediate aftermath of World War Two. On the one hand, the presence of the University and publishing houses ensures the continuity of an intellectual and academic tradition, essentially concerned with ideas, often in their social and political application, and distrustful of the histrionics of avant-gardism. At the same time, as the nineteenth-century novelist Henri Murger, the author of *Scènes de la vie de bohème*, testifies, the Left Bank, in its student and Beaux-Arts traditions, played host to a nineteenth-century bohemianism that proved no less durable. What is interesting is that while the intellectual tradition remains geographically stable, attached to the cultural institutions on which it depends, the bohemian tradition is far more volatile and shifts across the city, dependant on the constantly changing structure of the urban fabric. In particular, its movement is connected to the growth of centres of transient populations, either in the developing centres of pleasure in the modern city or in the areas surrounding railway stations, which provide not merely the essential infrastructure for bohemian existence in terms of cheap studios, accommodation, restaurants and cafés, but also the indispensable frontier between the bourgeois city and the *classes dangereuses*[2] that constitutes the marginal space in which bohemian activity takes place. It is therefore possible to chart the movement of Parisian cultural centres through the migration of bohemianism from the Left Bank to Montmartre, and from Montmartre to Montparnasse, before it rejoins the intellectual tradition in post-war Saint-Germain-des-Prés, with a brief detour through the 'aristocratic' bohemianism of the bar Le Boeuf sur le toit in the 1920s. Such an itinerary sheds considerable light not just on the nature of Parisian cultural activity in the twentieth century but on the development of the city itself.

In the beginning was the *Mur*, the Wall, probably one of the single most significant factors in the cultural development of Paris. Montmartre already had a long history as a *lieu de plaisir* for the Parisian population: the village on the hilltop (*Butte*) with its vineyards and leafy taverns was a popular object of summer excursions, while the *quartiers* of Les Porcherons and La Nouvelle France, stretching from the present-day Place du Havre to the faubourg Poissonnière, had acquired already by the early eighteenth century a more seedy reputation for drinking and prostitution.[3] The construction, in 1784, of the Mur des Fermiers Généraux (the tax-collectors' wall) was crucial in institutionalizing this split between upper and lower Montmartre and in establishing Montmartre as a whole as the major *lieu de plaisir* of the capital. The Mur des Fermiers Généraux was both a physical and a fiscal wall, designed to separate the urban population of 600,000 Parisians in an area of high customs tarifs from the relatively cheap outlying districts beyond the city. All the way round the city the Wall was accompanied on the inside by the *chemin de ronde* (circular road) and on the outside by the *boulevards extérieurs* (outer boulevards), with regular points of access at the *barrières*, or customs posts. Because of the differential in duty payable on, among other things, alcohol within and beyond the Wall, the areas surrounding the *barrières* outside the Wall became important *lieux de plaisir*, as did the *boulevards extérieurs*, populated by dance-halls, drinking establishments and, later, places of popular entertainment. The geography of pleasure in the nineteenth- and twentieth-century city is closely allied to the Wall: one of the best-known and most popular dance-halls, for example, the Bal Bullier, was at the *barrière* at the end of the Boulevard Saint-Michel, on the site of the current restaurant and café, the Closerie des Lilas; the

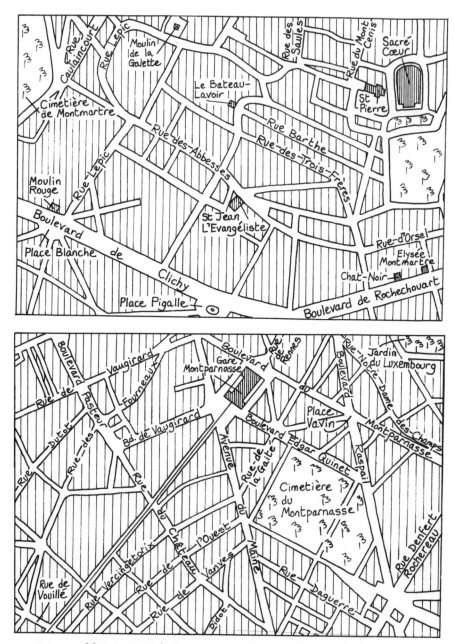

Montmartre and Montparnasse at the turn of the century.

dance-halls, cafés and theatres of Montparnasse are situated along the old
boulevard extérieur, now the Boulevard du Montparnasse, and at its
barrière on the current Place Pablo Picasso, formerly the Place Vavin; as
late as 1900, the anonymous author of the *Guide secret de l'étranger
célibataire à Paris* (The secret guide to Paris for the foreign bachelor)
draws attention to the cabarets and small theatres on the Boulevard de
l'Hôpital.[4] It was on Montmartre, however, that the cultural impact of the
Wall was the greatest, establishing the Place Blanche, the Place Pigalle and
the Place Clichy as major pleasure-centres, together with the Boulevards
des Batignolles, de Clichy, de Rochechouart and de la Chapelle. The Law
of 1860 that annexed the *Communes Limitrophes* and extended the city to
the fortifications on the present Boulevards des Maréchaux had the effect
of consecrating the *barrières* and *boulevards extérieurs* as *lieux de plaisir*
within the city while maintaining their marginal status on the frontiers
between the bourgeois capital and newly developed artisanal or working-
class districts. It was this marginality that was crucial to the attractiveness
of Montmartre and Montparnasse as pleasure centres; as a guide to the
Exposition Universelle of 1855 remarked:

From time immemorial, the rich society of Paris adopted a neutral space where
all classes could rub shoulders, see each other, talk to each other, without making
any more contact than the pursuit of pleasure demanded.[5†]

At the same time, this marginality translated itself into the criminality
essential to the creation of the 'Montmartre du plaisir et du crime'
(Montmartre of pleasure and crime).[6]

The key factors in the creation of this marginality were both demographic and cultural. Demographically, the most important factor was
the position of Montmartre between 'deux faisceaux de voies ferrées, à
l'est celle de la Chapelle, à l'ouest celle des Batignolles' (Two networks of
railway lines: La Chapelle to the east and Batignolles to the west).[7] Not
only did this ensure a significant working-class population, employed by
the various companies, but, through the Gare Saint-Lazare, the Gare du
Nord and the Gare de l'Est, it provided a constant flow of travellers,
giving to the area a sense of transience. In particular, it is essential to recall
the importance of the Gare de l'Est as the capital's major military railway
station and that of the Gare Saint-Lazare as the suburban station linking
Paris with the racecourse at Maisons-Lafitte. Culturally, as Chevalier

---

†*De tout temps la société riche de Paris a adopté un endroit neutre où toutes les classes
peuvent se coudoyer, se voir, s'entretenir, sans pour cela se lier plus que le besoin du plaisir
ne l'exige.*

reminds us, 'l'événement' (*the* event) was the migration in the winter of
1881–82 of the two Left Bank impressarios Emile Goudeau and
Rodolphe Salis from the Latin Quarter and the foundation of the first
Montmartre music-hall cabaret, Le Chat Noir at 84 Boulevard de
Rochechouart. This marked a significant shift of the Parisian *bohème*
from the Left Bank to the Right and a new, crucial alliance between
bohemianism and commercial entertainment. Salis's cabaret, which
involved *chansonniers* (satirical entertainers), music and silhouette-plays,
gave rise to multiple imitations, the 'théâtricules de Montmartre' (the
little theatres of Montmartre):[8] L'Enfer, Le Bagne, L'Abbaye de Thélème,
Les Frites Révolutionnaires, and, the best-known, Aristide Bruant's Le
Mirliton. These cabarets were rapidly accompanied by the creation of the
dance-halls that grew out of the Montmartre tradition of *guinguettes*, the
most famous of which was La Moulin de la Galette: the Elysée-
Montmartre and the Moulin Rouge, which, in its turn, transformed itself
into the modern music-hall, with imitators such as the Casino de Paris and
the Folies-Bergère. By 1900 lower Montmartre had become the centre of
the Parisian entertainment industry, with dance-halls, music-halls, cabarets, the Cirque Médrano and the establishment on the Boulevard de
Clichy of the world's largest cinema, the Gaumont-Palace.

It was this national, and international, reputation of Montmartre,
boosted by the Exposition Universelle of 1900 and the nation-wide
'Tournées du Chat Noir' (Chat Noir tours), that led to the establishment
of the Butte de Montmartre as a centre of bohemia and the artistic avant-
garde. The Impressionist painters had already flirted with the area in the
last years of the nineteenth century, attracted by the cheap accommodation, the ready availability of studio space, and subject-matter such as
Renoir's *Moulin de la Galette* or Lautrec's *Moulin Rouge*. For a young
provincial, such as the future inter-war poet and novelist Francis Carco,
it had become the natural *quartier* to colonize on a first visit to Paris.[9] It
was also a natural location for the establishment of an avant-garde
movement, such as the Cubists in the ramshackle studios of the Bateau-
Lavoir, though it is worth recalling that the historic meeting between
Picasso and Apollinaire in 1904 took place in Austen's Fox Bar near the
Gare Saint-Lazare. The Bateau-Lavoir, with its shifting population of
artists and writers, including Picasso, Van Dongen, Braque, the poets
Max Jacob and André Salmon, and the inter-war novelist Pierre Mac
Orlan, came to define a certain cultural production of the Belle Epoque,
encompassing both avant-garde and more traditional means of
expression, and reliant on the cheap social infrastructure of Montmartre,

as well as upon the proximity of the *lieu de plaisir* in lower Montmartre and the centre of the Parisian press in the Faubourg Montmartre. From 1906 to the outbreak of World War One, the Butte de Montmartre played host to an extraordinary diversity of cultural activity, encompassing the creativity of the avant-garde, presided over by Apollinaire, the bohemians represented by writers such as Mac Orlan, Roland Dorgelès, author of the best-selling *Les Croix de bois* (Wooden crosses) and Carco, and caricaturists like Gus Bofa, Chas Laborde and Poulbot, the inventor of the archetypal Parisian street-urchin. The meeting-point between these different strands of cultural activity, often overtly antagonistic, was the Lapin-Agile on the rue des Saules, which brought together not merely representatives of different artistic tendencies, but also artists, bohemians, workers and criminals, a mixture recorded in Mac Orlan's *Le Quai des brumes* and Dorgelès's *Le Château des brouillards*.

What is remarkable about this cultural mixture is not merely its extraordinary vibrancy but its temporary nature: by the outbreak of World War One most of its major players had left: writers like Mac Orlan, Carco or Dorgelès, sickened by the memory of poverty, all too easily romanticized into the notion of 'la vache enragée' (starvation), had moved away, particularly to Passy, albeit retaining a sentimental, albeit ambiguous, attachment to the *bohème* of the 1900s; the avant-garde moved on, either in the cases of Picasso or Van Dongen through upward mobility, or, in the case of Modigliani, through a poverty unable to cope with rising prices in Montmartre, to Montparnasse. They left behind them a highly resilient literary avant-garde, represented by Pierre Reverdy's poetry review *Nord-Sud*, itself a recognition of the Métro link between Montmartre and the centre of the capital, and the Surrealists in the rue de Fontaine. In the 1930s Montmartre became synonymous with a certain tendency of cultural production that was, in one sense, both aesthetically and politically reactionary, with novelists like Louis-Ferdinand Céline and Marcel Aymé and artists and caricaturists like Vlaminck, Laborde, Daragnès and Ralph Soupault deploring the cosmopolitan nature of the city below and increasingly celebrating the 'France profonde' (essential France) represented by the village on the Butte. It is these survivors from the pre-war avant-garde who come to constitute the 'Ecole de Montmartre' (Montmartre School) in the inter-war years and who exert a powerful influence on young right-wing culture in the years after the Liberation.

By the end of World War One, the cultural centre of gravity of Paris had shifted away from Montmartre, but by no means back to the Quartier

Latin. The *années folles* (crazy years) of the 1920s were centred on not one, but two cultural locations: Montparnasse, for the artistic avant-garde, and the Right Bank venue of Le Boeuf sur le toit for the right-wing, mondain, intelligentsia. The significance of Le Boeuf sur le toit, 'ce bar éclairé brutalement' (this brutally-lit bar),[10] established at 28 rue Boissy d'Anglas, lies in its alliance with a certain Right Bank popular culture associated with the Champs-Elysées, and particularly with the Bal Mabille, and in its ability, under the influence of the poet, novelist, artist and film-maker Jean Cocteau, to unite a particular *mondain* bohemian-ism, deriving from the world of theatre and ballet, in particular Diaghilev, and a number of writers who were essentially allied to the political right: Cocteau himself and his partner, the young novelist Raymond Radiguet, but also the novelists Paul Morand, François Mauriac and Joseph Kessel. In addition, it played host to a cross-partisan avant-garde, with com-posers like Darius Milhaud, sculptors such as Zadkine, and the outriders of the literary avant-garde, such as Blaise Cendrars and René Crevel. In particular, its clientele included Surrealists like Aragon, together with worrying fellow-travellers Jacques Rigaut and Drieu la Rochelle, both of whom were obsessed by suicide. As Mauriac records:

The Christian, even the bad Christian if he has kept faith, possesses a sense, an antenna, to detect amongst those who surround him the evil which never pardons. I did not know that Raymond Radiguet, that marvelous trained owl, motionless and unseeing on his stool in the *Boeuf sur le toit*, was on the point of dying. I did not know the Drieu la Rochelle or René Crevel would kill themselves, but I saw with the eyes of the spirit a glow, a sign, suspended over those charming heads. . . .[11]†

In the inter-war years there was a powerful Right Bank culture, deriving from an essentially Proustian legacy, which was to maintain a cultural importance that lasted into Vichy and into the post-war period, particu-larly through its influence on the new generation of the 'Hussards', Roger Nimier, Antoine Blondin and Jacques Laurent.

In his memoirs of 1964, *A Moveable Feast*, Ernest Hemingway records his period spent as a young penniless writer in Paris immediately after World War One and emphasizes the dominance of the *quartier* of

---

†*Le chrétien, même le mauvais chrétien s'il a gardé la foi, possède un sens, une antenne pour démêler chez ceux qui l'entourent ce mal qui ne pardonne pas. Je ne savais pas que Raymond Radiguet, celle merveilleuse chouette dressée, immobile et aveugle, sur son tabouret du Boeuf sur le toit, était en train de mourir. Je ne savais pas que Drieu la Rochelle, que René Crevel se tueraient, mais je voyais avec les yeux de l'esprit au-dessus de ces têtes charmantes un lueur, un signe . . .*

Montparnasse as an international artistic and intellectual centre: 'In those days many people went to the cafés at the corner of the boulevard Montparnasse and the boulevard Raspail to be seen publicly, and in a way such places anticipated the columnists as the daily substitutes for immortality.'[12] Unlike Montmartre, the borders of Montparnasse are less easy to define. For the author of a guide-book like Clive Holland's *Things seen in Paris* of 1926, the definition of Montparnasse is broad enough to encompass the Latin Quarter and its surrounding quartiers: 'The Latin Quarter of Paris is not easy to define, but it may be roughly considered to comprise the area covered by the Boulevard St.Michel, or as it is usually called the Boul. Mich., and the Odeon quarter of the Boulevard Montparnasse from the Gare Montparnasse to the Place de l'Observatoire'.[13] More precisely, Montparnasse may be said to be bounded on the north-west by the rue de Vaugirard, on the north-east by the rue d'Assas, on the east by the avenue du General Leclerc and the avenue Denfert Rochereau, and on the south by the rue d'Alésia and its extension into the rue de Vouille and the rue de la Convention. As such, it occupies parts of the 6th, 14th and 15th arrondissements and has as its main arteries the avenue du Maine and the Boulevard Raspail, both running diagonally from north-west to south-east, the Boulevard du Montparnasse, from west to east, and the rue de Rennes linking the focal point of the Gare Montparnasse with (further north) the Boulevard Saint-Germain and the city centre. In addition to the railway station, now part of the Maine–Montparnasse development, its major crossroads is the Place Pablo Picasso, formerly the Place Vavin, lined with the cafés La Coupole, Le Dôme, Le Sélect and La Rotonde.

In fact, Montparnasse owes its artistic success in the 1920s to its socially heterogeneous nature, which enabled it, well before World War One, to become established as a modest *quartier de loisirs* (entertainment district) within the capital. Like Montmartre, Montparnasse benefited from the same social development that followed the establishment of the Mur des Fermiers Généraux in 1784, with its accompanying boulevards.[14] The Wall, as we have seen, maintaining high customs tariffs for the city and relatively low prices for, among other things, wine, outside the capital, led to the creation of *lieux de plaisir* – taverns, *guinguettes*, dance-halls – all along its perimeter. It was for this reason that, as in the case of Montmartre, a similar pleasure industry was developed where the Wall ran to the south, along the present-day Boulevard du Montparnasse. In particular, it gave rise to a number of taverns and *guinguettes* in the rue de la Gaîté, and, especially, as we have seen, to the establishment of the most famous *bal* in Paris, the Bal Bullier, where the Boulevard Saint Michel meets the Boulevard Montparnasse and the Boulevard de l'Observatoire, on the site of the present-day Closerie des Lilas. In other words, from the end of the eighteenth century onwards, Montparnasse constituted a powerful link, through pleasure, between the capital and the *quartier*.

As the nineteenth century progressed, this link was maintained, as was its original nature. With the annexation of the outlying villages in 1860, under the Law of 26 May 1859, Paris expanded to the south as far as the fortifications, now constituted by the 'boulevards des Maréchaux' (the Marshals' Boulevards), the Boulevards Brune and Lefebvre, and absorbed the previously independent communes of Vaugirard, Plaisance and Petit Montrouge. As Albert Demangeon points out, 'These *quartiers eccentriques* (outlying districts) were, par excellence, the habitat of the *classes populaires* (lower classes)',[15] and Montparnasse, along with the *quartiers* of Santé, Petit Montrouge, Plaisance, Javel and Grenelle, was populated by workers and clerks.[16] Essentially, the avenue du Maine came to act as a border between the heavily working-class districts of Vaugirard, Plaisance and Petit Montrouge, dominated by the Chemins de Fer de l'Ouest and by the slaughterhouses on the rue de Vaugirard, but sustaining a thriving and diverse artisanal industry, and the districts towards the Cimetière du Montparnasse and the Jardin du Luxembourg which, while populated by clerks, were also inhabited by the bourgeoisie, particularly along the boulevards themselves. It is for this reason that, by the end of the nineteenth century, Montparnasse had become recognized as one of the Parisian centres 'du plaisir et du crime',[17] a significant interface between the capital's bourgeoisie and its *classes dangereuses*. A novel such as Charles-Louis Philippe's *Bubu de Montparnasse* (1901) plays on its audience's recognition of a social reality by evoking the career of a Parisian pimp, Bubu, a native of the *quartier* of Plaisance who graduates to the aristocracy of the underworld and who use the bars of the avenue du Maine as their headquarters, just as this aristocracy's Right Bank counterparts dominate the Place Pigalle.

In the case of Montparnasse, the *crime* represented by the prostitutes and the pimps of the avenue du Maine goes hand in hand with the *plaisir* of a burgeoning entertainment industry. The rue de la Gaîté, already a centre of *guinguettes* in the early nineteenth century, saw a development throughout the century of popular theatres, such as the Gaité-Montparnasse, and, in the twentieth century, the Théâtre Montparnasse of the celebrated director Gaston Baty. At the same time, the *quartier* witnessed the growth of cinema, notably with the Pathé Cinema in the rue de la

Gaîté, though on nothing like the same scale as in Montmartre or on the Grands Boulevards.[18] What is important about this aspect of the early development of Montparnasse is that it not only illustrates the ability of the main arteries, the former 'boulevards militaires', to develop a thriving context for popular culture,[19] but that it establishes the district as a significant 'quartier d'acculturation du Paris prolétarien' (a district of cultural adaptation for working-class Paris),[20] and one that serves as an 'intermediary stage between local centres and . . . the centre of the capital'.[21] In other words, within the context of the city as a whole and its overall identity, the cultural activity of individual and discrete areas can, given the right circumstances, radiate out and inform the life of the larger organism. What begins as a localized form of entertainment becomes an indispensible facility for the city as a whole, and a defining characteristic of it. In the case of Montparnasse, this fragile connection with the city is ensured both by the establishment of the Gare Montparnasse, a major mainline station linking the capital with the west, and in particular Brittany, which in its turn leads to the establishment of a Breton culture in the *quartier*, and a significant suburban commuter station, and the growth of the Cimetière du Montparnasse as one of the two major Parisian cemeteries, along with the Cimetière du Nord in Montmartre. With the railway station and the cemetery, Montparnasse achieves a role within the life of the capital that goes beyond its specific operation as a *quartier*, which, in its turn, is reflected in the growth of cheap hotels, cheap restaurants and, in particular, the cafés that will become the centres for the artistic activity of the immediate pre-war and post-war periods. The guidebooks of the early 1900s show Montparnasse as a significant, but by no means dominant, *lieu de plaisir* in comparison with the Grands Boulevards and Montmartre.[22]

If the 1920s constitute the high point of the success of Montparnasse as a national and international centre of high culture, the seeds of this success were already present in the pre-war era. There was a close and often ambiguous relationship between pre-war Montparnasse and the Latin Quarter of the capital's student population, to the extent that, as we have seen, some guidebooks go so far as to confuse the geographical limits of each district. What is important, however, is that not only is there a significant overspill of student culture into the popular culture of pre-war Montparnasse, particularly on borderline territory such as the Bal Bullier, but also implantation of intellectual activity, more closely associated with the cafés on the Boulevard Saint-Germain, but extending in the 1900s to establishments such as the Closerie des Lilas. Once again, the importance of the centres of higher education, with their student population and intellectual publishing activity, proves to have been an important factor in both the development and the evolution of cultural centres.

At the same time, Montparnasse before World War One had been a major centre of attraction for emigrés, artistic or political, often from Eastern Europe. William Wiser records, somewhat luridly, that

Before the Russian Revolution the favourite café of Menshevik and Bolshevik conspirators had been *La Coupole*, on the boulevard Montparnasse at place Vavin. Political outcasts like the fiery intellectual Leon Trotsky sat at its table fanning the hopes of fellow exiles, while Lenin, awaiting his hour, preferred to play chess at a corner table.[23]

More important than the political exiles, however, was the artistic influx from Eastern Europe into Montparnasse. Again, Wiser comments:

Refugees of one diaspora or another – Lipchitz, Zadkine, Soutine, Chagall – followed their troubled paths to the new ghettos of Montparnasse. The displaced painters and sculptors sought light and cheap living space: at *La Ruche* on the rue Dantzig they found both, and the reassuring company of fellow artists of predominantly Eastern European origin.[24]

'La Ruche' (the beehive) was an artists' colony established on wasteland near the slaughterhouses of Vaugirard by an amateur sculptor Alfred Boucher. Following the Exposition Universelle of 1900 he assembled a disparate collection of redundant pavilions to be used as studios and living accommodation, the most remarkable of which was Eiffel's circular iron and glass *halle aux vins* (wine market) which, once transported to the rue Dantzig and with its hive-like shape, gave the name La Ruche to the whole development. What is important about La Ruche, apart from its intrinsic artistic innovation, is that it consolidated the growth of artists' studios in the 13th and 14th arrondissements and heralded the arrival of the avant-garde from Montmartre.

In fact, it was the decline of Montmartre as a centre of the literary and artistic avant-garde that propelled Montparnasse into international prominence at the end of World War One. In this way, it was the beneficiary of a cultural ebb and flow throughout the capital in the course of the nineteenth and twentieth centuries, from the Latin Quarter of Murger's *Scènes de la vie de bohème* in the Second Empire to the Montmartre of the Belle Epoque and back to the Left Bank just before and during World War One. Inevitably, it was to fall victim to just such an evolutionary process as the Parisian cultural centre of gravity shifted in the 1930s back to the Latin Quarter and Saint-Germain-des-Prés.

As we have seen, the avant-garde had emigrated to Montmartre at the turn of .˙.ⁿ century, attracted by the village-like atmosphere of the Butte, its cheap lodgings and restaurants, its studio space and the vibrant social and artistic life of the Place Clichy and the Boulevard de la Chapelle. However, by the outbreak of war, most of the major figures of this avant-garde had abandoned the Butte, either because, like Picasso or Kies van Dongen, they were now rich enough to escape the squalor and hardship of the Bateau Lavoir, or, paradoxically, as in the case of Modigliani, because they could no longer afford to live in a district that was gradually gentrifying. For whatever reason, there was also a prevailing sense that Montmartre had outlived its usefulness as a centre of artistic innovation. As one of its most faithful chroniclers, Francis Carco, recalls:

Mac Orlan had got married; he had left Montmartre and most of our friends, profiting from the welcome extended them by Gus Bofa at *Le Sourire*, went less to the Butte and more to the Boulevards and newspaper offices. We only saw Roland Dorgelès in a taxi. . . . It was the end.[25]†

And he concludes: 'Montmartre n'était plus' (Montmartre was no more).[26]

Significantly, avant-garde Montparnasse was the creation of the great artistic impresario of Montmartre, the poet Guillaume Apollinaire, who had already launched Cubism in the Montmartre of the Belle Epoque. As Carco comments:

Montparnasse was created by Apollinaire, who took us to see Baty (at the Théatre Montparnasse) and was treated royally everywhere. His presence in this district, where the mixture of races provokes disquieting undercurrents, created a kind of 'union sacrée' of the arts, fixing it and crystalising it. . . . As a neighbour of his cousin Paul Fort, whose domaine comprised the Boul'Mich', Bullier, the Luxembourg Gardens and the Closerie des Lilas, he traced the limits of his fief and, from the café of the Deux-Magots. . . , extended it along the rue de Rennes and the boulevard Raspail until it crossed the boulevard du Montparnasse. He even sent out scouts as far as Plaisance, where Douanier Rousseau lived, and for a time established his headquarters in the pleasant rue de la Gaîté.[27]‡

†*Or Mac Orlan s'était marié; il avait quitté Montmartre et la plupart des camarades, profitant de l'accueil que leur faisait au* Sourire *Gus Bofa, fréquentaient moins la Butte que les Boulevards et les salles de rédaction. On ne vit plus Roland Dorgelès qu'en taxi. . . . C'était la fin.*
‡*Montparnasse est né d'Apollinaire qui, le premier, nous entraînant chez Baty, se vit partout fêté. Sa présence en ces lieux où le mélange des races provoque un inquiétant remous, créait comme une union sacrée des arts, la fixait, la cristallisait. . . . Avant qu'on n'y prît garde, voisinant avec son cousin Paul Fort, dont le domaine comprend le long 'Boul'Mich', Bullier, le Luxembourg et la Closerie des Lilas, il traçait les limites de son fief et, du café des Deux-Magots . . . l'étendait par la rue de rennes et le Boulevard Raspail*

In the wake of Apollinaire, the poets and the painters abandoned Montmartre and joined the nascent artistic community created already by such developments as La Ruche. Most, like the painter Modigliani, who lived in the rue Campagne-Première, had left a Montmartre that they associated only with poverty for an area that offered ample studio space in the form of artisanal workshops, cheap accommodation and the abundant café and restaurant life associated, among other things, with *quartiers* surrounding busy railway stations. In the inter-war years, Montparnasse was home to Chagall, Modigliani, Kisling, Foujita, Friesz, Matisse, Picasso, Pascin, Miro, Max Ernst, Giacometti and Kandinski.[28] They congregated in the busy brasseries on the Place Vavin, and even the poorest of them could afford to eat regularly at Marie Wassilieff's *cantine* on the avenue du Maine.[29]

It was this combination of inexpensive lodgings and food, an artistic community and a healthy popular cultural life centred on dance that attracted émigrés, not merely from Eastern Europe but also, and in far greater numbers, from the United States. Essentially, American visitors fell into one of only two categories: the rich, who congregated in the western 8th and 16th arrondissements, and the bohemian poor who clustered along the Left Bank and, in particular, in Montparnasse. As Hemingway recalls, what attracted him to establishments like the Dôme or the Coupole was that 'the big cafés were cheap then, too, and all had good beer and the aperitifs cost reasonable prices that were clearly marked on the saucers that were served to them'.[30] With the exchange rate in the 1920s in the dollar's favour, even the poorest American visitors could afford an extended stay in Montparnasse, especially if, like the Hemingways, they lived in a 'flat over the sawmill at 113 rue Notre-Dame-des-Champs'.[31]

Where both categories of American could come together, however – the rich and the poor – was in the dance culture of establishments like the Coupole, which operated as both a brasserie and dance-hall, and served not merely as the stage for some of the oddest excesses of the 'Crazy Years' but also as the indispensable meeting-point between respectability and bohemianism that defines any major cultural centre. As Clive Holland comments on the Dôme:

---

jusqu'au croisement de ce boulevard avec celui du Montparnasse. N'avait-il point déjà poussé ses éclaireurs vers Plaisance où habitait le douanier Rousseau, et fait durant un temps son quartier général de l'aimable rue de la Gaîté?

If one wishes to gain a little insight into the Bohemia of today one cannot do better than to spend an evening at the *Café du Dôme*. . . . The *Dôme* is the café of all others, perhaps, to which most celebrities visiting Paris seem to gravitate sooner or later. . . . One meets at the *Dôme* many curious types who are doing strange things for a living. On one occasion a man who has trundled a wheelbarrow from Moscow to Paris en route for Madrid . . .[32]

In the end, it was this kind of tourism that did for the artistic community of Montparnasse, as it had done to a large extent for that of Montmartre and as it was to do in the late 1940s for Saint-Germain-des-Prés. Wiser records that by the end of the 1920s the 'overcrowded *terrasses* on the Place Vavin were less a sanctuary of the arts than a tourist stop for new hordes of poseurs',[33] and cites the journalist Harold Stearns denouncing the Sélect as 'a seething madhouse of drunks, semi-drunks, quarter-drunks and sober maniacs'.[34] The delicate ecology of a *lieu de loisirs* depends on relative cheapness as it does on the even interaction between differing social categories. It is this that fosters the artistic activity. But when that balance shifts in favour of the affluent outsider, with the inevitable economic consequences, the artistic activity is bound to move on.

At the same time, the rapid decline of Montparnasse can be attributed to more precise causes. The Wall Street Crash of 1929 and the subsequent Depression cut off the flow of American would-be bohemians. The worsening international situation in the 1930s, together with the rise of the Front Populaire government in France, restored to the French intellectual a prominence based on the written word and sustained polemic. The new culture of 1930s Paris was literary, and it gravitated to the University district and the publishers' *quartier* of Saint-Germain-des-Prés. As such, it contrasted strongly with the painter-dominated culture of the avant-garde movements that occupied Montmartre and Montparnasse, and no longer had any need for its studios or its frivolities. Montparnasse returned in large measure to the role of subsidiary pleasure centre it had played before World War One and which it still continues to exercise.

The cultural centre of gravity moved on – in fact, it moved back: to the Latin Quarter and Saint-Germain-des-Prés. Herbert Lottman's lengthy study of the 'Rive Gauche' emphasizes its importance as a centre of left-wing, committed, intellectual culture throughout the inter-war years and the immediate post-war period, with the assembly hall of the Mutualité at the eastern end of the Boulevard Saint-Germain as one of its key loci. It is important to add, however, that even during Montmartre's bohemian phase it retained a role as a centre of non-aligned poetic activity, with figures such as Apollinaire, Paul Fort and Léon-Paul Fargue, and that, during the inter-war years and beyond, it reflected *engagé* (committed) intellectual life at both poles of the political spectrum. In the 1930s, while the Groupe Octobre, led by the poet Jacques Prévert, and fellow-travelling intellectuals colonized the Café de Flore and the Deux Magots, the Brasserie Lipp on the opposite side of the Boulevard Saint-Germain was the headquarters of Action Française intellectuals, such as Thierry Maulnier's team of the review *Combat*.[35] More than Lottman acknowledges, the Left Bank was evenly split during the inter-war years and beyond, between intellectuals of the right and the left, and the division of cultural space between left and right in Saint-Germain-des-Prés reflected that balance of political forces.

In the years immediately following the Liberation, Saint-Germain-des-Prés came to constitute a major cultural centre in Paris, perhaps the last of its kind, but a centre that reunited both left- and right-wing intellectual activity and high and popular culture. Of those on the left, the Existentialists occupied the Flore and the Deux Magots, whilst dissident Communists, such as Marguerite Duras, Edgar Morin and Dionys Mascolo, constituted the Groupe de la rue Saint-Benoît. The right continued to occupy the Brasserie Lipp, while also transforming the Rhumerie Martiniquaise, between the Carrefour Saint-Germain and the Place de l'Odéon, into a major cultural centre, in which the 'Hussards', particularly Nimier and Blondin, rubbed shoulders with left-wing libertarians such as Boris Vian. At the same time, with Vian fulfilling the same role as that played by Apollinaire in an earlier avant-garde, Saint-Germain-des-Prés became the centre of popular cultural activity, strongly allied to a youth culture, through the importation of American dance and, particularly, both New Orleans and be-bop jazz. This was accompanied by a resurgence of cabaret performance, through Vian himself, the avant-garde group Les Frères Jacques, closely allied to the ex-Surrealist novelist Raymond Queneau, and the growth of 'la chanson Rive-Gauche' (Left Bank song), represented by Juliette Gréco, Mouloudji, Léo Ferré and Georges Brassens, whose repertory, often through the mediation of the composer Joseph Kosma, brought high cultural figures such as Aragon, Prévert, Queneau and even Sartre, into a broader cultural domain. The very ambiguity in the term Existentialism, which denotes a technical philosophy, a literary mode, a moral code and an unrestrained exuberant lifestyle, encompasses the blend between high culture, bohemianism and popular culture that characterized the cultures of Montmartre and the Montparnasse and which was soon, probably definitively, to disappear.

For a brief period, from 1945 to 1952, Saint-Germain-des-Prés assumed the mantle of Montmartre in the Belle Epoque and Montparnasse in the 1920s, as a conjuncture of vibrant popular and high culture. Indeed, it almost consciously imitated the *années folles* of the 1920s in the second post-war period, with the same blend of high cultural literary, artistic and intellectual activity and a more generally accessible popular and youth culture based on music, dance, café society and American cultural imports. It was for this reason that Saint-Germain-des-Prés fell victim to the same commercialization of cultural space that destroyed Montmartre, marginalizing its remaining writers and painters, and Montparnasse. In particular the growth of tourism, especially American tourism, drove Sartre and his friends from the Flore and the Deux Magots to the less central Bar de l'Hôtel du Pont Royal. This cycle of bohemianism, pleasure and tourism provides a powerful cultural dynamic in the city, but one which is ultimately fatal to cultural practitioners.

The shifts of cultural space in twentieth-century Paris demonstrate a number of key factors: the alliance between urban geography and cultural activity; the importance of the growth of *lieux de plaisir* for the fostering of bohemianism and high cultural activity, in particular the crucial role played by the Mur des Fermiers Généraux and the colonization of the *Communes limitrophes*; and the fragility of urban cultural centres, dependant on both urban and cultural evolution. What the cultural history of Paris illustrates is the close relationship between student culture, the University, popular culture, bohemianism and high culture, all held together in a complex and delicate ecology and highly vulnerable to urban trends beyond their control. Lottman's own conclusion, that the 'Rive Gauche' vanished as a cultural force with the widespread use of the telephone, to which might be added the development of the mass-media, especially television, coincides with more general sociological trends: the increasing professionalization of the intellectual class, recuperated by the university system, and the progressive demarcation between an industrialized popular culture and the avant-garde, led to a collapse of the traditional bohemianism of the nineteenth and early twentieth centuries. The motor force of that bohemianism – the plastic arts – fragmented, at least geographically, and the new cultural industries, particularly the cinema and the mass media, were less conducive to and less dependant on any particular urban locus. For the first half of the century, however, the growth of the city in its most concrete sense was also the growth of its culture.

3
Vénus noire: Josephine Baker and the Parisian Music-hall

JON KEAR

Josephine Baker brought with her presence the glimpse of another world. As she danced quivering with intensity, the entire room felt the raw force of her passion, the excitement of her rhythm. She was eroticism personified. The simplicity of her emotions, her savage grace, were deeply moving . . . then from her supple throat came a song, crystal clear at first, then with a hoarseness that caught at the heart. ANDRÉ DAVEN

In the mid-1920s and 1930s Josephine Baker became a major celebrity in Paris and arguably the most famous American star in Europe. In the course of her career she was to be transformed from a fairly raw, exuberant and frenetic black dancer, whose dancing was perceived to be a pure instinctive expression of her ethnicity, into a glamorous popular French jazz singer. In this essay I want to examine a cluster of themes concerning that fraught passage of rights and the presentation of Baker within Paris; to probe what accounted for her popularity and her controversy; to articulate Baker's fame within the historical context of issues and debates within Parisian culture and specifically within the context of the Parisian music-hall tradition. In so doing what I am primarily interested in is elaborating the terms in which Baker was made into a sign of 'otherness', a reciprocally defining sign that opened up a passage into the imaginary for her urban audience.

Though she was to achieve notoriety in Paris for her 'Primitive African' dancing, Baker was in fact an illegitimate 'half-negro' born into the slums of St Louis, Missouri, in 1906.[1] She grew up in impoverished circumstances in a racially segregated America, which witnessed violent race riots in east St Louis in 1917. Eager to escape, at the age of seventeen Baker enrolled in the chorus line of a travelling troupe with the jazz and blues singer Bessie Smith, and later that same year began dancing in the chorus of a modest but popular black vaudeville revue called *Shuffle Along* run by the black theatre entrepreneurs Sissle and Blake.[2] It was here that she began to attract attention for gauche but versatile dancing

Josephine Baker performing in *Un Vent de Folie* at
the Folies-Bergère, 1927.

and comedy improvisation. After the success of *Shuffle Along* she appeared primarily as a comedienne and dancer on Broadway in 'blackface' as one of the principals in Sissle and Blake's next production, the *Chocolate Dandies* revue.[3] Having acquired a growing reputation on Broadway as an all-round performer, Baker was transplanted to Paris in 1925 when she was recruited by Carol Dudley as a dancer for *La Revue Nègre*, an all-black revue booked to appear at the revamped Théâtre des Champs-Elysées.[4]

The importation of a 'down-market' all-black revue was part of the new strategy of theatre manager Rolf de Maré to reverse the post-war slump in theatre attendance, and was by no means an uncontroversial move, apparently dividing the management.[5] The theatre's elegant facade, decorated with bas-reliefs of *Apollo and the Muses* by Emile Antoine Bourdelle and its interior murals of *Isadora Duncan* by Maurice Denis, declared a neo-traditionalist allegiance to classicism, as critics of the revue noted. The idea of presenting an all-black revue was probably prompted by the success of Arthur Lyons's *Chocolate Kiddies*, a black jazz revue that ran successfully in Berlin for two years, and also by the success of *Showboat*, which had been presented in Paris some years earlier. The idea to stage the show, however, is usually credited to the Cubist Fernand Léger, whose African-inspired ballet *La Création du Monde*, a musical adaptation of Cendrars's *Anthologie Nègre*, had been staged by Rolf de Maré's ballet company, the Ballet Suédois.

An interest in black cultural forms had gradually developed in Parisian culture facilitated by the ethnographic Museum of Mankind and the international expositions held in Paris, which served as storehouses and showcases of non-Western cultural artefacts acquired through colonialism. The initial wave of interest in black culture was largely allied to the burgeoning connoisseurship of the panoply of forms that defined the *naïf* and *primitif*, the popular and the vulgar. Through the agency of competing formations of European avant-gardes, African masks and sculpture were integrated into a Nietzschean aesthetic of 'Dionysian barbarism'. Abstracted from their original cultural functionalism, these forms served as vehicles through which an oppositional aesthetic was constructed: an atavistic aesthetic of iconoclasm, vitalism and cultural renewal.[6] African artefacts were used as models to redefine and extend the language of modern art, their conventions being quickly absorbed within the formal innovations of early Modernism.

The second wave of interest in black culture was more diffuse and spurred by both the aesthetics of simultaneity and the increasing appetite for spectacles of the exotic. The staging of Roussell's *Impressions d'Afrique* in 1911, Tzara's *Le Cœur à Barbe* and the increasing collaborative ventures during the 1920s between avant-garde musicians, writers and painters within the milieu of the theatre (such as the aforementioned *La Création du monde* and Cocteau and Milhaud's *Le Boeuf sur le toit*) opened the way for a series of more populist variants.

A crucial component of this second wave was the importation of jazz music and dance into Paris, which gained momentum with the influx of black soldiers into Europe during World War One. Jazz entered the Parisian scene not simply as a specific cultural form but as a *mentalité*. Paul Guillaumin argued that modern man must become like the negro.[7] Cocteau invoked jazz as the soul of the 'Fauve epoch'. As this suggests, the many-faceted Parisian appropriation of black culture was largely ill-defined, African and American forms being conflated as part of the modernist aesthetic of the *L'Orde primitif*. *La Revue Nègre* was conceived to capitalize on these trends, particularly on the increasing popularity of jazz music and dance in Paris, and was timed to coincide with the Exposition des Arts Décoratifs, which in 1925 staged a major display of African culture, an event that initiated its appropriation into the vogue of Art Deco fashion. However, *La Revue Nègre* by all accounts began life as a fairly standard black American gospel and blues revue featuring a cast of 25 black American singers, musicians, comedians and dancers, headed by the blues singer Maud de Forest with songs by the black songwriter Spencer Williams.[8] During rehearsals in Paris the show was totally reworked. The stage managers, Rolf de Maré and André Daven, felt it wasn't sufficiently geared to Parisian tastes. The blues numbers were too spiritual, depressing even. They wanted a carefully choreographed effect of 'raw exuberance', they wanted black American jazz combined with dazzling African-inspired dancing, set against exotic backdrops. The original choreography was considered too tame and precise, dominated by tap and chorus-line dancing. Precision dancing was associated with a European tradition. Black dancers were supposed to be instinctive and rhythmical, agile and dextrous even, but incapable of co-ordinated discipline. Moreover, it wasn't quite exotic enough nor erotic enough for the Parisian music-hall.[9] They decided therefore to spice it up, in effect to 'blacken it up', employing the French choreographer Jacques Charles, a producer known for his fantasy spectacles at the Moulin Rouge, to refashion the show. As a result Maud de Forest was relegated to a relatively minor turn. Baker, whose exuberantly improvised dancing attracted Charles's attention, gradually assumed a more prominent role. She would eventually become not only the focal point of the performance, but the centrepiece of the accompanying publicity too, posing for Paul Colin who made the posters for the show and whose collection *Le Tumulte Noir* would immortalize it and Baker for the Parisian audience.[10] The grotesque quality of these prints of the company with their coarse exaggeration of large red grinning lips, bulging eyes and sparkling teeth as the defining features of the de-personalized Negro physiognomy, predictably reworked the formulaic caricature of blacks that proliferated within Europe from the eighteenth century on. Only gradually over the course of Baker's rising stardom would Colin's imagery of her become more studied and individualized.

Colin's prints weave together a modish fusion of Art Deco and Cubism, and as a result are a good index as to how the revamped show was pitched.[11] The revised *Revue Nègre* opened on 2 October 1925, and the audience on the preview and opening nights included a carefully selected group of tastemakers and trendsetters: luminaries such as the music-hall star Mistinguett, the painters Francis Picabia, Kees Van Dongen, Fernand Léger and Darius Milhaud (the composer of the music for Léger's *Le Creation du monde*). The writers Blaise Cendrars, Jean Cocteau and Janet Flanner, and the important art dealer and African art connoisseur Paul Guillaume, were also in attendance. Their presence helped set the tone for the making of *La Revue Nègre* into an event, and many of them helped publicize and popularize the performance.[12]

The show, unusually, was compèred by a black host and hostess and featured nine tableaux, comprising visual clichés of black life: Mississippi steamboats, Harlem night-clubs, the ghetto, the African jungle and so forth. The popular Mexican caricaturist Miguel Cavarrubias was employed to provide appropriately elaborate set designs. Baker appeared in numerous guises within these tableaux performing the Charleston, the new dance craze, or engaging in comedy routines. Sometimes she combined the two as when she crossed her eyes, bent her knees, put her finger on the top of her head and then spun herself like a top; this gesture became one of her signatures. The highlight of the show, however, was *La Danse Sauvage*, in which Baker and her partner, Joe Alex, dressed in mock-African costume – bare skin and feathers – performed a provocative erotic dance within an exotic jungle set, a

Paul Colin, poster for *La Revue Nègre*, 1925.

fantasy space populated with giant watermelons and more evocative of the Pacific than Africa.

Baker's dancing was an eclectic mix of difficult, unpredictable steps, some improvised and others carefully contrived by her French choreographers. Current dance crazes like the Shimmy and the Charleston were blended with what was described as a gyrating 'stomach dance'. Baker's performance was frenetic – energetically and spasmodically jerking, flinging and spinning herself across the stage in different directions, making contorted hieratic gestures and strange faces, shaking her rear, doing the splits, strutting and pouting in staccato movements. It was this 'savage dance', with its mock-Africana and Baker's willingness to appear semi-naked, that propelled her from obscurity into the limelight.

The revamped *Revue Nègre* became an immense critical and commer-

Josephine Baker and Joe Alex performing 'La Dance Sauvage' in
La Revue Nègre, 1925.

cial success. Its run at the Champs-Elysées was extended twice and
eventually it moved to the Théâtre de l'Étoile and then went on tour to
Brussels and Berlin. It was duly integrated into the Modernist pantheon.
The painter Jacques-Emile Blanche said it embodied the 'modern spirit',
Léger agreed, and Jane Renouardt called it 'a Cubist dance spectacle'.[13]
The appeal of the show was, however, broader based. The eclectic
tableaux and dancing of *La Revue Nègre* were designed to trigger the pre-
coded tropes of the fantasies of 'otherness' that were the customary trade
of the Parisian music-hall. They opened up the fantasmatic alterity of the
distant exoticized spaces beyond the city's horizons.

The critic Paul Achard, singling out Baker as the star of the show,
wrote:

We don't understand their language, we can't find a way to tie the scenes
together, but everything we've ever read flashes across our enchanted minds:
adventure novels, glimpses of enormous steamboats swallowing up clusters of
Negroes who carry rich burdens, a caterwauling woman in an unknown port,
. . . stories of missionaries and travellers . . . sacred dancers, the Sudan . . .

plantation landscapes, the melancholy songs of Creole nurses, the Negro soul with its animal energy, its childish joys, the sad bygone time of slavery, we had all that listening to the singer with the jungle voice, admiring Louis Douglas's hectic skill, . . . and the pretty coffee-coloured ragamuffin who is the star of the troupe, Joséphine Baker.[14][†]

This strategy of listing was a characteristic of the *Revue*'s reception, as if the diverse tableaux and its palpable discontinuities could only be approached through such critical manoeuvres. In these reviews an eclectic repertory of images is released; a mobile set of signifiers heavily inflected by colonialist fantasies, interweave, merge and disconnect in turn, as the critic ranges back and forth through time and place. There are references to eighteenth-century explorers such as Bougainville and La Péruse or more recent ones like Stanley and Livingstone, references to the Sudan, the Congo and the South Seas filtered through the tropes of the sublime. Yet, it was not simply a space of fantasy that was defined and occupied in these passages, but a space of community and definition. It is the invocation of the 'other' that sanctions Achard's use of the pronoun 'we' that opens the passage.

The specific descriptions of Baker's dancing harked on the animal energy, jungle rhythms and the 'dark gods' of Africa, drawing analogies between the dance and the promise of unrestrained sexual consummation. In 'Danses Nègres' (*L'Art Vivant*, February 1925) André Levinson described Baker's performance in the following terms:

There seemed to emanate from her violently shuddering body, her bold dislocations, her springing movements, a gushing stream of rhythm. It was she who led the spellbound drummer and the fascinated saxophonist in the harsh rhythm of the 'blues'. It was as though the jazz, catching on the wing the vibrations of this body, was interpreting word by word its fantastic monologue. The music is born from the dance, and what a dance! The gyrations of this cynical yet merry mountebank, the good-natured grin on her large mouth, suddenly give way to visions from which good humour is entirely absent. In the short *pas de deux* of the savages, which came as the finale of the *Revue Nègre*,

---

[†]*On ne comprend pas leur langue, on ne cherche pas à relier le fil des scènes, mais c'est toutes nos lectures qui défilent devant notre imagination ravie: romans d'aventures, chromos entretenus où d'énormes paquebots engloutissement des grappes de nègres chargés de riches ballots, une sirène miaulante dans un port inconnu encombré de sacs et d'hommes de couleur, des histoires de missionnaires et de voyageurs . . . les danses sacrées, le Soudan . . . des paysages de plantation, toute la mélancolie des chansons de nourrices créoles, tout l'âme nègre avec ses convulsions animales, ses joies enfantines, la tristesse d'un passé de servitude, nous avons eu tout cela en entendant cette chanteuse à la voix de forêt vierge, en admirant la science trépidante de Douglass . . . et ce joli gavroche café au lait qui est la célébrité de la troupe, Joséphine Baker.*

there was a wild splendour and magnificent animality. Certain of Miss Baker's poses, back arched, haunches protruding, arms entwined and uplifted in a phallic symbol, had the compelling potency of the finest examples of Negro sculpture. The plastic sense of a race of sculptors came to life and the frenzy of African Eros swept over the audience. It was no longer a grotesque dancing girl that stood before them, but the black Venus that haunted Baudelaire.[15]†

This passage covers many of the terms that would continually frame the perception of Baker. It is a list made up of overlapping contradictions as juxtapositions of contrast are left to stand in opposition. There is mapped out here both Eros and innocence, benevolence and threat, the natural body and the representational body; the travesty of the female black body assuming a masculinized 'phallic' form; an African sculpture come to life.[16] All of these terms were essential to illusion staged, and many would persist throughout her career. The last-mentioned idea, a black variant of the Pygmalion myth, would for instance frame the publicity stills of the photographer Madame D'Ora when she portrayed Baker in what have come to be seminal images of the performer. For all the stark simplicity of the photos, both are modelled after primitive artefacts: the portrait was modelled after a Tanagra mask, the nude after a Gauguin statuette.

The more knowing critics recognized that these signs deployed in the representation of Baker were fundamentally located in the 'dark recesses' of French popular culture, situating the fascination of this 'exotic' fantasy of 'otherness' within the tensions and repressions of Parisian metropolitan culture. As one critic noted:

our romanticism is desperate for renewal and escape. But unknown lands are rare. Alas, we can no longer roam over maps of the world with unexplored corners. We have to appease our taste for the unknown by exploring within ourselves the lands we haven't penetrated. We lean on our own unconscious and our dreams. As for reality we like it exotic. These blacks feed our double taste for

---

†*C'est d'elle, de son trémoussement forcené, de ses dislocations téméraires, de ses mouvements 'lancés' qu'émane le rhythme. Elle semble 'dicter' au 'drummer' envouté, au saxophoniste ardemment tendu vers elle, syllabe par syllabe, le monologue fantasque de sons corps en folie. La musique naît de la danse. Et quelle danse! La déhanchement de la bateleuse cynique et bon enfant, le rictus qui fait grimacer la large bouche, font place subitement a des visions dont toute bonhommie est absente. Ce bref pas de deux des 'sauvages' dans le finalé, avec Joé Alex, atteint à une grandeur farouche et une superbe bestialite. Certaine poses de Miss Baker, les reins incurvés, la croupe saillante, les bras entrelacés et éléves en un simulcré phallique, la mimique de sa face, évoquent tous les prestiges de la haute statuaires nègre. Le sens plastique d'une race de sculpteurs et les fureurs de l'Eros africain nous étreignent. Ce n'est plus la 'Dancing-Girl' cocasse que nous croyons voirs: C'est la 'Venus Noire' qui hanta Baudelaire.*

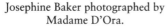

Josephine Baker photographed by
Madame D'Ora.

Josephine Baker photographed by
Madame D'Ora.

exoticism and mystery . . . we are charmed and upset by them, and most satisfied when they mix something upsetting in with their enchantments.[17][†]

Yet, this put the matter too lightly, for Baker's performances became a key reference point in a set of highly charged racial debates within Paris about the evolving direction of urban mass society. Her performances, as Phyllis Rose has remarked, acted like a litmus test for racial attitudes.[18] Robert de Flers, a member of the French Academy and reviewer for *Le Figaro*, described the show as the 'most direct assault ever perpetrated on French taste' and complained that this 'lamentable transatlantic exhibitionism makes us revert to the ape in less time than it took us to evolve

†*Notre romantisme d'aujourd'hui est avide comme l'ancien, de renouvellement et d'évasion. Mais les terres inconnues sont rares: nous n'en sommes plus, hélas! à rêver sur des mappemondes inachevées! Notre goût de l'inconnu, nous l'apraisons donc en cherchant en nous-même les terrains ou nous n'avons pas pénétré. Nous nous perchons curieusement sur notre inconscient et sur nos rêves, et pour ce qui est du réel, nous nous tourons vers l'exoticisme avec délices. Or ces etranges nègres flattent en nous notre double goût de l'exotisme et du mystère. . . . Nous les regardons, inquiets et charmés et nous sommes plus satisfaits quand ils mêle un peu d'inquiétude à nos enchantements. (C'est un spectacle auquel notre civilisation ni notre n'on rien à gagner, mais il est bien captivant.)*

from it'.[19]† A stream of racist literature popularized the idea that the dominance of Western civilization was imperilled, or drawing to a close.[20] This had ironically occurred, so it was argued, through the contamination of true indigenous French culture by alien cultures that France had been brought into contact with in its imperial mission to civilize and colonize non-Western countries. The argument about cultural contamination was interwoven with other longstanding discontents about the 'social and cultural dishevelment' that had occurred under the Republic. The French nation, it was argued, had been polluted and weakened through environmental hazards associated with the city, sexual contact across class lines and by interbreeding with other nations and 'inferior' races. For some the perceived process of decline was an inevitable part of the evolutionary cycle, even part of a process of cultural renewal, but the more zealous French patriots spoke apocalyptically of the approaching war of races or the eclipse of the West.

From the white supremacist perspective, European enthusiasm for black culture was symptomatic of the onset of a period of decadence and degeneration – a willed return to a lower form of life. To support this claim they drew on scientific treatises on physiology and anthropology. The objectification of the black body through the systems of statistical measurement in social anthropology consigned it to the lowest rung of the evolutionary ladder. Polygenetic evolutionary theory insisted on a separate line of white evolution. The notion of the purity of the race depended also on distinguishing its line of cultural evolution and the cultural forms appropriate to it from those indigenous to other cultures.

As Petrine Archer-Straw has argued, it was above all jazz dance that posed the most disconcerting spectacle.[21] The emulation of black jazz dancing was seen as posing a greater threat to Western civilization than jazz music, which could be contemplated abstractly and appropriated within Western forms, while dance involved imitation and the simulation of sexual intimacy. Black dance was perceived to be saturated with intoxication, frenzy, delirium and unbridled sensuality. For many critics the taste for black dancing was symptomatic of the anarchy and social dishevelment they felt pervaded contemporary French culture. André Levinson – the same critic who had praised Baker's performances –

---

†Il représente, en effet, l'offense la plus directe qu'ait jamais reçu le goût français. . . . Mais encore faut-il qu'il s'agisse de spectacles relevant d'un art quelconque et non point, comme il advient pour la Revue Nègre, d'un lamentable exhibitionisme transatlantique qui semble nous faire remonter au singe en beaucoup moins de temps que nous n'avons mis à en descendre.

lamented the dispiriting and corrupting influence of what he saw as the black jazz contagion and spoke of 'European idlers' who 'passively give themselves up to the enjoyment of the Negro dance without setting up any barriers to its atavistic, demoralising appeal'.[22]

The notion of degeneracy associated with the black race and its cultural forms heightened its appeal for many. Yet, whether valued as primeval and vigorous and capable of regenerating all aspects of a depleted Western civilization or as the sign of degeneration, the assessment of black culture rarely escaped being conscripted into this de-evolutionary debate. Hence the understanding of black culture was wholly circumscribed by its instrumentality for a Western system of values.

La Revue Nègre saw Baker acclaimed as a new star attraction in Paris, and she was quickly signed up to appear in a major new revue at the Folies-Bergère, with songs commissioned from Irving Berlin among others.[23] Baker's appearances at the Folies-Bergère marked a significant transition in her career. It was here that the characteristic trademarks of her performance and public persona were selectively redefined, the management drawing on components of her act in *La Revue Nègre*, but honing and crucially adjusting them to fit into the kind of entertainments the Folies provided. Yet, what the Folies-Bergère provided was in significant respects itself undergoing a critical transition: the Folies-Bergère was being redefined within the changing economic relations of the music-hall.

From the time of its transformation into an up-market musical hall under the management of Sari in the 1870s, the Folies-Bergère had specialized in the production of exotic orientalist kitsch, glamour and the plain bizarre. The acts that appeared there conformed to the standard fare of the music-hall, a diverse mixture ranging from vaudeville song and dance artistes to circus entertainers.[24] After Sari's death, following shortly after an abortive attempt to turn the Folies into a classical music theatre, The Folies-Bergère was taken over by the Allemands, who also ran the theatre La Scala.[25] Under their management it reverted back to being a musical hall, and under the directorship of Edouard Marchand introduced chorus girls and presented its first full-scale revues. Soon after it acquired its present name – La Revue des Folies-Bergère. This signalled a gradual shift from individual variety acts and touring companies to fully integrated and choreographed shows on the model of the better class of American burlesque revues featuring a selection of stars with lavish sets.

The Folies-Bergère produced popular culture for a bourgeois and haute bourgeois crowd that comprised tourists and the Parisian general public, dilettantes and cultural aficionados. Cultural sites like the music-hall, the circus and the night-club were to form an integral part of the iconography of early Modernism. Music-hall, which was structured discontinuously in terms of the succession from act to act – 'plotless drama' as e.e. cummings put it – was seen as a vibrant and exemplary modern form.[26] Hence there was no shortage of literary and artistic representations of the Folies-Bergère, nor was it neglected by the press. The Folies-Bergère had become a component part of the mythical image repertory of the alluring hedonistic pleasures of urban Modernity, embodying the intriguing ambiguities and superficialities of the pageant of modern life.

On stage, the Folies increasingly provided an eclectic spectacle renowned for its exotic acts from four continents. Like the international expositions it was part of the function of the music-hall to provide an image of Paris as an internationalist and multi-dimensional world; the expositions provided the economic and anthropological spectacle, the music-hall its fantasy equivalent, though in practice the two worlds blurred. In his book on music-hall written in the 1920s, Louis Léon-Martin claimed that

The whole world is at our disposal: Hawaii with its melancholy guitarists, the Orient . . ., America with its eccentrics, its girls and its dancers, India with its charmers and musicians. The limits of the possible are pushed back.[27†]

Off-stage, the spectacle centred on the promenoir where prostitutes notoriously practiced their trade. That too had become part of the allure of the reputation of the Folies-Bergère, part of its 'permitted disorder' and savour, though after a series of violent incidents the promenoir was eventually monitored and regulated. The ending of the sanctioning of this particular spectacle of sex was met with the shifting and intensification of the focus of sexual intrigue back onto the stage. Most top acts were now female, and the spectacle of the nude female on stage became an integral part of what the Folies-Bergère presented. Prior to 1907 the economy of eroticism had largely centred on equivocation, on the grey areas between seeing and knowing, on the gaps between garments, of skin-coloured outfits, on fetish, on provocative language and gestures. Masquerade and travesty had been staple elements of the ambiguities it exploited.

†*Le monde entier est à notre disposition: Hawaï avec ses guitaristes nostalgiques, l'Orient . . ., America avec ses excentriques, ses girls et ses danseurs, l'Inde avec ses charmeurs et ses mages, que sais-je? Les limites du possible sont naturellement reculées. Nous nous échappons dans le temps et dans l'espace.*

Increasingly, though, the 'artful' presentation of the disrobed body would be the centrepiece of what the Folies-Bergère offered its audience, the nude review gradually substituting ostentatiousness, glamour and the burlesque for the topical satire and verbal repartee that had previously played an important role within the music-hall.[28] Moreover, the 'nude review' represented a solution to the severe economic problems the Folies-Bergère faced. With one star per revue, the Folies-Bergère could cut overheads and build the show around one figure carefully presented with lavish sets. Flesh took the place reserved for the costly panoply of stars and became the main attraction. This confirmed a trend toward an accentuation on the visual that in part reflected a modernist sensibility, but also was part of the reformation of the Folies-Bergère made in order to cater increasingly to an international tourist trade.

From this snapshot we get some idea of what constituted popular culture at the Folies-Bergère and its shifting emphases. In certain respects Baker was easily assimilated into this internationalist spectacle as a variant of its orientalism. Baker represented both an 'exotic curiosity' and a spectacle of the nude – adding a new erotic black element. Though she was not the first black performer to appear at the Folies-Bergère, indeed the revue which preceded her, *Un Soir de Folie*, featured black dancers, she initiated the enduring tradition of the 'Negro' star as the centrepiece of the Folies' spectacle.[29]

Nevertheless, there were important alternations made to Baker's image to prepare her for performing at the Folies-Bergère. Baker's appearance was subtly, but thoroughly, reshaped. Helena Rubinstein's make-up accentuated Baker's eyes with black Kohl, applied a foundation called *Crème Gypsy*, which gave her skin a curiously distinctive ochre-brown colour, accentuated her lips with a dark lipstick to make them fuller, whitened her teeth for contrast, and brilliantined her hair, giving her a kiss curl in the middle of her forehead. The showcasing of Baker also differed from the usual run of nude stars at the Folies-Bergère. Baker's body was not as slender or lithe as were those of the white dancers at the Folies, and hence the presentation of her body was different: not the elegant and dainty movement of the white Folies dancer but the gauche, frenetic and effervescent movements of a woman whose body was produced as an ethnic spectacle.

Baker's debut at the Folies was in a show entitled *La Folie du Jour*, which opened with a series of tableaux about fashion, tourism and Paris shop-windows. This sequence was a reverse strip featuring eight women representing scantily clad Americans who leave more decorously dressed

Poster showing Josephine Baker in *La Folie du Jour*, 1926.

than they were on their arrival. Baker's entrance predictably offered a marked contrast to this image of Paris and its chic urban sophistication. She appeared as Fatou, a native girl in an elaborately simulated jungle set, making her entrance by walking backwards on all fours. In this scene she proceeded to slither along and down the limb of a felled tree and into the life of a white explorer as he lay dreaming beside the riverbank at twilight.[30] Barely clad black male singers sang softly and played the drums. Baker then performed a solo and more explicit variant of the *danse sauvage*, naked except for a banana skirt, whose girdle of phalluses rose suggestively as she wriggled her hips.

The banana outfit was designed especially for her (she apparently greeted it with laughter), but it became a trademark, an almost inescapable signature, taking on various novel inflections in the course of her

Josephine Baker in a performance of *La Folie du Jour*, *c.* 1926.

career. This girdle of phalluses hanging from her waist like so many scalps identified her as sexually active, an aggressively promiscuous vamp, a prey turned hunter, sexually available but with the added *frisson* of the threat of castration. It belonged to the image repertory of exotic licentiousness of the Folies, part of its strange tawdry mixture of clichéd erotica and travesty. Yet its meanings were ethnically coded. It is a myth enshrined and popularized in the fantasies of early travel literature that record the masculine and even animal-like sexual appetite of the native black woman.[31] The black female was defined as primitive both by temperament and physiology and likened to the lower classes of prostitute. When Picasso chose to rework Manet's notorious image of prostitution, *Olympia*, with its candid sexual address, he chose to substitute a black body for the white body of Olympia, as Gauguin had before him.[32]

The emphasis on the rear in Baker's dancing had similar ethnic as well as sexualized encodings. Certainly, it referred to the repertory of pornography, in which the buttocks were a particular focus of fetishization, but it also referred back to the famous public displays of Saartjie Bartmann, the so called 'Hottentot Venus' in the nineteenth century, whose steatopygia (protruding buttocks) was perceived as marking her as atavistic and sexually intensified.[33]

However, this staging of a transgressive libidinal economy of the body had other reference points. It allegorized the imagery of the 'new urban woman' economically and sexually emancipated, an imagery permeated with fantasies of unlicensed sexual availability but there was also ambivalence about the moral and social implications of what 'she' represented. Interestingly, in this regard the sexually ambiguous position Baker occupied generated its own effects of hybridity. When Baker sang she was sometimes positioned as the lover of the city, a role usually reserved as constituting a masculine subject position.[34]

Baker's second sequence in the revue followed an hour later, after a satire on aspiring *nouveau-riche* pretensions in a period set simulating the palace of Versailles. Baker's entry was again contrastingly set in the jungle, this time staging a myth of origination. The sequence opened with the descent of large globe like a great bejewelled egg, covered with flowers, that slowly descended from the top of the theatre onto the stage, whereupon it cracked open to reveal Baker curled up inside dressed in feathers and a grass skirt. She then proceeded to dance – at a frantic pace – the Charleston on a mirror that was lit in such a manner that it refracted and multiplied her shadow across the backdrop and auditorium. In this

Postcard of Josephine Baker performing
at the Folies-Bergère, *c.* 1926.

sketch Baker was pursued by a besotted professor, played by the Folies'
comedy star Dorville, whom she eludes, eventually substituting a black
male dancer in her place – a substitution that the myopic professor
appears not to notice.

The show received a mixed press – e.e. cummings, articulating the
performance through the aesthetics of simultaneity, wrote:

By the laws of its own structure, which are the irrevocable laws of juxtaposition
and contrast, the revue is the use of everything trivial or plural to intensify what is
singular and fundamental. In the case of the *Folies-Bergère*, the revue is a use of
ideas, smells, colours, Irving Berlin, nudes, tactility, collapsible stairs, three
dimensions and fireworks to intensify Mlle Josephine Baker.[35]

This passage captures well the modernity of the spectacle that Baker represented for her avant-garde admirers, but its insights were true only up to a point. For though it was the Folies' function to particularize Baker, establishing signatures for her and thereby fully integrating her into the music-hall star system, her identity was neither as unified nor as regionally situated as were those of her white contemporaries, whose image usually rested on their unique singularity or their belonging to a particular identifiable milieu.[36] Baker's image, for all the limitations of racial determination, was more readily refracted, duplicated and relayed through a shifting chain of significations. It was precisely these refractions that led cummings to become enthralled. His enthusiasm for Baker's performance was met with predictably heated criticism from an anti-pornography group and from those Parisian critics like Gustave Fréjaville who saw themselves as the defenders of traditional and nationalistic values that the music-hall was perceived to embody. 'There's no need to regret that the text of this revue is not always of the highest quality', wrote Fréjaville. 'Its audience hear badly, understands little, and the French ears destined to receive this trash are so few in number that there's little need to worry about them.'[37]

The 1927 Folies show, *Un Vent de Folie*, was to harden opinion. More than ever the Folies-Bergère was given over to a purely visual spectacle with Baker playing a more prominent role – most of the comic repartee was now erased. The performance predictably centred on shifting contexts and dramatic costume changes. Many sequences formulaically revisited those of *La Revue Nègre*, such as one in which she appeared dressed as a 'ragamuffin' on a plantation. In another she danced the Charleston. The banana skirt with its girdle of phalluses appeared again, though in a spangled, more 'hard-edged' variant. The main innovation involved the incorporation of film into Baker's performance. The producer Louis Lemarchand, influenced by Piscator's experiments with multi-media in Berlin, chose to present a sequence in which Baker danced the Black Bottom on stage while a projected film of her doing the same dance appeared behind her.

During her time at the Folies-Bergère, 'Joséphine', as she familiarly began to be called – a presuming form of address which purposely connected her to the 'Impéatrice Joséphine Bonaparte' – became more than a fashionable celebrity, she became a Parisian craze.[38] Her admirers included avant-garde painters and writers, all of whom flocked to see this phenomenon. Eventually, she was to pose for artists such as Giacometti and Picasso, the latter portraying her in 1927 as Nefertiti. Alexander

Calder made wire sculptures in tribute to her. Her particular fame was symptomatic of a more general phenomenon gaining momentum. Black jazz and dance became 'the rage', cultivated in Paris in what was variously described as *nègrophilia, nègropathie* or even '*virus noir*'.[39] 'Le Jazz Il est nous aujourd'hui' (Jazz is us today) wrote André Coeuroy, and one of the introductions to Paul Colin's *Le Tumulte noir* stated that today 'nous nous nègrifiames' (We negrify ourselves).[40]

Yet, Baker's fame also had its own specific momentum, a fame carefully stage-managed by her long-time associate and press agent, the self-styled Count Pepito di Albertini, 'the no account count', as the singer Bricktop called him. The marketing of Baker to her Parisian audience involved the grand-scale mythologizing and commodification of her image. Later, she would state that her chameleon-like personality had been entirely fabricated by her press agents. Albertini worked hard at keeping Baker's name in the press, feeding the gossip columns with stories of her alleged promiscuity and her high society conquests. In one publicity stunt Count Pepito and Baker even staged a fairytale 'Count and the showgirl marriage', which was quickly disclaimed after press investigations revealed not only that his title was phoney, but that Baker was still legally bound to an American she had married in her youth. The more successful strategies of Baker's publicists ran to the endorsement of cosmetics and other commodities. There was a moving Baker doll, slick Bakerfix hair pomade and endorsements of, among other things, 'Water Lilly cream', whose caption declared 'You too can have a body like Joséphine Baker if you use Valaze water-Lilly cream'. There were endorsements for Pernod and even a short-lived Joséphine Baker magazine. In December 1926 Albertini secured the financing for Chez Joséphine – a night-club – on the rue Fontaine in Montmarte, where she appeared nightly after performing at the Folies-Bergère, and it was here she began her singing career. The first of several dubious biographies was published in the following year by Marcel Sauvage, illustrated with 30 of Paul Colin's prints. Moreover, she also secured recording and film contracts that same year, marking her entry into the new technologies of mass media. Undoubtedly, the move into film was intended to broaden the scope of her audience not only within France but across Europe and America. Yet Baker's film career quickly faltered.[41] Her first cinematic début was a remake of the Cinderella story, entitled *La Sirène des tropiques*, directed by Mario Nalpas with a screenplay by the renowned Maurice Dekobra that included suggestions from Albertini. It was a light comedy, geared to display Baker's talents as a dancer and comedienne.

Paul Colin, cover for *Joséphine Baker's Magazine*, 1927.

Baker played an innocent girl from the tropics who goes to Paris; there she dances and is transformed into an elegant woman by means of beautiful clothes. In one scene typical of the film's somewhat parodic theme of racial transmutation, she falls into a flour bin and turns white. The film was an excruciating failure by all accounts, but the story has an uncanny irony to it. For that on-screen transformation rehearsed and parodied the actual off-stage modifications to the image of Baker during the late 1920s and early '30s.

Gradually, as the 1920s drew to a close, the fashion of *nègrophilia* began to subside. Realizing the novelty of her act was wearing thin, Baker began to work toward an alternative image. Yet this was no simple passage of rights such as other Parisian music-hall and cabaret stars were to make.[42] The transformation of Baker's image was inflected by the intensification of xenophobia and racial animosity at the end of the decade. In 1928 Baker temporarily left Paris, embarking on an extensive second European tour, taking in much of Northern and Eastern Europe. On her previous tour, in 1925, prior to her taking up her contract at the Folies-Bergère, she had enjoyed much success, particularly in Berlin, being exposed to the Neue Sachlichkeit.[43] Her return tour three years later was to expose her to the growing tide of nationalism and racism fuelled by economic depression and high unemployment. The tour continually attracted violent protest. First stop was Vienna, where she was heckled and where right-wing groups picketed her performances. In Budapest there were more demonstrations, whilst in Zagreb members of the Croatian clerical party threw ammonia bombs in a demonstration inside the theatre. Some dates were cancelled. The experience left a lasting impression upon her.[44] During this same period Albertini and Baker, in collaboration with the writer Félix de la Camara, wrote *Mon sang dans tes veines* (My blood in your veins), which was published in 1931. This novel is a clumsy meditation on the issue of racial discrimination, and in particular on racial purity. The narrative turns on a car accident that results in the white protagonist, Fred, undergoing a blood transfusion. On discovering that the donor had been Joan, the daughter of his parents' maid, the hapless Fred cancels his marriage to his xenophobic fiancée, who promptly declares him to be a 'black white man'. In taking up the 'blood issue', the novel provided a controversial move. Despite overwhelming scientific evidence to the contrary, purity of blood line was considered to be the somatic determinant of race for white supremacists; adulteration of blood line was frequently cited in accounts of the degeneration of the West.[45] Yet, if the book provided a critique of the mythical premises of racial purity, the taboo of 'miscegenation' remained in place; the anticipated plot development – a romantic union of Fred with Joan – conspicuously fails to materialize. This taboo crucially delimited her short-lived film career. In the film *Zou Zou*, as in *La Sirène des tropiques*, Baker played the romantic lead, but with the debilitating constraint of never winning her man. In Baker's films her reward is invariably Parisianism instead; acceptance as a French citizen and the passage of rights from naïvety to sophistication are constant themes of these films.

In 1929, after an absence of two-and-a-half years, which Baker spent travelling and touring, she returned to Paris. In interviews preceding her performances she emphasized that she considered France to be her country, that she adored France, and even that she was French. More poignantly, she stated that France was the only country where one could live in peace.[46] The Charleston and the banana skirt were to be things of the past. Albertini amplified, that he wanted to show a wholly new Joséphine Baker. No longer would she be a curiosity, but instead would be recognized as an artist; indeed, he predicted she would be a great French star.[47] The transformation from black dancer to Parisian chanteuse was initially staged in a one-off farewell performance before her European tour in 1928. In this performance she first appeared to the audience dancing, dressed in a 'ragamuffin costume'. She then suddenly disappeared from stage re-emerging shortly after in an evening gown to perform a song in French. The transformation was greeted with rapturous applause. Her return to the music-hall some years later was intended to be the consummation of that transformation.

During her time away Baker, under Albertini's guidance, had reworked both her appearance and her act. She had slimmed down from 137 to 115 pounds and altered her costumes and make-up, further lightening the pigmentation of her skin. In addition, she had her voice trained and learned to speak French fluently. If the early Baker represented an ethnographic spectacle, the revelation of raw primitive nature spontaneously and unselfconsciously revealing itself through the frenetic qualities of her dancing, the new Joséphine signified the taming and conversion of that fantasmatic 'otherness' of black nature into white popular culture. Press commentaries that once focused on the elaboration of her savage mystique now praised her professionalism and poise. Baker's act was henceforth primarily a demonstration of that process of conversion or translation. Yet that integration could never be complete, but was residually permeated by the fantasies of 'otherness' that circumscribed her place within the music-hall. Her performance henceforth was the symbolic enactment of a form of ambivalence – a central ambivalence that pertains to the desire inherent in the colonialist, for, as Homi Bhaba has put it, 'a reformed recognisable Other, as a subject of a difference that is almost the same, but not quite'.[48] Indeed, Baker's image was now refracted through a series of contradictory images and subject positions that grew ever more stark.[49] Her return performances were staged at the up-market Casino de Paris, where she temporarily displaced Mistinguett, the long-standing Queen of Parisian music-hall, in a show entitled *Paris qui Remue*. Despite its name, *Paris qui Remue* had little to do with Paris in a literal sense, invoking Martinique, Algeria, Indochina, Equatorial Africa and Madagascar. To promote the show the producer Henri Varna bought a leopard for Baker, to act as both a novel 'fashion accessory' but also as an *alter ego*. It was significantly named Chiquita, despite being male, and sported a diamond collar around its neck. If Baker had chosen the Casino to parade her new-found Parisianism, the Casino in turn had hired Baker for the 1930–31 season to coincide with the colonial Exposition in Paris whose theme that year was the harmonization of the colonies with its French rulers. Baker, whose act now in

Postcard of Josephine Baker in the 1930s.

some respects embodied that theme, was so identified with it that she was initially chosen as Queen of the Exposition until it was pointed out that the United States was not a colony.

This division of belonging that interpolated Baker became integrated into her performance through the song that became her theme song, and which she first performed in her opening season at the Casino de Paris, *J'ai Deux Amours* (I have two loves).

The song was written as part of a sketch called 'Ounawa', which concerns the love of an African girl for a French colonist and her anxieties about the choice she must make between her feelings for him and her fears of having to leave her homeland for Paris in order to be united with him. It thematizes the division between racial and national identity and the lure of Paris with its freedoms and dangers. Yet its original meanings were to be overwritten by the particular resonances it acquired as a personal dramatization of Baker's displacement and desire to be integrated into the Parisian milieu.

J'ai Deux Amours, Mon pays et Paris,
Par eux toujours, Mon cœur est ravi . . .

ran the original lyrics. Baker, however, discreetly substituted the line *Mon pays c'est Paris* for *Mon pays et Paris*. Her countless performances of this song captured on numerous foot-reels, was both an act of compliance to the demands of an audience for whom this song had come to acquire a special meaning and a demand for acknowledgement of her status as 'une Française noir', as she put it; it became in effect appropriated as a symbolic claim to citizenship.[50]

That lure of Paris for Baker as for many black jazz musicians was the lure of freedom from the oppressive racial conditions in America.[51] Yet, this relative freedom and opportunity accorded to black artistes in Paris was contingent and acquired at the cost of another form of bondage – ambivalently placing themselves in the service of mirroring the projected images that Parisian culture offered them. This cracked mirror was not without its own ironies: black artistes cast as the 'other' simultaneously mimed and mocked these differentials, enacting a kind of cleaving of subjectivity, achieving Parisianism through a form of masquerade. To paraphrase Luce Irigaray, Baker, unable to unpick the seams of her disguise, gilded it.[52]

4

'Le Cinéaste de la vie moderne':
Paris as Map in Film, 1924–34

TOM CONLEY

*Le vieux Paris n'est plus (la forme d'une ville
Change plus vite, hélas, que le coeur d'un mortel).*

These monumental lines that end the second stanza of 'Le Cygne' stand, many say, among the first and freshest expressions of the modern city in French literature. In the panel of *Les Fleurs du mal* entitled 'Tableaux Parisiens', Baudelaire displaces an urban vision of a Paris modernized into the immutable tradition of the eclogue and landscape. Ushering into literature a spatial sensibility that lyrical verse had never known, Baudelaire turns industrial zones, squalor, and the rubble of renovation into the raw material of poetry. At the beginning of 'Le Cygne' the voice mourning the changing face of the romantic city has just crossed 'le nouveau Carrousel', a site, adjacent to the Louvre, that had recently been razed in the midst of Haussmann's transformation of Paris. The narrow and jagged streets that spilled onto the Carrousel (rue de Chartres, rue du Doyenné, and the rue des Orties) had been a slum offering refuge to a number of malcontents, like Baudelaire himself, who counted among a number of dissident artists at odds with the politics of the new regime under Napoléon III.

In his rich socio-historical study of the complex mental spaces represented in 'Le Cygne', Richard Terdiman observes that the inhabitants of the quarter between the Louvre and the Tuileries comprised a strange mixture of disaffected individuals who could identify neither with the new political order nor with the labour force that up until then had been subsisting in the same squalor. 'The writers and painters sought to disown their middle-class social origins – but *without* consenting to fusion with the workers whose class figured the only alternative to the increasingly dominant bourgeoisie itself'.[1] With Haussmannization came a city newly sanitized; urban renewal promised the extradition, from the centre of Paris, of *both* the labour class and the dissident intellectuals who lived in familiar worlds of poverty. Writers, artists and poets were doubly deterritorialized by being deported from the welcome space of alienation in and about the older streets between the Louvre and the Tuileries. They were being exiled from the utopian isolation of exile. No wonder, then, that the populace and the poet are collapsed, at the end of the poem, into the memory of *Méduse*-like survivors of a shipwreck, 'matelots oubliés dans une île', floating on the horizon of the modern city. 'Le Cygne', a literal sign of the times, thus registers the advent of the new through the description of an erasure of a space vital to migrant Parisians in the recent past. At the same time, the immutable melancholy of the poem is caught in the bric-a-brac of novelty, of

> *palais neufs, échafaudages, blocs,*
> *Vieux faubourgs. . . ,*

that even makes suspect any feeling of nostalgia that would be felt in the aftershocks of Haussmann's new wrecking of the city.

Baudelaire's memory of the pulverization of both the areas about the Louvre and the Romantic ideolect is recalled here to serve as a threshold for other city views. Later views of Paris use the 'Tableaux Parisiens' to mark contrast with and an affinity for the myth of the beginnings of the new city. If the tradition of the 'new' had begun in 1857, and if Baudelaire and Flaubert conveyed its tensions as no other writers had ever done, it stands to reason that later city views would use 'Le Cygne' and urban planning of the 1850s as points of reference or as an intertextual element in an ongoing dialogue between the vanguard and urban space.

MODERN PARIS THEN AND NOW

With the advent of new media, especially cinema, the composite shape of Baudelaire's lyric – at once a classical poem and a tableau, an image of Paris filtered through the memory of 'Le radeau de la Méduse', a volley of images in random order, a grandiloquent and even pompous, oratorical lyric – has special appeal. As Walter Benjamin intuited in his *Illuminations*, Baudelaire's city poetry was the first to translate the shock and pleasure of exile through an art of collage and scattering of images that betrays a movement of constant deterritorialization. Baudelaire's Paris conveys the experience of disaffected pleasure. The capital of France is never seen from a point of view that overlooks its entirety, that can pretend to map out its surface area, or catch a glimpse of a total order. The city is seen from the eyes of the *flâneur* whose glimpses and flashes in the midst of his movement in the streets turn the distracted and innocuous impressions of everyday life, a continuum of social contradiction, into a 'micropractice', a carefully chaotic register of events that resists the control of urban planners.

Such, it seems, is the appeal of the new cinema of the city in the aftermath of the First World War. Film forcibly refers back to the scenes of city life that Baudelaire had first chronicled, but it uses the new medium further to fracture the spatial experience of the cultural and economic centre of France. The grounding paradox of its innovation may be located in its replication of a space whose control Haussmann had plotted out in the time of Baudelaire, but that was undergoing tremendous alteration with the advent of the automobile filling the boulevards and a growing mass of people circulating in the streets. What Haussmann had intended to produce for logistical ends, in the form of avenues carved out of the city to enhance the rapid deployment of soldiers for counter-insurrectional warfare, was in reality a Paris being redesigned for a technology yet to be invented. On broad boulevards the car could speedily cross the city as carriages had never been able to do. And with increasingly perspectival views of city space being made – boulevards ending at vanishing-points – a different set of pictorial relations of the city could be obtained. For the sake of its self-promotion, cinema could not fail, either, to reproduce touristic views through the display of places and streets that Baedeker and other guides had already memorialized. But at the same time, it was able to offer alternative views of common space through its own means.[2] In its early relation with Paris, cinema thus conveyed an inherited 'diagram' – if Foucault's and Deleuze's vocabulary of co-ordinations of power and space are appropriate – but it was also, if it had been aligned with the political aesthetics that Baudelaire inaugurated and, in turn, with what Benjamin later embodied, a tactical force able to change the diagram by means of its own strategic language.[3]

As film records the city it also changes it as no other medium had formerly been able to do. It inscribes a difference of time into the immutable images of tourism, and it redefines the modernity that began with Baudelaire's vision of the capital city in the age of Napoléon III. Historians inform us that in its silent and early sound phases, cinema told stories, it entertained, it celebrated and explored its own mechanism as an 'image-movement'. But as a mechanism affecting broader processes of acculturation, like urban planning, it reproduces diagrams that fix in place conflicting ideas about the constitution of social space. Just as maps had served as blueprints for establishing and circulating ideas about state and nation since the age of Louis XIV, so too cinema could be used to show, by the stunning virtue of its inherently dialogical process, where and how viewing subjects could discover the place that film was assigning them in the social world of its narrative. No less, as a diagram, it could make spectators infer how they ought to fit in an organization of space *outside* of the theatre in which were projected familiar images of Paris.

No wonder, then, that in the blitz of an illumination, Benjamin would simply imply how cinema acquires a power of control that is not unlike the remapping of Paris that Haussmann had caused. With the new gridding came the bonus of rechannelling the daily lives of most of Paris's citizens. The map of Paris redirected its inhabitants in a way that bears analogy to what corporate heads of automobile and oil companies did to Los Angeles at the end of World War Two. As in urban planning, so too in cinema: the entrepreneurial Louis Feuillade had realized that the serial film, when shot in and about local spaces of the city, could fascinate spectators enough to make them marvel over the invisible conspiracies of evil machinations taking place in spaces that were being afforded new and silent aura in the shots of abandoned streets and empty buildings in the middle years of the First World War.

THE MAPPING OF MIND, SPACE AND AIR

Cinema in the years following World War One put forward in immediate and graphic ways the critical relation that the medium had held (and, no doubt, still holds) with cartography. It displays itself as a series of maps that are read in the light of a propensity to mobilize ideology, in other words to function as blueprints of visible formations that bind subjectivity to a consciousness of space. Instances from three films can be used to launch and test this hypothesis. First, René Clair's *Paris qui dort* (The crazy ray, 1924), a study of the Eiffel Tower and the streets of Paris in daily, accelerated, and arrested time, offers bird's-eye views of the urban space of Paris visualized as a map. Because the narrative tells of time being stopped (thanks to the invention of a global editing machine by a mad Dr Crase), what we see from the top of the Tower is so distant that nothing can be said to move in its spaces. Immobile, the extreme long shots of the city form a backdrop against which a group of characters – Parisians in exile in their own city – while away the endless time they have on their hands. At two points, however, Clair offers a view of the gridded pattern of the iron beams. A black configuration of crisscrossed lines is seen against the sky, in *contrejour*, without any allusion being made to its place in the diegesis. The shot has no point of view that would tell us who

'The abstraction of the latticework of I-beams . . .',
from René Clair's 1924 film *Paris qui dort*.

is really beholding the abstraction. A distracted glance at the shot might indicate that Clair is merely marking an affiliation with the most recent 'poète de la vie moderne', Apollinaire, who only a decade earlier had inaugurated *Alcools* with an invocation to the Tower ('A la fin tu es las de la vie ancienne . . . O bergère . . .'), and to *l'esprit nouveau*, implicitly extending into Clair's cinema an allusion to the *Querelle* that the monument had emblematized throughout much of the twentieth century.[4] The isolation of Clair's view *denies* the literary allusion that would have had a redemptive or mollifying effect. Because the deixis of the montage is so weakened in the film (no point of view or visual origin of the shot can be established in adjoining takes), the spectator can infer that the design intensifies the mapping tendency marked elsewhere in the film. The abstraction of the latticework of I-beams turns into a controlling web in which the players find themselves caught. The purely aesthetic treatment of the tesselations of rivetted steel beams turns into an underdetermined image referring to the graticules and rhumblines of an equipollent grid that, because it is cast about the sky and flows all over the frame, is seen extending about and over the world below. Clair's shots of the iron tracery can also allude to a neo-Cartesian plan of the kind that the author of the *Discours de la méthode* attributed to the fantasy of an 'ingénieur', both a cartographer and an evil genius (*un malin génie*), plotting out an orthogonal plan of a new city on the *tabula rasa* of a plane surface.[5] The grid, which becomes a real subject of *Paris qui dort*, would thus be aligned with the quincunx pattern, known for its use in the conquest of space, that is now gridding the imagination of the spectator who beholds the configuration. The framing of the details of the Eiffel Tower confirm in a glance a consciousness of the power that diagramming and cartographical strategies are imagined being brought to the control of subjectivity.[6] In Clair's film it is all the more efficacious insofar as the director associates the logic of spatial centuriation with the ways that film, as a 'spiritual automaton' in the service of Fascism, will colonize the minds of an infinite number of viewers. The Tower itself plays a role in the strategy of control. One of the opening shots of the film shows the base of the structure through an iris shot. Later, the players circulate in front of it. Its arched form is replicated in the mad Dr Crase's electronic oscillator that sets two buttress-like arcs over a truncated conic section that bears affinity with the Tower itself. The machine that stops and starts movement, the projector, is associated with the Tower.

The cinematic consciousness of the mapping impulse is, as Clair makes the point, paradoxically stronger when it is seen in the most fleeting or distracted ways. Recalling Gilles Deleuze's taxonomy of montage in his book *L'Image-mouvement* (1983), we can note that the French school of poetic realism of the 1930s preferred the long take and the establishing shot of extended depth of field to the alternating patterns or rhythmic creations of the American and Soviet schools. An intensified sensibility of atmosphere, of a molecular (which the philosopher opposes to an earthen or molar) condition of life prevails. French cinema, Deleuze adds, has a special propensity for on-site locales where the volatility of both air and water induce the movement and ambience of change or variation that comes from *within* the environment and not from the hands of the camera operator and the editor. Montage is delicate, it inheres in the mutability of forms themselves and cannot be attributed to a specifically cinematic cause. Just as Lumière's camera captured the delicate motion of a breeze in the trees over the terrace where 'baby is being fed' (in the film of 1895 of that title), montage of the early sound years depends on water and air to promote the illusion of movement and change, the water films of Vigo, Renoir and Grémillon serving to exemplify Deleuze's category.

But at the same time – without detriment to Deleuze's reading – it can

'The Tower . . . through an iris shot'

'The players circulate in front . . .'

'The mad Dr Crase's electronic oscillator . . .',
three stills from René Clair's *Paris qui dort.*

be said that in these films wherever water flows, like a repressed dimension of history, the legacy of cartography returns. The controlling instance tied to the presence of Paris and the effects of thematic cartography are marked in oblique but powerful ways. Two classic films can serve to clarify the point.

THE EIFFEL TOWER DENIED

First, in *L'Atalante* (1934) — a story of life on the barges that work up- and downstream the canals of France linked to the coastal ports — Paris, in the most literal sense of the term, figures as a perspectival object.[7] The newly wed Juliette (Dita Parlo), married to Captain Jean (Jean Dasté), leaves her family and her native rural soil to begin a conjugal life on the water. The marriage seems to be fuelled by her desire to see Paris, the city of her childhood dreams.

In a shot that announces that Paris will soon figure on the horizon of the film, Juliette is seated in a position, before a conic section of a gramophone, assuming the pose of the dog on the RCA logo affixed to the machine. The woman-as-dog listens to a 'master's voice', *off*, that announces the autumn fashions on display in Paris. Mere utterance of the toponym whets an appetite to see how the city will be viewed from the canals and the waters of the Seine. In a shot that follows, we see on the lower part of the frame the deck of the boat, the antithesis of the Eiffel Tower. The monument that would identify the city in a long shot is absent. All we see is a flagpole aiming skyward. Later, when the crew announces their arrival ('On est à Paris! on est à Paris!'), Juliette clambers on desk, a basket of wet laundry in her arms, to behold nothing but the diurnal sky above.

Paris never arrives when it is heralded. The shot in which the knobbed pole juts skyward, responds on the image-track to what is indicated as the coming of Paris on the sound-track. In the disjunction, a paradoxical network of urban shapes is brought forward. In his exhaustive biography of the director Jean Vigo, Jean Salès-Gomez reports that the producer of the film wanted the director to organize the plot around a 360 degree panoramic view of the city taken from the top of the Eiffel Tower.[8] Vigo adamantly refused to include the shot, no doubt because it would have been detached from the material ambience of the film and the points of view of workers toiling in the lower depths of the social pyramid. The director, it appears, wanted to make a film that looks skyward from an immanent perspective, that conveys from the point of view of the labourers the sense of the crushing social contradiction that prevailed during the Great Depression. Here the latent allusion to the Eiffel Tower is concretized in the figure of the pole. The latter reinvents the view that would have been taken from above to what is seen from below. A touristic *point de repère* is denied. And when Paris does appear in the film, it is seen in a sequence spliced between two episodes in the quarters 'le père Jules' (Michel Simon) inhabits, a world of bric-à-brac in which Juliette obtains real pleasure in her frolics with the first mate. The Paris we see between the episodes in the cabin is the canal Saint-Martin, cutting through the 10th arrondissement, that is anything but touristic. The sequence taken in the canal Saint-Martin specifies the labour expended when the men push the barge into the lock and pull it by its mooring rope in the channel below. The site invokes a world of labour and con-tradiction that Boris Kauman's camera catches in the countertilted shots that contrast ripples of water with stone, between which the human subjects are forced to walk along a narrow line. The camera often draws a diagonal line bisecting the frame, of which one half is defined by bricks and pavement, the other by fluid waves. The oneiric world of atmosphere is continually opposed to that of brick, mortar and macadam. The workers' *habitus* is located at the impossible juncture of the two elements, a point that the narrative will later stress when Captain Jean descends a granite sea-wall and runs out to the water where no resolution can be found.

On the other hand, the implicit cartography of the canal indicates more than the fact that the route that takes the *Atalante* out to Le Havre has nothing to do with Paris, Notre-Dame or the Eiffel Tower. The mapping of the Seine yields evidence of a crushing historical contradiction. Jean-Baptiste Colbert, Louis XIV's minister for finance, had developed the canal routes throughout France to foster commercial growth. From 1760, planners from the Ecole des Ponts et Chaussées had mapped out a new hydrography that would, in the name of progress, develop water-ways to democratize the distribution of goods for the nation at large.[9] In *L'Atalante* the lyrical illusion of vapour, steam, fog and shimmering water is seen within a pre-ordained, inherited system of conduits that the film rehistoricizes in terms that run counter to the ideology of progress incrusted in three centuries of canal projects. Rather than aiding the cause of economic progress for the people as a whole, the canals in which the narrative unwinds betray the outlines of a controlling diagram imputed to be the cause for the creation of inhuman zones of rubble, poverty and bleakness of the kind that the camera records so carefully around Corbeil and along the Seine from Paris to Le Havre. Thus, when the final shot of *L'Atalante* – an aerial view at a distance of several hundred feet – shows the boat cutting its way upward on the water, the uncanny, non-established vantage-point of the observer responds to what would have been a panoramic shot of Paris seen from the Eiffel Tower. Now an ichnographic view of the barge, the shot virtually detaches the vessel from the surface of the water, giving the impression both of an apotheosis of both the film and the ship, of the *Atalante* and *L'Atalante*. The vessel chugs skyward (if we behold the image as a scenographic view), detaching itself from the physical ground of the river and shores to which it had been moored. The shot confirms how the boat figures in a visual dialogue of bodily and geographical fragmentation. Throughout the film, amputation and re-attachment of bodily members (notably a pair of hands in a jar of formaldehyde) inspire the narrative, the visual jokes and the painterly origins in Van Gogh's art of the 1880s.[10] But at the same time, the implicit cartography of the film and the history responsible for the creation of a network of waterways bring an urgent and forceful political dimension to the lives of the three principal characters.

Paris, the absent centre of the narrative, is correlative to the sight of *nothing* that the crazed Captain Jean discovers at the end of the voyage, at the moment, after having climbed down the sea-wall, he first runs away from and then, in the next shot, toward the camera, in search of a visible place, a ground of meaning, implied to be in the vanished figure of Juliette. When Paris disappears from the geography of labour in *L'Atalante* it becomes clear that the civil ideology of a national centre and circumference is scattered. The itinerary of the boat is confined to man-made river-beds and canals that indicate a history of social contradiction at the basis of the 'poetic' illusions of mist, fog, vapour and shimmer that fuel the lives of the workers. The most everyday effects of aesthetic beauty in the industrial landscape are scarred by the co-opting of 'progress' that had been at the basis of the network of canals in which the film was made.

With their attention drawn to potamography, the director and camera-man topple the icon of national strength generally represented by maps of rivers and waterways. Since the time of the earliest atlases of France, the cause of the nation had been emblazoned in its rich fluvial commerce heralded through what was projected by a balanced distribution of navigable rivers. The centre of Paris, idealized as a boat cutting the waves on an eternally upstream passage on one of France's greatest rivers, is called into question when the barge *cannot* be seen as an allegory of the city. Though it 'floats but never sinks' (according to the legend in the emblem of *Ivory Soap*), the boat has nothing to do with the centre of the nation, thus refusing the comparison that it continually invites the spectator to make, if indeed the film moves from hearth to home and cosmos in its affective journey.[11] The city is meant to be skirted throughout the film.

BOUDU, 'SAUVÉ DES EAUX', BUT CAUGHT IN TRAFFIC

Paris figures no less evasively in Jean Renoir's *Boudu sauvé des eaux* (1932), in which the presence of the Seine, the inner city, the *quais*, and the Ile-de-la-Cité are clearly marked. Much of the narrative unfolds in Edouard Lestingois's bookshop located on the East Bank, opposite the south-east wall of the Louvre by the northern shore of the Seine. The shop is ostensibly near the Pont des Arts, but from within it looks out on a space that bears resemblance to a perspective from the second floor of the Institut de France. Books and knowledge are connoted by the spatial relation of the Left Bank and its prominent sites facing a museum containing countless treasures of art stolen from the four corners of the world.

Books are taken up in the narrative and citations from them appear everywhere in the dialogue, while pictures and *tableaux vivants*, no less cited, from recent and classical art, comprise much of the image-track. Two literary allusions are outstanding. One is to an elegant copy of Balzac's *La Physiologie du mariage*, and the other to an early edition of Baudelaire's *Les Fleurs du mal*. Before the narrative gets under way, Emma Lestingois asks the maid, Anne-Marie Chloë, if she has packaged the copy of Baudelaire for a client who is expected at the shop. The remark appears innocuous when, after a long duration, a moustached gentleman wearing a bowler hat crosses the street along the *quai*, approaches Boudu, who loiters distractedly in the shop's dooway, puffs smoke from his cigarillo at Lestingois's name painted on the glass panel of the door, and asks, 'Excusez-moi, Monsieur, mais auriez-vous là une édition des *Fleurs du mal* de Baudelaire?' To which the scruffy interlocutor yaps, 'Mais vois-tu pas que c'est une librairie, pas un magasin de fleurs!' The joke is simply too stupid and too laboured to be dismissed with the same quizzical perplexity drawn on the face of the man who asked Boudu for his Baudelaire.

The reference confirms that the film is in dialogue with the first representation of modernity of Paris – the city-poems of *Les Fleurs du mal*. The bric-à-brac, specifically the descriptions of the dust and rubble of the city by the Louvre in the elegy for Andromache, that deplores a space in which accelerated upheaval resists all allegorization, constitutes a more plausible allusion in the greater context of *Boudu*. A distance is marked between the pompous 'modernity' that Baudelaire had described and the compression of automotive effects of the city in 1932.

In this sequence viewers note that the first 'authentic' images of Paris begin from a view of the Louvre behind the sight of a boat chugging upstream, belching black smoke from its single stack. Until that point the narrative had been taking place in Lestingois's bookshop, in which an iron beam divided the space of the frame into two equal units. The smokestack begs the viewer to apprehend a similar division of space, except now the beam is partially vaporized in the black fumes that waft skyward. Like Boudu's cigarillo in the later sequences involving the purchase of *Les Fleurs du mal*, the atmospheric condition of the city is stressed over and above the site itself. The smoke cues the fluid qualities of the air and the river, suggesting that the mercantile activity associated with the Seine is both an industrial nightmare and an ambience where water and movement, far from being co-opted by enterprise, are repressed in the commerce of used art and literature. The critique of progress as a function of river traffic is clear, here spilling into the world of Lestingois as near to the Louvre as real sylvan space is to the eclogues the merchant quotes in front of his mistress.

The film tells us that we are never in a city that can be allegorized in the way that Baudelaire and Balzac had done in their verbal maps of the city for their readers. Boudu commits suicide for a reason that defies explanation. Because he lost his dog? Because he is crushed by the traffic and din of the Quai d'Orsay in a post-Haussmannian world? Or was he merely a moving form that established an interval between a surface of written shapes in motion and a flurry of moving objects that seemed to flatten the hero in the reduced depth of field shown through a telephoto lens? The answer to the question that the narrative poses is no doubt less important than the articulation of a history of city spaces that Renoir locates between nineteenth-century literary sources and the on-location photography of Paris by the Seine.

The site of the film, the *scène* of the Seine, where Lestingois and Boudu meet for the first time, is fugaciously present throughout the film. The hero returns to the water (he follows 'le fil de l'eau', sighs Lestingois with fig-leaves about him, next to his wife and mistress in the penultimate shot of the film), but the water itself, like Paris, seems to be the overriding ocular attraction. When Lestingois scans the river and its environs from his apartment, he seems to see a map taking shape before his eyes. Finding what he desires, he extracts Boudu from a scenography of the modern city. Paris *hic et nunc* becomes the object of the bookseller's telescopic gaze, a Paris vastly different from what he purveys in his second- and thirdhand editions of literary classics.

EPILOGUE

Boudu sauvé des eaux marks a fairly decisive break between two views of Paris. For Renoir, Baudelaire, who had been an official herald of the modern city, now figures as a quaint and antiquarian poet of the cityscape. The film of 1932 indicates that unbeknownst, or despite itself, the seventh art taps into – and brings to a pictural surface – what might be called a 'geographical unconscious'. In the images it offers of a highly local area of the city, *Boudu* maps out an intricate but deeply embedded set of spatial and historical relations. Paris avers to be a place of conflict in which a sense of time and movement, felt to be anachronistic, is designated as a post-Romantic literary heritage. It is displaced by the medium of cinema that records the speed, noise and chaos of a city that is both immobile and in a perpetual rush. Wherever a character goes, he or she encounters an inhabitable situation, whether in the anal passages of the bookshop or in the incontinent circulation along the *quais* by the Seine. The relief from urban pressure that the river would offer is located in the midst of the commercial traffic. Adjacent to the shop but insulated from it, its flow is likened to the very character of the camera (and Boudu, its icon) recording the closed social space of Lestingois's milieu.

Renoir's film effectively complicates (even though it was completed two years before) the social and physical geography of Vigo's *L'Atalante*. In that film Paris figures as a central absence right where, in most maps of the rivers and canals of France, it had marked a central presence. The site is conscientiously denied in order not to bring tourism to its portrayal of social contradiction. In the bargemaster's office (in Le Havre, the infernal heaven and terminus of the itinerary) a worker sighs, speaking to no one, 'nous sommes rien, rien du tout', thus confirming how, in view of the labours of the river sailors, Paris is no different from Corbeil. Like the film itself, the river cannot furnish illusions enough to fuel the everyday lives of labourers who toil under capitalism. Vigo gives us a social map that reaches back to the designs of Colbert but whose contours are heightened by class conflict. In *Paris qui dort* René Clair shows us that cinema itself is a diagram in a Foucauldian sense: the views of Paris in the film are those not of a history of the city but of the ways that filmed representations of its spaces can be deployed for strategic control. A film-map, it offers a glimpse of the city both in and outside of time, a city past and future, arrested and accelerated, but a city subject to forms of control that Baudelaire would never have fathomed.

5

City Space, Mental Space, Poetic Space: Paris in Breton, Benjamin and Réda

MICHAEL SHERINGHAM

The Parisian field to be explored in this essay could be said to enjoy special privileges since it possesses both longevity and the capacity to generate or incorporate immensely varied modes of apprehending and construing the city. It owes this in part to its insistently interrogative and subversive nature, to the way it questions and undermines fixed views and orthodox perspectives, whether literary, sociological or historical, advancing instead the case for indirection or obliquity in the articulation of urban, specifically Parisian reality. This field could be called 'poetic' since a poet, Baudelaire, stands at its fountain-head, and other poets – Nerval, Apollinaire, Breton, Queneau and Réda – are closely associated with it. Yet its vitality has little to do with genre, literary history or literature *tout court*, and its widespread impact and resonances – in philosophy and theory (Benjamin, Lefebvre, Certeau), film (Godard, Rivette), anthropology (Rouch, Augé) – stem less from literary works than from the dissemination of ways of figuring the relationships between the traversal of urban space, the exploration of subjectivity at grips with its external context and the operations of language, in other words for encouraging productive interaction between city, mind, history and text. My discussion will focus principally on the Surrealists (especially Breton), on Benjamin, and on Réda.

Seen from the vantage-point of Apollinaire and Surrealism (this was in effect Benjamin's perspective in the late 1920s) Baudelaire's astonishingly productive engagement with the city, in the 'Tableaux parisiens' of *Les Fleurs du mal*, the prose poems (a genre now customarily associated with urban experience) of *Le Spleen de Paris*, and such essays as 'Le Peintre de la vie moderne' (The painter of modern life), can be seen to have two principal aspects. The first centres on the notion of modernity. Baudelaire's famous review of the Salon of 1846 culminated in an appeal for art to engage with what he called the heroism or the 'epic side' of modern life. Pointing out that each age has its own passions and forms of beauty, and arguing that great art always combines the eternal with the transitory, he urged the artist to recognize that Parisian life offered subjects as grand and poetic as those of antiquity, and that what he called 'le merveilleux' permeated the contemporary urban environment if only one could recognize it.[1] An artist who did recognize this, according to Baudelaire, was Constantin Guys, famous for the rapidity of execution he brought to depictions of contemporary fashions and high society, and Guys became the anonymous subject of a remarkable essay, 'The Painter of Modern Life'. Here Baudelaire celebrates Monsieur G. for the ability to extract the eternal from the transitory, and to isolate the poetic dimension of modernity from the simply modish by dint of a capacity, grounded in an essentially childlike vision, to crystallize on paper fleeting impressions garnered while in the midst of everyday life. Too passionate and obsessional to be a dandy, though possessing some of the dandy's refinement and independence, cerebral, but too enamoured of the visible and the tangible to be a pure philosopher, Baudelaire's ideal artist is a passionate observer and a 'parfait flâneur' who is most at home when out in the street, picking up the electric energy of the crowd but remaining incognito, registering the kaleidoscopic patterns of life in all its grace and detail.[2]

As a prospector of modernity the Baudelairean artist develops the *flâneur's* sense of connoisseurship and curiosity to a pitch of obsession. A little further in this direction lies the hysterical persona of the poet whose exchanges with the city have a more extreme and existential character. In some of the key poems of the 'Tableaux parisiens': 'Le Cygne', 'Les Petites Vieilles', 'Les Sept Vieillards', and many of the prose poems, the city street becomes the stage for an encounter between self and other, individual consciousness and figures who mirror its labyrinthine recesses and perplexities. The desire of the painter of modern life to marry the crowd ('épouser la foule') becomes something more intense, '[an] ineffable orgy, [. . . a] holy prostitution of the soul which gives itself entirely, poetry and charity, to the unforeseen which reveals itself, to the unknown which happens along'.[3][†] Urban space becomes the arena in which the poet can explore the impact of the external world on his own subjectivity, as in 'Les Petites Vieilles' (The little old women), where instead of settling for a single register or perspective the poet shifts alarmingly from one to another, presenting the old women he encounters in his urban prowls now as wholly external paraphernalia of the city

---

†[. . .] *cette ineffable orgie, [. . .] cette sainte prostitution de l'âme qui se donne tout entière, poésie et charité, à l'imprévu qui se montre, à l'inconnu qui passe.*

streets, now as dimensions or possibilities of his own being: 'my teeming heart exults in all your sins / and all your virtues magnify my soul!'[4]†

The two aspects I have isolated: on one hand the notion of a 'modern life' perceptible only to those with the antennae to receive it, and on the other the dramas of identification played out in city space, have in common a protagonist who makes it his business to be out in the city streets. Both aspects thus involve a connection between urban experience and individual self-discovery or attunement to the spirit of the age. In the work of Apollinaire, whose seminal poem 'Zone' (1913) stands with T. S. Eliot's *The Waste Land* (1922), also full of Baudelairean echoes, as a cardinal expression of the twentieth-century poet's sense of the city, the two features of Baudelaire's inheritance are amply represented. The self-styled 'Flâneur des deux rives' (Stroller of the two river banks) was an avid collector of Parisian curiosities, introducing readers of his newspaper column 'La Vie anecdotique' (Anecdotal life) to all manner of trifling but strange urban events and locations. In the haunting 'Souvenir d' Auteuil' (Memory of Auteuil) for example, the *flâneur* takes us round a series of municipal depots, including the Hôtel des Haricots, where rows of disused street-lights resemble a primeval forest. Like the poem, the journalistic column becomes a space in which to seek one's bearings amid the flotsam and jetsam of experience.[5] As impressario for the Fauves, the Cubists, the Futurists and a bevy of other avant-garde groups and individuals, Apollinaire continually sought to identify the new spirit, 'l'esprit nouveau', convinced like Baudelaire that it should be the common mission of poet and artist to take the pulse of contemporary life and to find forms appropriate to its articulation. For Apollinaire the central feature of early twentieth-century modernity was the impact of technology and its products: new modes of transport, new styles of building, new forms of experience. The challenge here was not only to develop *poetic* styles and forms that could reflect these new realities, but to respond more profoundly to the existential disorientation occasioned by the need to jettison established categories of belief and understanding. While some of Apollinaire's work suggests uncritical enthusiasm for whatever was new, his best poems, at least among those that deal directly with urban experience, present a remarkable blend of formal innovation and subjective exploration. In such poems as 'La Chanson du mal-aimé', 'Le Voyageur' or 'Zone', a free-verse poetics of fragmentation and juxtaposition converts itineraries in urban space into mental journeys

†*Mon coeur multiplié jouit de tous vos vices! / Mon âme resplendit de toutes vos vertus!*

involving past and future as well as present. The aspiration to an identity purged of its debilitating attachment to extinct desires leads to affirmations of solidarity with the brave new world of steel, electricity and rapid motion, but the need to come to terms with the past rather than simply negate it leads to the constant recrudescence of past scenes, so that the present in which the poet–protagonist writes and reflects becomes a shifting, conflictual zone of turbulence. This zone of present experience, a space that plays host to past and future versions of self, is quintessentially in Apollinaire that of the city street, and it is the street that will be the central forum of the Surrealist engagement with Paris.

ANDRÉ BRETON: SUBJECTIVITY IN THE CITY

In Surrealism, the differing, if by no means antithetical, ways of valuing Parisian experience we have adumbrated in Baudelaire and Apollinaire can conveniently be identified with differences between Aragon and Breton. Aragon's *Le Paysan de Paris* (Paris peasant), which played a decisive role in the germination of Benjamin's Arcades project (the *Passagen-Werk*), stands alongside Breton's *Nadja* (also important for Benjamin) as a seminal contribution to the Surrealist vision of Paris.[6] As the opening 'Preface to a modern mythology' makes clear, Aragon's starting-point is the very Baudelairean notion of a modernity incarnated in transient urban phenomena. The brilliant descriptions of the then recently demolished Passage de l'Opéra, a typical example of the glass-roofed arcades erected a century earlier to provide sheltered shopping on two storeys, and of the late nineteenth-century Buttes-Chaumont park, with its artificial hills, lakes and precipices, are really imaginary forays into the collective unconscious as it makes itself visible in the artefacts and rituals that characterize these two 'sacred' sites. Yet if *Le Paysan de Paris* is the *locus classicus* of a certain Surrealist vision of Paris, the work of Breton, where the theme of Paris is present in a more widespread way throughout the writer's career, provides a richer, subtler contribution to the poetic construction of the city. Largely this is because Aragon mythologizes Paris in a manner consistent in many ways with a tradition running from Villon through Restif de la Bretonne and Hugo to the twentieth century, while Breton develops the other strand, identified earlier in Baudelaire and Apollinaire, where the streets of Paris play a catalytic role in the exploration of *individual* mental space.

This is not to deny that individual subjectivity is implicated in Aragon's urban meanderings. Nor indeed that Breton's apprehension of Paris has a mythic or historical component. A remarkable text, dating from 1950,

'Pont-Neuf', famously proposes a detailed 'interpretation' of the topography of central Paris according to which the geographical and
architectural layout of the Ile de la Cité, and the bend of the Seine where it
is situated, are seen to make up the body of a recumbent women whose
vagina is located in the Place Dauphine, 'with its triangular, slightly
curvilinear form bisected by a slit separating two wooded spaces'.[7†] At
one level this 'reading' is presented in terms of the psychology of forms, as
an instance of how we respond to physical features of the environment in
ways that reflect our own psychological make-up. But Breton also goes to
some length to show that our response to urban sites is not exclusively
conditioned by physical stimuli but also by historical resonances enshrined in street names, in snippets of antiquarian knowledge often
manifested architecturally, and, more esoterically, in *'what took place
here' ('ce qui a eu lieu* ici'). Yet if the resonance of past events and
personalities – particularly, for Breton, those associated with such
pursuits as alchemy, intrigue, revolution or poetry – still affect the
atmosphere of the streets and monuments where they took place, thus
over-determining the factors capable of affecting an individual in the
present, it may also be the case that these historical resonances were
themselves prompted in the first place by the physical features of the site.
Hence, if the Place Dauphine and environs were for long a place of
passion and licentiousness, this may be accounted for by the erotic
reading mentioned above. In this vein Breton argues at some length that
the decision in the seventeenth century to locate a new bridge across the
Seine (the Pont-Neuf) at the western tip of the Ile de la Cité rather than at
the Notre-Dame end, which would have been more logical given the aim
of relieving traffic crossing the river along the main north–south axis, can
only be explained by the powerful attraction exerted by the erotic heart
of the capital. The 'force' to which the individual passer-by may respond
as he or she circulates in Parisian space is thus the product of a dialectic of
historical and physical textures, but in advancing and illustrating this
thesis Breton also makes it clear that the individual subjectivity of the
respondent is crucial. More importantly he indicates that the role of the
encounter with, and imaginative response to, urban space is ultimately to
provide insights into the individual as much as to the city. What attracts
or repels us as we circulate in the Paris streets may be conditioned by
historical and physical features, but what it reveals is the topography of
our own subjectivity:

†*Sa conformation triangulaire, d'ailleurs légèrement curviligne et de la fente qui la bissecte
en deux espaces boisés.*

The steps which draw us, year after year, without external constraint, to the same parts of the city testify to the way certain aspects, which in an obscure way present themselves as either benign or hostile, progressively impinge on our sensibility. A walk down a single street, of sufficient length and variety – the rue de Richelieu for example – if we focus our attention, can provide, between two street-numbers which could be specified, alternating zones of well-being and disquiet. No doubt a highly significant map should be drawn up *for each individual* which would indicate in white the places he is prone to haunt and in black those he avoids, the rest being divided into shades of grey according to the greater or lesser degree of attraction or repulsion exerted.[8†]

In proposing an analogy and a reciprocal connection between the inner space of individual subjectivity and the outer space of contingent locations and events, this passage typifies Breton's view that personal identity and destiny are made manifest in a process of interaction with outer experience. As far back as one goes in Breton's work one encounters a view of the city street as an area of possibility. The street is quintessentially the place where *something can happen*:

The street, which I thought capable of transmitting its surprising detours to my life, the street with its worries and its looks, was my true element: there, as nowhere else, I could breathe the wind of eventuality.[9‡]

The equation between circulation in Parisian space and circulation in mental space is a consistent feature of Breton's 'automatic' writing from the publication of *Les Champs magnétiques* (Magnetic fields) in 1920 onwards, and here, both implicitly and often explicitly, the textual space engendered by the act of writing in a way designed to suspend the control of rationality and other censoring agencies, and to mobilize creative energies within language itself, is also implicated. In the automatic prose poetry of *Poisson soluble* (Soluble fish), Parisian environments are frequently the setting for the dazzling processes of individual metamorphosis that consistently feature in these narratives:

†*Les pas qui, sans nécessité extérieure, des années durant, nous ramènent aux mêmes points d'une ville attestent notre sensibilisation croissante à certains de ces aspects, qui se présentent obscurément sous un jour favorable ou hostile. Le parcours d'une seule rue un peu longue et de déroulement assez varié – la rue de Richelieu par exemple – pour peu qu'on y prenne garde, livre, dans l'intervalle du numéro qu'on pourrait préciser, des zones alternantes de bien-être et de malaise. Une carte sans doute très significative demanderait pour chacun à être dressée, faisant apparaître en blanc les lieux qu'il hante et en noir ceux qu'il évite, le reste en fonction de l'attraction ou de la répulsion moindre se répartissant la gamme des gris.*
‡*La rue, que je croyais capable de livrer à ma vie ses surprenants détours, la rue avec ses inquiétudes et ses regards, était mon véritable élément; j'y prenais comme nulle part ailleurs le vent de l'éventuel.*

'A Kiss is so quickly forgotten.' I heard this refrain go by during the long walks in my head, in the province of my head and I knew nothing of the rest of my life, which unfolded on its blond track. To want to hear beyond oneself, beyond this wheel, one spoke of which, ahead of me, barely skims the cart-tracks, what folly! I had spent the night in the company of a frail and alert woman, tucked away in the long grass of a public square, towards the Pont-Neuf. For a whole hour we had laughed at the vows exchanged, to their surprise, by the late-night strollers who came in turn to sit on the nearest bench. We stretched out our hands towards the nasturtiums flowing from a balcony of the City-Hotel, with the aim of abolishing in mid-air everything that makes a ringing sound as it shudders, like the ancient coinage which was exceptionally the currency that night.[10]†

Liberation from the usual co-ordinates of space, time and logic is associated with love, or eroticism, which triggers a switch onto a mental or imaginary plane. At one remove from the ordinary path of existence (which goes on all the while), the narrator is both independent of everyday reality and still a participant within it. This ambivalence is partly figured through the way the urban setting (characteristically indicated by very specific topographical references) is subverted by the encroachment of the natural world, which makes the city a hybrid environment containing, or continuous with, the non-urban world outside it. Ambivalence also stems from temporal dislocation in so far as the historical past of the city (present here through the reference to cart-tracks and ancient coinage) is seen to be still extant below the surface. In the mini-narratives of *Poisson soluble* the poet constantly slips in and out of the historical present, journeying from the city to the countryside and back again, abolishing the barriers separating city centre, *banlieue*, *faubourg*, and city proper, observing 'the boulevard like a salt marsh under its luminous signs',‡ or 'the Paris landscape nightingale of the world [which] varied from minute to minute'.[11]* In the rest of the text cited above, the narrator follows the Seine at dawn to a 'white village' that turns out to be a picture, and then to a second village, Ecureuil-sur-

---

†'*Un baiser est si vite oublié' j'écoutais passer ce refrain dans les grandes promenades de ma tête, dans la province de ma tête et je ne savais plus rien de ma vie, qui se déroulait sur sa piste blonde. Vouloir entendre plus loin que soi, plus loin que cette route dont un rayon, à l'avant de moi, effleure à peine les ornières, quelle folie! J'avais passé la nuit en compagnie d'une femme frêle et avertie, tapi dans les hautes herbes d'une place publique, de côté du Pont-Neuf. Une heure durant nous avions ri des serments qu'échangeaient par surprise les tardifs promeneurs qui venaient tour à tour s'asseoir sur le banc le plus proche. Nous étendions la main vers les capucines coulant d'un balcon de City-Hotel, avec l'intention d'abolir dans l'air tout ce qui sonne en trébuchant comme les monnaies anciennes qui exceptionnellement avaient cours cette nuit-là.*
‡*Le boulevard pareil à un marais salant sous les enseignes lumineuses.*
**Le paysage de Paris rossignol du monde variait de minute en minute.*

mer, where he and his partner disappear. While maintaining narrative continuity, the text insistently disavows referentiality not only by means of fantasy and incongruity but by drawing attention to linguistic generation. The lovers' bench ('banc') at the beginning is echoed by 'shoals of fish' ('bancs de poisson'), and the 'cover' ('couverture') of the village (as picture) features a 'a flighty young lady skipping on the edge of a grey laurel wood' ('sorte de lorette sautant à la corde à l'orée d'un bois de laurier gris'), where the phonetic echoes in the words *lorette/l'orée/ laurier*) lay bare the arbitrariness of the textual elements.[12] (It should be noted in passing that the *lorette* is a specifically nineteenth-century, and urban, category.)

References to Paris consistently feature in Breton's automatic texts as the starting-point for scenarios of liberation and self-annihilation engendered by the break with referential codes and the adoption of linguistic and discursive play. It is as if the city of Paris were always already half imaginary, half linguistic, a territory of desire as much as of reality. In particular, the street, aired by the wind of eventuality, figured as an ever-changing space, and hence a zone of infinite possibility, offers itself as a place of metamorphosis where the individual past, and the restricted identity or *état civil* which goes with it, can always be abrogated by virtue of the multi-levelled historical and physical associations in which the street consists. The city-street, in other words, imparts to the individual subject something of its own sameness-within-difference.

Nadja, published in 1928, two years after Aragon's *Le Paysan de Paris*, is the first of a series of autobiographical narratives in which Breton recounts events in his life that seemed to substantiate his evolving theories, central to the activities of the Surrealist movement, with respect to what he called 'le hasard objectif' (objective chance). This is the generic term for a category of experiences where the unfolding of individual existence seems conditioned by factors outside the fields of obvious causality or conscious volition. Breton's encounter with the enigmatic young woman, Nadja, and the fairly brief period when he sees her regularly, are punctuated by surprising episodes of telepathy and coincidence which challenge our conventional view of reality and point to the existence of unsuspected pathways linking individual subjectivity and external events. *Nadja* emphasizes that just as the liberation of language depends on the surrender of conscious control over utterance, so access to the occult pathways of experience may be propitiated by an attitude of openness and availability to experience that finds its cardinal expression in the practice of aimless wandering in uban space:

Meanwhile, you can be sure of meeting me in Paris, of not spending more than three days without seeing me pass, toward the end of the afternoon, along the Boulevard Bonne-Nouvelle between the *Matin* printing office and the Boulevard de Strasbourg. I don't know why it should be precisely here that my feet take me, here that I almost inevitably go without specific purpose, without anything to induce me but this obscure clue: notably that it (?) will happen here. I cannot see, as I hurry along, what could constitute for me, even without my knowing it, a magnetic pole in either space or time. No: not even the extremely handsome, extremely useless Porte Saint-Denis.[13][†]

The kind of urban *errance* (wandering) described here, which is undoubtedly Breton's central contribution to the poetics of the city, has its specific ecology. It has often been pointed out that Breton's Paris is clearly delimited, conditioned by residence in the rue Fontaine in the north of the city not far from Montmartre, and by various enthusiasms and prejudices. But if certain locations (such as the Tour Saint-Jacques, associated with alchemy) are favoured, and do indeed have a sacred 'aura', these serve essentially as landmarks within a latent field of energy that is manifested primarily through events such as encounters with people or objects, coincidences, unusual or uncanny occurrences, which tear the customary fabric of experience. The Paris of *Nadja* is a city of signs – luminous advertisements, billboards, printed ephemera, notices – and Breton treats Nadja (in a way arguably prejudicial to her needs as a human being) as a sort of Ur-sign, a pointer to a level of reality to which the city itself rather than Nadja is the key. Viewed at first as a free spirit, a 'génie libre', Nadja, whose erratic behaviour leads to her incarceration in an asylum, fades into the background while Breton is buoyed up by a new love that Nadja is deemed to have heralded.

Beginning as a quest for identity (the opening words are 'Who am I?'), *Nadja* progressively establishes a view of experience as cryptogram: 'Perhaps life needs to be deciphered like a cryptogram.'[14][‡] In many respects this vision, and its connection with the city, is more fully realized in *Les Vases communicants* (1932), where the communicating vessels of the title are dreams and waking life, or more fundamentally the

---

[†]*On peut, en attendant, être sûr de me rencontrer dans Paris, de ne pas passer plus de trois jours sans me voir aller et venir, vers la fin de l'après-midi, boulevard Bonne-Nouvelle entre l'imprimerie du* Matin *et le boulevard de Strasbourg. Je ne sais pourquoi c'est là, en effet, que mes pas me portent, que je me rends presque toujours sans but déterminé, sans rien de décidant que cette donnée obscure, à savoir que c'est là que se passera cela (?). Je ne vois guère, sur ce rapide parcours, ce qui pourrait, même à mon insu, constituer pour moi un pôle d'attraction, ni dans l'espace ni dans le temps. Non: pas même la très belle et très inutile Porte Saint-Denis.*

[‡]*Il se peut que la vie demande à être déchiffrée comme un cryptogramme.*

unconscious and reality. Breton advances a resolutely materialist view of dreams indebted to Freud's theory and practice, but also critical of it in some respects, which he illustrates by prolonged analysis of a recent dream partly concerned with his guilt at the way he treated Nadja, and with the breakdown of his relationship with the woman who supplanted her. The point of the analysis is to show that the dream can be entirely explained with reference to real events, that all its elements derive from lived experience, and that the function of the dreamwork is to contribute to the resolution of conflicting elements in the subject's life. Rather than a parenthesis the dream is a movement 'in the pure sense of a contradiction which leads forward'.

In the middle part of the book, as in the central section of *Nadja*, Breton turns his attention to a specific period in his recent past and in this case subjects it to minute analysis. While the context is again experiences that take place in Parisian space and the focus once more on coincidences, meetings, parallels and strange events, the argumentation is more circumstantial, and the attention to detail more pronounced. Breton now has a case to prove. Waking life and dream life, he argues, are not opposed but complementary. To demonstrate this he seeks to show how, during a period when his personal situation left him at a low ebb, positive psychical forces asserted themselves by infiltrating his everyday life, subjecting it to the logic of the dreamwork. In the course of the analysis these positive forces, which will later be designated by the generic term *desire*, are strongly associated with three fields: libidinal energy, subjectivity and the city. Having explained the reasons for the sense of abandonment he felt at this time (April 1931), Breton notes how at one stage he was saved from despair by 'woman' in general, incarnated by the generic 'Parisian woman' constituted by women glimpsed in the streets. Subsequently, specific women, notably a German tourist and a working-class girl who turns out to be only sixteen, occupy prominent positions in the networks of repetition and substitution that characterize Breton's life at this point. The two women are initially linked because, like Nadja, they have extraordinary eyes, a fact that constantly surfaces in the convolutions of Breton's narrative. When the young girl fails to meet him in the Café Batifol, Breton recalls that his first visit to this establishment had been in pursuit of another woman with strange eyes. Deciding to attend a play the girl had mentioned seeing with her mother, Breton finds that the name *Batifol* features prominently in the opening act. A woman (named Parisette) whom Breton dines with instead of the young girl, turns out to know a certain *Jeanson* whose name echoes that of *Samson*, author of an article Breton had read just before, while the latter name connects with the original girl because her eyes had reminded Breton of those of Moreau's *Dalila*.

And so on. As he traces out the patterns linking events, names, people and places, or things read, seen and imagned, which marked his life between the 5th and the 24th of April 1931, Breton notes that everything is as in a dream *except* that 'here I am in reality moving around Paris'.† In this portion of waking life, as in a dream, desire is at work:

the exigency of desire in quest of the *object* of its realisation makes hay with external facts, egotistically retaining only what may serve its cause. The futile activity of the street is scarcely more irksome than tangled bedsheets. Desire is at work, carving up the rapidly changing fabric, then deftly setting its fragile thread to work between the pieces.[15]‡

The thrust of Breton's demonstration is that at a point when he was psychically endangered, desire, the agent of subjectivity, came to his rescue. Not by providing a haven from the world of reality (a dream world) but by operating on given reality: 'le torrent du donné' (the torrent of the given). All the ingredients are real: 'La Café Batifol n'est pas un mythe' (The Café Batifol is not a myth), the real world was there all the time, but 'I was desperately striving, with all my power, to extract from the *milieu*, to the exclusion of all else, what could contribute to the rebuilding of myself.'[16]* At this 'particularly irrational' juncture in his life Breton's subjectivity was paramount. Yet the real world had by no means ceased to exist for him. Rather, under the sway of desire, it became a fragmented, unstable, labyrinthine field, a territory of bric-à-brac ready to be conscripted in the cause of psychic process and reparation.

In *Les Vases communicants*, as in *Nadja* and subsequently in *L'Amour fou*, the great purveyor of materials for the processes of the psyche to derive energies and modes of representation is the city of Paris. And indeed, by the end of *Les Vases communicants*, Paris emerges increasingly as the privileged mirror of subjectivity, in all senses its capital. There is nothing fortuitous about the Parisian setting of Breton's 'dream-

†*Là je me déplace réellement dans Paris.*
‡*L'exigence du désir à la recherche de l'objet de sa réalisation dispose étrangement des données extérieures, en tendant égoïstement à ne retenir d'elles que ce qui peut servir sa cause. La vaine agitation de la rue est devenue à peine plus gênante que le froissement des draps. Le désir est là, taillant en pleine pièce dans l'étoffe pas assez vite changeante, puis laissant entre les morceaux courir son fil sûr et fragile.*
Je tentais désespérément, de toutes mes forces, d'extraire du milieu, à l'exclusion de tout le reste, ce qui devait d'abord servir à la reconstitution de ce moi.

phase': only this city could have provided the psychic support he needed. And we should not be surprised at the amount of topographical and circumstantial detail Breton provides (despite the fidelity to his anti-realist refusal of descriptions), for example the numerous street names that enable us to reconstruct his itineraries. Paris is not incidental to the construction of subjectivity or desire presented in *Les Vases communicants*, it is of its essence, and the emphasis on the tangible reality and factitiousness of the city, far from being at odds with the project of rendering subjective experience, binds subjectivity to its objective correlative, Paris itself. The apotheosis of Paris-as-subjectivity comes in the third section of *Les Vases communicants*, which culminates in a long disquisition on the disastrous neglect of subjective existence. A lyrical evocation of Paris seen at dawn from the heights of the Sacré-Coeur extols the nocturnal city as the embodiment of 'the general essence of subjectivity, that immense field, richest of all, [which] is left to lie fallow'.[17][†] Encompassing dreams, the unconscious and the whole realm of feeling or affect, the terrain of subjectivity requires exploration like the streets of a nocturnal city whose 'unconscious powers' call for profound meditation and deciphering.

The labyrinthine windings of desire and the dialectical interplay of subjectivity and topography also feature prominently in two famous chapters of *L'Amour fou*. One chapter concerns the chain of events surrounding Breton's meeting with Jacqueline, who was to be his second wife, during a walk through Paris at night, which, Breton subsequently found to his amazement, reproduced almost exactly a Parisian itinerary outlined in an automatic poem he had written some ten years earlier.[18] The second involves a visit to the flea-market with the sculptor Giacometti, when both men were fortuitously drawn to purchase objects that, in manifold ways teased out by subsequent analysis, furnished symbolic 'solutions' to underlying psychological conflicts present at the time in each individual.[19] In both cases the city plays an active role as intermediary between internal and external reality. Paris offers itself as the place of recovered subjectivity, as the harbinger of lost identity. If the question of identity is always to the fore in Breton's negotiations with the city, if non-purposeful circulation in urban space is seen as a path towards the discovery of an authentic, sublimated dimension of selfhood, this reflects the fact that for Breton identity is conceived in terms of difference, as

[†]*L'essence générale de la subjectivité, cet immense terrain et le plus riche de tous est laissé en friche.*

something played out on another stage, in another dimension, at another level. With its endlessly varied spaces, vistas and itineraries, its combination of exteriors and interiors, its multiple layers of history that make each street a palimpsest, the city's inherent theatricality provides the ideal stage for the Surrealist pursuit of identity.

WALTER BENJAMIN AND THE MEDITATIVE FLÂNEUR

The Surrealist dimension of Benjamin's massive unfinished opus on Paris, the *Passagen-Werk* or Arcades Project, is well known. Benjamin began work on it in the late 1920s, partly under the impact of Aragon's *Le Paysan de Paris* (1924) and Breton's *Nadja* (1928), and it was Aragon's brilliant evocation of the Passage de l'Opéra that inspired Benjamin's central insights into the arcades he describes as being 'buried deep in great cities like caverns preserving the fossils of an extinct animal – the consumer of the pre-imperial epoch of capitalism', and as 'the home of the collective dream'.[20] In Breton's *Nadja* it was the emphasis placed on experience, and particularly what Benjamin labelled 'a profane illumination, a materialistic, anthropological inspiration', that provided food for thought, as did the Surrealist writer's seminal perception of 'the revolutionary energies that appear in the "outmoded", in the first iron constructions, the first factory buildings, etc'.[21] In a recent study it has been argued that Benjamin's indebtedness to Surrealism is greater than hitherto acknowledged, and in particular that through the twelve-year evolution of the *Passagen-Werk* he remained attentive to developments in Breton's post-*Nadja* explorations of the interface between the city's streets and the subject's 'ghostly' identities.[22] Equally, the German editor of the *Passagen-Werk* highlights two strands in Benjamin's thinking whose interconnections are Surrealist in origin: attention to concrete details – objects, dress, architecture, stray pieces of information – and a fascination with the dream state.[23]

If Surrealism provided Benjamin with one of the starting-points for his work on Paris, he nevertheless always indicated the differences between his project and that of the Surrealists. With regard to *Le Paysan de Paris* Benjamin observed:

Delimitation of the tendency of this work in relation to Aragon: while Aragon persists in remaining in the field of dreams, what counts here is to find the constellation of awakening. Whereas with Aragon there remains an impressionistic element – 'mythology' – and this impressionism is to be held responsible for the many empty philosophemes in the book, here the aim is to dissolve 'mythology' in the space of history.[24]

As we noted earlier, however, Breton also had serious reservations about the mythologizing character of Aragon's *Paysan* (stemming partly from the Baudelairean 'mythology of modern life'). In *Nadja* and *Les Vases communicants*, attention to precise spatial and temporal detail marks a concern for the minutiae of subjective experience as it unfolds in urban space, and this favours liberation from the customary limitations of habitual consciousness. Similarly, at many points in the *Passagen-Werk*, Benjamin, while by no means sharing the individualistic concerns of Breton, represents the interaction of subject and city in ways which not only have clear affinities with Surrealism but contribute more widely — and centrally — to the tradition under discussion here.

As ever with Benjamin it is appropriate to begin with the *flâneur*. However, just as Benjamin himself progressively elaborates the figure of the *flâneur* or urban stroller by contrasting his relationship to the city with that of other types of city-walker, so it is vital in my view to discriminate between a number of versions of the *flâneur* to be found in Benjamin's writings. In the nineteenth-century literature on the *flâneur*, particularly in the *Physiologies*, which he found particularly rich and symptomatic, Benjamin encountered distinctions between the *flâneur* and the *badaud* or idler, who simply gapes; between the *flâneur* and the *promeneur*, who is more purposeful, and so on.[25] In building up his own portrait Benjamin regularly takes issue with the established legend or myth of the *flâneur*, notably with regard to the question of knowledge. Where the mythical *flâneur* of the *Physiologistes* (including Balzac) possesses an encyclopaedic knowledge of faces and streets which makes him an expert, Benjamin plays down this expertise in order to emphasize instead the *flâneur's* hidden motives, his more complex interactions with the city's labyrinth.[26] The Benjaminian *flâneur* differs from the *voyageur* who believes that historical knowledge can give access to the *genius loci*. For him it is the *fait divers*, a highly localized event that took place *on this very spot*, or the snippet of detailed information which counts.[27] But if the *flâneur's* fascination with clues links him to the figure of the detective, his motives are more personal, and have less to do with ratiocination.[28] At one point Benjamin suggests that *promeneur* becomes *flâneur* at the point where he is prey to hysterical tears provoked by the irruption of the past in the present.[29] Indeed temporality is fundamental to this figure, whose attitude is also conditioned by a desire to divorce himself from his own past, profiting from the anonymity of the big city.[30] At one point Benjamin refers to the *flâneur* as someone who takes refuge in the shadow of the city. Like the *promeneur solitaire* of Rousseau, the *flâneur* cherishes his 'oisiveté' (idleness) and enjoys self-contemplation, but for Benjamin he differs in that he is still intensely preoccupied with the *outer* spectacle.[31] And unlike the *promeneur philosophique*, the *flâneur* needs the crowd – even if he prefers to remain incognito.

The notoriously elusive character of Benjamin's thought, and its historical evolution, together with the immensely complex composition and publication history of the *Passagen-Werk* and its offshoots, tended in the past to encourage a certain legend or myth of the Benjaminian *flâneur*. There are traces of this, for example, in Christopher Prendergast's excellent discussion of Baudelaire's prose poems where he compares the mobile, ironic stance of the Baudelairean walker-narrator with the more rigid attitudes that are said to characterize the Benjaminian *flâneur*.[32] Basing his reading mainly on the texts available before the publication of the Arcades project notebooks, Prendergast presents the *flâneur's* position as one of either *control* or *jouissance*, superiority and detachment or vicarious pleasure deriving from voyeuristic non-involvement.

Interestingly, the notion of the *flâneur* as one who engages in voyeuristic objectification of the other has often been focused back on to the Surrealists. Breton's narrator in *Nadja*, for example, is often seen to exemplify the unattached observer who looks at city life as a spectacle to be consumed, while retaining the freedom to withdraw his interest at will (Benjamin himself noted the passage where Breton candidly affirmed that he felt 'closer to the things that Nadja is close to than to her'). But if this critique is partially valid, it misses much that Benjamin himself detected in *Nadja* and it is also much less applicable to Breton's subsequent accounts of city-wandering. Moreover, the view of the *flâneur* as voyeur does not do justice to the aspects of this figure perceptible in a passage such as the following:

For the *flâneur* the street brings about a metamorphosis as it leads him back through past time. He goes down a street. For him each street has a downward slope, if not towards the Mothers, at any rate into a past which may be all the deeper for not being his own past, his private past. [. . .] His footsteps call forth a surprising echo, the gaslight on the tiled floor casts an ambiguous light on this double ground. The figure of the *flâneur* makes his way along the stone roadway on two levels as if he were animated by a clockwork mechanism. Inside, where the mechanism is hidden, a song issues from a music box as if from an old toy: 'From my childhood / From my childhood / A song always follows me.' Thanks to this melody he recognises his surroundings; a childhood speaks to him, which is not the past of his own youth, the most recent, but a childhood lived through earlier. What does it matter whether this childhood was that of an ancestor or his own? He who wanders at length and without aim in the city streets becomes intoxicated. With each step, walking acquires a new force. Shops, cafés, women who smile, constantly appear, and the next street corner, a distant square in the fog, the back of a woman walking ahead of him exert an ever more irresistible attraction. [. . .] Paris created this type. The strange thing is that it wasn't Rome. What is the reason? In Rome does day-dreaming itself follow already-established itineraries? Is the city too rich in temples, monuments, closed squares, national sanctuaries, to enter wholesale into the dream of the passer-by with each paving-stone, each signboard, each step and each coach-door? [. . .] A landscape [. . .] that is indeed what Paris becomes for the *flâneur*. More precisely, he sees the city split itself clearly in to two dialectical poles. It opens up to him like a landscape and it encloses him like a drawing-room. This too: the anamnestic intoxication which accompanies the *flâneur* wandering in the city not only finds its nourishment in what the eye can see, but can also latch onto straightforward knowledge, inert facts, which then become things that are lived through, experiences.[33]

The first thing to note here is the connection between motion and metamorphosis. The *flâneur's* movement, ordained not by overall purpose or direction but by a willingness to have his progress determined by whatever turns up, transforms the city street, endowing it with an extra dimension, another level. For the *flâneur*, as Benjamin puts it brilliantly, all streets slope down and back, if not to the 'realm of the mothers', then to a past, youthful rather than archaic, which is not personal yet has the quality of lived experience. It is the walker's footsteps which call forth this 'surprising echo' or response, making the ground double and the *flâneur's* progress something that takes place simultaneously on two levels. By virtue of this, the *flâneur* recognizes his surroundings as somehow familiar, and it is this experience he finds intoxicating, which propels him onwards and makes him reluctant to stop as he is solicited by stimuli on all sides. In harmony with something running deep down in the city's heart the *flâneur* feeds not only on what he sees but draws sustenance from simple facts, bits of local lore or legend that cease to be merely inert and take on the character of lived experience.

Obsessional and narrowly focused as his attitude might seem, the *flâneur's* behaviour, under this description, certainly does not consist in sovereign detachment, nor is voyeuristic *jouissance* either the aim or the prize. A number of the traits encompassed here, including the sense of moving simultaneously on two planes and the way the historical past ('what took place here' – a similar phrase is found in Benjamin and Breton) is made pertinent and available to lived experience, have direct counterparts in Surrealist texts such as *Nadja* and *Les Vases communi-*

cants. But in this guise the *flâneur* is neither a mythologist nor a voyeur but a subject engaged in a multi-faceted interaction with the city.

These aspects are further developed in passages concerned with the 'méditatif' (meditator), an important avatar of the Benjaminian *flâneur*. The category of the *méditatif* features prominently in Benjamin's discussions of Baudelairean allegory. If allegory is what will preserve Baudelaire from the 'abyss' of myth, meditativeness is a half-way stage on the way towards allegory.[34] Meditativeness is in part a defence mechanism against disruptive experience. The meditator differs from the *penseur* (thinker) in that the former does not reflect directly on a phenomenon but dwells on his own reflection on it.[35] To meditate, to turn something over in one's mind, is to draw experience into the realm of one's mental space, which is also the realm of affective memory ('ressouvenir') and of the image. Meditative thought 'is placed under the sign of memory', and it 'places the image at its service'.[36] Part of the 'ivresse' of the *flâneur* lies in pursuing resemblances, and superimposing one experience on another, in response to the 'clins d'oeil' (winks) that space keeps administering. For Benjamin the theme of meditativeness brings out the phenomenology of *flânerie*, its characteristics as a *state* that has a number of phases like those triggered by taking a drug.[37] The mode of reflection that constitutes meditation is presented in somatic terms as a mental activity that responds to the body's experience, its susceptibility to bombardment by external stimuli. The meditative is an important category in Benjamin's delineations of the *flâneur* because it brings out the abolition of the boundary between inner and outer which is a vital aspect of the experience of *flânerie*. Meditation is a mode of thinking that, rather than sealing mind from body, abstract thought from sensory experience, amalgamates them in a wider space. It is by dint of 'meditativeness' that for the *flâneur* the experience of 'reading a street name at night can be the equivalent of a transmigration'.[38] Drawn into the subject's mental space, the street name is not simply a practical, historical or picturesque datum. It can trigger (as Proust will amply testify) a parallel journey, by no means exclusively mental since it will draw on the body's memory as well, into the folds of a past experience that is both collective and individual, personal and impersonal.

Benjamin's crucial position in the field of discourse about Paris which we are considering has been greatly bolstered by the recent publication of the *Passagen-Werk* notebooks.[39] In providing a more comprehensive view of Benjamin's thinking over a period of some two decades, the *Konvoluten* indicate the complex layering of Benjamin's thought, revealing many analogies with the Surrealists, particularly Breton, and with later phases of Parisian wandering and writing. If the theatricality of Parisian space, the interaction of historical memory with present experience, the kinds of subjectivity fostered by exchanges with the city, are among the topics that could be pursued at length in a comparison of Breton and Benjamin, they could also form the basis of extensive comparison with the work of a contemporary writer, Jacques Réda.

JACQUES RÉDA: TRAVELS IN THE CITY

The big city is generally where you travel to or depart from, on a journey elsewhere. If to travel is to be in transit, on the move, betwixt and between, the edge of the city marks the end of travel, its cessation. Of course the traveller may explore cities, but this is an interlude; *travel* will be resumed when the city is once again left behind, for the journey onward or the return. It follows that to adopt the mind-set of the traveller *within* and with reference to the city, and particularly with reference to one's own city, is to do something perverse, subversive, unsettling. It is to break with the utilitarian order, habits and protocols that characterize urban existence. It is to play a game whose rules we invent for ourselves.

Since the publication of *Les Ruines de Paris* (a title that deliberately echoes Baudelaire's *Le Spleen de Paris*) in 1977, most of Réda's writing, in verse and prose, has been concerned with journeys of one sort or another, and several books have focused exclusively on Paris and its immediate environs. I intend to discuss one of these, *Châteaux des courants d'air*, published in 1986.[40] The book's back cover carries a useful description of the work, written, it is safe to assume, by Réda himself. We are told that the poet's third itinerary in the 'nébuleuse parisienne' will take him from the 15th arrondissement to the 14th, via the Luxembourg gardens and the Place Saint-Sulpice over the Pont-Neuf to the Gare de l'Est and thence on a circular tour of all the city's railway termini. Picking up, perhaps unconsciously, the image of the nebula, with its connotations of space travel, Réda sees his work as combining precise personal observation with 'the state of weightlessness' required by *flânerie*, to produce a particular kind of textual space. To underline the special character of this hybrid space Réda switches from prose to verse. But instead of the freewheeling *vers-libre* familiar from earlier city poetry, he gives us an unorthodox sonnet in rhyming couplets and a metrical form based on an unusual fourteen-syllable line that preserves some of the rhythm of spoken French but at the same time emphasizes constraint and the exercise of a particular faculty or discipline matching that of *flânerie* itself:

> If this book isn't a poem it's a novel:
> Each character a monument encountered
> By chance in the spiralling drift
> Of an eye alert less to architectural splendour
> Than to the secrets Paris harbours beneath her brow.
> But what of the walker's own hidden designs?
> It's hard to know if he's making an inventory or losing himself
> As he goes from gardens to church and then from station to station:
> Becoming in his turn, among these castles full of draughts,
> A space of mental passage where the city is lost,
> And refound, enjoying perhaps its metamorphosis
> Into pages where sometimes verse stalks amidst the prose,
> With a furtive air (the reader mustn't be shocked)
> Just as the wandering wind is heard gliding down the street.[41][†]

As an extension of *flânerie*, writing propitiates the interaction and exchange between *promeneur* and city. The former's spiralling progress (inspired in fact by the city's own shape) is determined less by a concern to celebrate architectural beauty or to make an inventory of what he sees than by a desire to read the city's mind, to penetrate the secrets under its brow. But this itself is perhaps no more than a cover for the pursuit of the *promeneur's* own designs, which, if they remain hidden, may perhaps be inferred from the places to which he is drawn – large, empty, open to the four winds – and from the kind of attention he brings to them, as well as from the fact that he is constantly on the move. Réda's poem establishes an important connection between his lack of clear purpose, which makes his writing partly a quest for its own *raison d'être*, an understanding of what lies behind it, and the way, in his *flânerie*, he feels himself becoming a 'lieu de passage mental' where the city itself is repeatedly lost and found. The enjambment 'métamorphose / En pages' entertains first the notion that the city revels in the very process of metamorphosis itself (a theme we will find often in the text), and second, its transmutation into

†*Si ce livre n'est pas un poème, c'est un roman | Dont les personnages seraient chacun un monument | Que rencontre, au hasard de sa promenade en spirale, | Un oeil moins curieux de splendeur architecturale | Que des secrets dissimulées sous le front de Paris. | Mais quels desseins le promeneur lui-même a-t-il nourris? | On ne sait plus très bien s'il inventorie ou s'égare | Ainsi de jardin en église et puis de gare en gare: | A son tour devenu, dans ces châteaux des courants d'air, | Un lieu de passage mental où la ville se perd, | Se retrouve, se plaît peut-être en sa métamorphose | En pages où parfois des vers circulent dans la prose, | D'un pas furtif (il ne faut pas effrayer le lecteur), | Comme se glisse dans la rue un air de vent rôdeur.*

text. At this point the oscillation between prose and verse, a feature of some of the texts in *Châteaux*, is presented less as an apt way of celebrating or capturing the city than of mimicking a general principle of surreptitious, furtive, almost imperceptible presence, as of a wind blowing down a street or a *promeneur* uncertain of his credentials.

Central to *Châteaux des courants d'air*, and to the modes of city travel practiced by Réda, is a shifting set of parallels between circulation in physical space, circulation in mental space and circulation in textual space, and hence between city, mind and text. But this does not make the city merely a pretext for enactments of self. The secret designs of the *promeneur* reveal themselves to involve anonymity and self-dissolution, a desire to become no more than an instrument serving to reveal the city's own reality. The moves and gambits of the *promeneur* serve to vary the angles at which the city is refracted through the prism of his mind, moods and words. The opening text emphasizes that it is the walker's own moves that prompt the city to reveal itself to him. He has to set things in motion by the primordial act of setting off on a journey in the city, finding pretexts for new itineraries. But if things go well the perceptions subsequently to be recorded will have stemmed from a symbiosis of such a kind that it is apparently the city's own reflections on itself which have been registered. No doubt this is an illusion and a device – a kind of extended prosopopoeia where the inanimate is given the power of speech. But it is based on a salient feature of the city that matches the *promeneur*. Like him the city exists in time, is constantly changing, possesses a history. Réda's writing always suggests that it is the city's constant metamorphosis which is at the heart of its reality. Monuments, streets, *quartiers*, utilities, institutions, customs are all, at any given time – that of any particular foray we might make – at some point in a process of mutation. This may be rapid or gradual, incipient or long-established, spectacular or unobtrusive, consistent or inconsistent with previously established patterns of development. But above all, this mutability makes the city a differential space made up of innumerable processes through which individual components are changing in appearance, function or importance but also changing in relation to each other. Seen this way the city is not so much the sum of its parts as the latent principle of a mutability whose impact may be registered the moment we decide to focus on it. If *this* is the city, then to apprehend its mobility, its play of differences, will require a corresponding mobility on the part of the witness. Réda's writing often conveys the sense of responding to the city's pressing desire for an act of witness that can reveal it to itself. This is what he means by turning himself into a 'lieu de passage mental' where the city 'se plaît peut-être à sa métamorphose'. The city needs to find expression by being filtered through the homologous zone of the *promeneur's* mind, and the *promeneur* feels compelled to externalize what the city is doing to (and in) his head. In doing so he also realizes a clearly marked desire for self-dissolution – escape from self – which, while being a personal trait in the writer, chimes both with certain ways of theorizing about writing itself, and with the experience of the city.[42] The city manifests itself in endless traits which confer on it, by analogy, certain kinds of personality but do not alter its profound anonymity. To identify with the city is to aspire to the pure anonymity of metamorphosis, of being nothing other than an endless turnover of perceptions and connections.

It is in fact moving home rather than walking that sets things in motion in the opening text of *Châteaux*. Although he only moves a few hundred metres in the same arrondissement, Réda observes that the southerly direction of his move matches the 'mouvement giratoire' (gyratory motion) of the city itself as it spirals outwards from Notre-Dame in a shape reflected (or created) by the organization of the twenty arrondissements. His new vantage-point gives him an insight into another aspect of the city's movement, the existence of thoroughfares, like the one running parallel to the bend in the Seine from the Pont Mirabeau to the Pont de Tolbiac, which, sometimes under different names, cut across several arrondissements creating connections between quite disparate sectors of the city (in this case the deserted Citroën factory, the hidden gardens of Alésia, the valleys of the Parc Montsouris and the 'farouche autonomie' (fierce autonomy) of the Butte-aux-Cailles). Such avenues, another example being the rue des Pyrénées, add a particular 'dimension mentale' to the 'corps de la ville':

streets in perpetual motion as in dreams, where it's the city which dreams itself, navigating in all directions through the strata of rock, life and memory which make up its layers, progressively reinventing the laws of its unstable gravitation.[43][†]

This passage is typical of the kind of reversal we noted earlier. A physical datum (long streets) prompts a series of recognitions that are then represented as belonging to the city itself, which has given them concrete expression in the phenomenon under description. This shift – from how

---

†*Rues en perpétuel mouvement comme dans les rêves, où c'est la ville qui se perd et navigue en tous sens à travers les strates de pierre, de vie et de mémoire qui forment son épaisseur, réinventant à mesure les lois de son instable gravitation.*

Paris might be conceived to how it might conceive of itself – is echoed by
a shift from seeing Paris as a 'ville imaginaire' (imaginary city) to seeing it
as a 'ville imaginative' (imaginative city) actively involved in self-
invention, even, Réda adds wryly, mythomania:

(all these places where she things she's Shanghai, Chicago, Conakry) ever in
quest of herself behind the reassuring brow presented by the monuments of her
glory.[44†]

Réda's next move in this passage involves a further reversal whereby the
promeneur or witness becomes an extension or projection of the city
rather than vice versa:

little by little her metamorphoses take effect on the walker. In his turn he feels he
is being imagined, borne along like a wandering, reflective antenna of the city in
its changing moods.[45‡]

This notion of the 'promeneur promené' is central to Réda's apprehension of the city and to the poetic logic of urban wandering. Whimsical
and anthropomorphic as it is, a passage like the foregoing, in addition to
being brilliantly observed and executed, communicates a profound desire
for a particular kind of rapport with the city, and via the city with the self.
To feel oneself so *absorbed* by the city is to enjoy a feeling of inclusion
and participation. In becoming one of the city's antennae, the observer
feels as if 'my head, which it contains, becomes the space which the city
surveys' – the city is now the 'promeneur'. And so:

here he is, fused with the streets, with the slow, spreading gyration the city
performs continuously on her invisible axis, that of time where – as is proclaimed
in the motto on her coat of arms – she floats and does not sink, linking to her own
perennity those strollers whose destiny, and perhaps secret design, is to
disappear.[46*]

A number of the texts in *Châteaux* end on this note of inclusion, fusion,
dissolution or absorption of the subject into the city. One of the
promeneur's arts is to find points of entry into the city's secret channels.
Réda favours features that link parts of the city together, underlining its

---

†(*Tous ses endroits où elle se prend pour Changhai, Chicago, Conakry), sans cesse en
quête d'elle-même sous le front rassurant que nous tendent les monuments de sa gloire.*
‡*Peu à peu ses métamorphoses influent sur le promeneur. Il se pressent à son tour, imaginé,
promené comme l'antenne vagabonde de la ville dans ses humeurs passagères.*
**Le voici confondu avec les rues, avec la lente, expansive giration que la ville opère
continûment sur son axe invisible qui est le temps, où – comme l'énonce la devise de ses
armes – elle flotte et ne sombre jamais, liant à sa pérennité ces promeneurs dont le destin et
peut-être le dessein secret sont de disparaître.*

hidden unity in diversity, as in the case of the long arteries mentioned above, or railway and Métro lines. Derelict areas, *terrains vagues*, building sites screened by palisades have a particular appeal because they provide breathing space and pauses for thought to gather. To concoct a route around the city – as Réda does in *Châteaux des courants d'air* – motivated not by official itineraries but by a strong associative logic is to make manifest its hidden cohesiveness. The perception of resemblances and associations prompted by visual appearance, particularly as modified by temporal factors such as times of day or atmospheric conditions, is paramount. But the lore of the city, the wealth of assorted practical and historical information in the possession of an educated citizen is also often to the fore, as in Breton and Benjamin.

Cultural memory plays an especially important role in the sequence entitled 'D'une rive a l'autre' (From one bank to the other), which features samples of four generic spaces – a garden (the Luxembourg), a church (Saint-Sulpice), a bridge (the Pont-Neuf), and an arcade (the Passage Véro-Déodat). The text on the Luxembourg gardens illustrates the strong allegorizing tendency in the city-walker's engagement with his surroundings. Not especially interested in the niceties of official history (the precise identity of the eighteen queens and 'grande dames' represented in sculpture) Réda nevertheless sees every detail of the garden's layout as emblematic and identifies its contribution to his overall sense of the garden as 'une vraie patrie spirituelle' (a true spiritual homeland). The account of Saint-Sulpice mentions all the obvious features, including the Delacroix frescoes described by Baudelaire and the statues of great churchmen in the square. But the striking thing about Réda's text is the way he combines historical and topographical reference with entirely personal impressions in a synthesis which succeeds in placing the emphasis neither on objective facts nor on private associations but on what one could call the human specificities of this particular place, the particular imprints it might leave on an open mind. Characteristically, throughout Réda's evocation of Saint-Sulpice one has the impression that he is taking us at once on a tour of a physical space we may know well ourselves and on a tour of his own mental space as refracted through its responsiveness to Saint-Sulpice. This is especially perceptible in a long final paragraph that describes the changing impressions of the facade as the sun sets, 'the slow metamorphoses of its substance brought about by contact with the setting sun',[†] where the church appears narrowly to

---

†*Les lentes métamorphoses de sa substance au contact du couchant.*

avoid total obliteration as it is consumed by purifying fires in accordance with its capacity to stand as the precarious materialization of 'le génie de l'église' (the genius of the church).[47]

Réda approaches the Pont-Neuf obliquely via his indignation at the permission granted to the sculptor Christo to wrap it up for a week, a criminal act in so far as it represented symbolically the occlusion of a site with unbroken links to the origin of the city in Roman times. For Réda the sturdy Pont-Neuf, resembling teams of oxen labouring in opposite directions, has since the seventeenth century acted as a fixative preserving 'the slow daydream of History' ('la lente rêverie de l'Histoire') against the kind of dissolution threatened by Christo.

The slow daydream of History, along the Seine which has none, has deposited, superimposed, its proofs of stone and, in people's minds, dark piles of anonymous memories and knowledge one thinks one has forgotten, but on which one leans as on the parapet of the Quai de Conti, to abandon oneself to the sweetness of the evening which suddenly becomes still.[48†]

Playing on the opposition between time and the timeless, history and its absence, motion and immobility, transience and permanence, the physical and the mental, this passage gives forceful and original expression to the idea that the monuments among which we casually linger in the city are concretizations of a history that is also deposited, less securely, in our mental reflexes and passive knowledge.

To write about the Parisian passages or arcades is inevitably to pay homage to Aragon and Benjamin, but Réda's account of a visit to one of these, while appropriately phantasmagoric (it is one of the more narrative texts in *Châteaux des courants d'air*), homes in on the rather sinister, abandoned quality of the passages, their 'loss of aura' in Benjamin's phrase, rather than on the marvellous. In fact Réda's text also constitutes an allegorical reflection on the limits, the precariousness of his own stance. In the end he presents himself as a ghost who haunts only an image of the places he traverses, and compares himself to the legendary crew of figures in portraits who, it is said, under cover of darkness, step down from their pedestals and canvases in the Louvre to enjoy a limited and secretive freedom.[49] The meditation seizes first on the checker-board tiled floor the passages have in common, which, set diagonally, makes the

†*La lente rêverie de l'Histoire, le long de la Seine qui n'en a pas, a déposé, superposé ses preuves de pierre et, dans les têtes, des entassements obscurs de souvenirs anonymes et de savoir qu'on croit oublier, mais sur lesquels distraitement on s'appuie comme sur le parapet du quai de Conti, pour s'abandonner à la douceur du soir tout à coup immobile.*

movements of the rare passers-by resemble moves in a game of live chess. For Réda the passages convey a feeling that one is being observed from on high, but with an indifference that serves to suggest both one's freedom (one can make any move one wants) and its futility. More positively, the notion of chess moves conjures up a fantasy whereby not only all the other surviving passages, clustered in a small group of arrondissements in central Paris, but also certain adjacent buildings become available to imaginative scrutiny, allowing the 'accès phantasmagorique' of the image-making *flâneur*.[50] Seen from this mental vantage-point these other spaces – the musty theatres round the Palais-Royal, the Bourse, the Banque de France, the Bibliothèque Nationale and the Hôtel des Postes – are revealed to possess family resemblances: emptiness, theatricality, darkness, alternations of frenetic activity and quiescence, noise and silence, endless repetitions and series – of gestures (in the theatre), objects (in the library), financial transactions (at the Bourse), messages (at the post office).

What is striking in this text is the way it emerges as an allegory of Réda's imaginative access from one space to others, and more especially from one dimension into others. His footsteps in the passage, as he moves a few paces to right or left or tries a knight's move, seem to enable corresponding exploratory movements in other zones, which, if he can link them by imaginative exploration, allow his 'entrée en communication'. But the allegory also reveals the dangers of a game that has only one player. As he emerges at nightfall, Réda's final perception of the passages turns them into a series of railway coaches relegated to the sidings and making up one long train which at night is switched on to a single-track line going nowhere: 'I was the only passenger of this convoy going nowhere, and I could make my way for a long while yet, in my mind, through a world where all barriers melted away giving me access to an interminable impasse'.[51†] An 'interminable impasse': a melancholy conclusion, but only a provisional one since the text ends with the enchanting sight of the great window – 'la rosace illuminée' – of the Gare de l'Est, galvanizing the *flâneur* onwards to a tour of the capital's 'univers ferroviaire' (railway universe).

THE ONCE AND FUTURE CITY

Having largely thus far looked at Breton, Benjamin and Réda discretely, I now want to consider more directly the general field of discourse about

---

† *J'étais le seul voyageur de ce convoi sans destination, et je pouvais avancer longtemps encore, en esprit, dans un monde dont toutes les cloisons s'évanouissent pour m'ouvrir une interminable impasse.*

Paris to which they may be said to contribute. When some of its basic constituents have been reviewed I will examine whether this discursive and practical field has any future. Central to it are questions of knowledge, power and possession. For the dominant discourses since the mid-nineteenth century, the project of 'knowing Paris' could be construed in terms of description, regulation and emulation. Rastignac's 'It's between us now!',[†] addressed to the city at the climax of Balzac's *Le Père Goriot* from the heights of the Père-Lachaise cemetery is the exact literary reflection of the crucial linkage between the rise of capital, the growth of the city, and the possibility of individual fortune. An immediate contrast can be made with the line, also addressed to Paris, which concludes the projected epilogue Baudelaire wrote for the second edition of *Les Fleurs du mal*: 'You gave me your mud and I turned it into gold'.[52‡] Rather than wanting to emulate the city whose attributes he identifies in a long enumeration, Baudelaire represents himself as an alchemist who has sought to distil the quintessence of the city. Both the Balzacian novelist and the Baudelairean poet lay claim to superior knowledge about Paris. The difference lies in the alignment with other modes of cognition. While Balzacian knowledge (strongly identified with power) participates in the dynamic of the age, the Baudelairean slant is tangential, oblique, ironically dispossessed. Balzacian knowledge is rooted in description and anecdote, while Baudelairean knowledge eschews these in favour of less palpable qualities. In the important preface he wrote for his prose poems Baudelaire evokes the quest for a literary style, a rhythmical prose capable of rendering the 'innumerable connections' that characterize 'giant cities' and especially of communicating their impact on the city-dweller prone to 'the lyrical movements of the soul, the undulations of reverie and the somersaults of conscience'.[53*] In thus linking the urban to questions of textuality and subjectivity Baudelaire certainly switches the prime emphasis from the observable characteristics of the metropolis itself (very few of which are described in the poems) on to the repercussions of city life in the individual. But the subjective existence thus foregrounded is wholly bound up with its *exposure* to the city. The subjectivity explored in the prose poems is in no sense a haven from urban reality; on the contrary it is the city's place of resonance and recognition. The prominent narrator–*flâneur* of the poems is generally

†*A nous deux maintenant!*
‡*Tu m'as donné ta boue et j'en ai fait de l'or.*
**Aux mouvements lyriques de l'âme, aux ondulations de la rêverie, aux soubresauts de la conscience.*

abroad in the city streets, exposed to the shocks and stimuli of the crowd, aspiring, like the Painter of Modern Life, to resemble a 'kaleidoscope equipped with consciousness', a mental space able to register the endlessly changing patterns of experience. This mode of subjectivity, rooted in the rapid interchange between the mind, the senses and a constantly shifting environment, is intrinsically urban, and it founds a category of experience that cannot be subsumed into existing models. In the two-way encounter between mind and city, a process unfolds that affords a specific type of cognition, and the Baudelairean stance towards the city is explicitly epistemic, fuelled by a drive towards a knowledge that cannot be separated from this interactive process.

Baudelaire, then, may be said to announce the possibility of a mode of experience in which questions of language (how is this experience to be articulated and preserved?), questions of subjectivity (*who* am I in the city?), and questions of space (how can I best approach the city?) intersect. And it is the further extensions of this possibility, as it informs a rich tradition in European thought and poetry, which we have investigated in Breton, Benjamin and Réda. For Breton, knowing the city is dependent on attunement to a particular wavelength, a process involving the adoption of an attitude of lyrical expectancy and availability to experience. The quasi-scientific, documentary tone Breton adopts in his reports on the fruits of his urban wandering reflects the sense of operating at the frontiers of knowledge. In a number of places in the *Passagen-Werk* Benjamin makes it clear that one of his central concerns is with the articulation of a particular dimension or category of experience – *Erlebnis* (or lived experience) rather than *Erfahrung*. The *flâneur* aspires neither to knowledge or possession. Like the Surrealist surrendering to the flow of unconscious thoughts, or aimlessly wandering the streets, he cultivates a kind of 'oisiveté' (idleness), a suspension of purposive activity that favours the eruption of phantasmagoric experience, where the spectacle of outer events becomes imbued with subjective resonance.[54] As in the case of Baudelaire and the Surrealists, resemblance and analogy are crucial. 'Resemblance is the organon of (lived) experience':[55] prey to 'the demon of analogy' (Mallarmé), the *flâneur* wanders through a city that has become a 'forest of symbols' (Baudelaire) or a cryptogram (Breton). The work of Réda is fully continuous with this tradition of a non-anecdotal, non-sociological, non-mythological, but profoundly allegorical approach to the city, rooted in the solitary experience of an obsessive but idle subject. To be sure, Réda's writing is more descriptive than that of the other writers we are considering, but his descriptions rarely seek to inform; rather, description is a way of trying to keep in play an elusive but vital form of experience that has been engendered by the adoption of an inherently unteleological stance.

For all three writers the experience of urban wandering involves temporal dislocation. But if the future is suspended as the present becomes suffused with the past, we always remain in a border zone, between now and then, and between the city's own historical archive and that of the individual. Similarly, at the level of identity, the exploration of individual subjectivity goes hand in hand with the revelation of the city's own reality. Magnetized by the city the urban *promeneur* goes on and on, seeking encounters that may prove revelatory (Breton); absorbing street names that act like 'intoxicating substances which make our perception richer in strata', and turn the city into a 'linguistic cosmos' (Benjamin); or constantly experiencing self-dissolution through the uncanny feeling that one's mind has become a conduit through which the city gives expression to its own sense of itself (Réda).

For all these writers Paris is a hall of mirrors, a place of recognitions, a metaphor for inner space, but with the proviso that the 'inner' cannot be separated from the 'outer' — that experience, identity, temporality, are only given through relation and interaction between subjectivity and objectivity, mind and world. This inherently phenomenological emphasis should alert us to the prevailing ethos that informs the poetic tradition of Parisian wandering. Solitary and individualistic as it might seem, this tradition in fact construes Paris as a place of relations; an organic totality which, in its very heterogeneousness, holds forth the (ever-deferred) promise of unity. Central to this tradition is the way it opposes ways of reducing the city to its constituent parts — objectifying its *quartiers*, dissecting its *métiers*, celebrating its piecemeal charm or metonymically extolling the whole city through one of its many aspects. Opposing such positivism, the Baudelairean tradition construes Paris as a site of melancholy but ever-hopeful experience that questions and subverts the reductive categories of the architect, the planner, the politician or the orthodox *littérateur*. Here Paris becomes the name of a dimension of experience where totality is imminent but never actual, a zone of possibility for which the city streets are the ever full, ever vacant, setting.

If the Parisian poetic field first delineated by Baudelaire has subsisted through a series of shifts and transformations to find striking new forms of expression in the writing of Réda, is it none the less an irrelevant anachronism in the age of McDonald's and Microsoft? Is Réda the last *flâneur*, a throwback to a superseded cultural phase? A recent book by

Jean-Christophe Bailly suggests that such a verdict could be premature. *La Ville à l'oeuvre* (The city at work) reflects the widespread concern for the future of cities that has placed architecture, planning and urban ecology at the centre of contemporary concerns. This is the context in which the ideas of the Surrealists (and the Situationists who emulated them), of Benjamin and Certeau, find continued or enhanced resonances. Bailly is a poet and essayist, an *écrivain* who writes about cities. 'Urban reality is sick', he observes.[56] But if so, he continues, we need to think hard about what it consists of in the first place. Back to basics: what *is* a city?

> The city exists as a mass and disperses itself in seeds, but what engenders it, making it exist and develop, is the movement of the people who traverse it. The law is simple: the more aberrant and capricious the movement, the less it is submitted to restrictive canons which serve to hem it in, the more the city has the chance to be identified, revealed, distracted. [. . . .] Traversed in this way, 'ionized' by the manner in which it is crossed, [. . .] the city is lit up from within.[57†]

Bailly emphasizes the liberating quality of urban space. 'La fonction urbaine' (the urban function), as he calls the basic essence of the urban, serves to create identity and community by facilitating access, making symmetries and resemblances, and encouraging common endeavours.[58] But 'the urban function' is under threat from the tyranny of bad architecture, soulless planning and indifference to what makes cities work, notably the basic unit of urban language, the *street*, and the 'ruissellement de paroles' (stream of words), the endless stories, which animate it. Keeping the street and the city alive depends on understanding their grammar and generating the new utterances on which they thrive. And for Bailly the principal agency of this process is walking, what he calls the 'grammaire générative des jambes' (generative grammar of the legs).[59] Like Réda, he insists that it is movement around it which engenders the city: what counts, Bailly says – echoing Michel de Certeau's analyses and his similar metaphorics of language and walking – is the 'micro-history of trajectories': it is these which make up the city's archive of memories, its 'dépot d'images' (store of images). In terms that again echo Réda, Bailly stresses the active interpenetration of personal

†*La ville existe en masse et se disperse en grains, mais ce qui l'engendre, ce qui la fait être et devenir, c'est le mouvement de celui qui la parcourt. La loi est simple: plus ce mouvement est dans l'écart, le caprice, moins il est soumis aux canons restrictifs qui cherchent à l'enserrer, plus la ville a de chances d'être identifiée, révélée, distrait [. . .] La ville ainsi parcourue, ainsi 'ionisée' par la démarche qui la traverse [. . .] s'éclaire de l'intérieur.*

and collective memory, seeing the city as 'a memory of itself which invites penetration and at the same time infiltrates itself in the active memory of the individual who traverses it'.[60†] The city-walker who is conscious of the space he traverses can become a participant in the palimpsest of the city, part of its archive. Indeed for Bailly, as for Benjamin, the act of deciphering urban signals is what he calls 'an immediate form of experience'.[61] There is urgent need to restore and perpetuate cities at the level of their *imaginaire*, in a struggle against various forms of dispersion. At the end of the book Bailly underlines the utopian strain in his lyrical analyses. But he insists that if 'urban reality is sick' we need to maintain a spirit of utopian projection, to keep insisting on the endless capacities for *meaning* a city offers and the wider patterns – however provisional and precarious – into which these meanings can cohere. The discourse and practice of Paris inaugurated by Baudelaire has proved flexible and resilient because it is rooted in abiding anxieties and aspirations. If it still has a future this is because, more than ever, the city – and Paris quintessentially – is the arena where vital connections between space, language and subjectivity are played out. Still in opposition, wilfully archaic in some respects, the discourse of the *promeneur*, the knowledge and pleasure it sponsors, may continue to offer hope and resistance.

†*Une mémoire d'elle-même qui s'offre à être pénétrée et qui s'infiltre en retour dans la mémoire active de qui la traverse.*

6

The City and the Female Autograph

ALEX HUGHES

In recent times, feminist geographers and social theorists[1] have criticized the way in which analysis of gender issues in the city, feminist analysis included, has tended to conceptualize the metropolitan environment oversimplistically, in terms of artificially discrete, public/private, productive/domestic, urban/suburban, male/female spheres. They acknowledge that 'the notion of a city divided in two by the gender-specific relations of production and reproduction was an elegant model [. . .] through which the modern Western city could be viewed'.[2] They argue, however, that the straitjacketing dichotomies of this model – dichotomies that generate the perception that women remain restricted to the home/suburban space, while activity within the public world, the world of the urban market-place, is largely limited to men – are 'cultural constructions rather than accurate descriptions of sociospatial reality'. Such constructions are influenced, besides, 'by particular experiences and values . . . which speak not to all women but only to some'.[3]

The argument that 'the segregation of public and private, male and female domains appears strongest as a guiding fiction'[4] serves to give the lie to stereotypal notions of the organization of cities, and of the (non)place of women within them. However, it does not mean that women have easily inserted themselves into the urban, public, androcentric spheres of modern Western civilization, or have found these spaces to be exclusively accommodatory or empowering. In her study of nineteenth- and twentieth-century urban experience, *The Sphinx in the City*,[5] Elizabeth Wilson argues that engagement with the city has certainly afforded women of this century and the last access to (sexual) freedom, and to the 'carnivalesque aspects of life', which the urban environment normalizes.[6] Concomitantly, it has drawn them into public existence, by drawing them, for instance, into the industrial and consumerist domains. On the other hand, Wilson indicates, the authenticity of that public existence is partially offset by the fact that the consumerist zones of the modern city space, constellated as they are by emporia catering for a female clientele, are ambiguous entities – 'public yet aimed at the intimacy of the private interior'.[7] What is more, an emblematic mode of the 'public life' into which cities have inserted women is – or at least has been – prostitution. This phenomenon helps to illuminate the sense of vulnerability that, even today, female city dwellers still experience in the streets and also explains why, in the past particularly, 'rigid control of women in cities has been felt necessary'.[8] The application of the kinds of control to which Wilson alludes has meant that in the metropoli of the West, 'women, along with minorities, children, the poor, are still not full citizens in that they have never been granted full and free access to the streets'. They have been obliged therefore to 'flourish in the interstices of the city, negotiating [its] contradictions in their own particular way'.[9]

Wilson's analyses of the woman/city relation in the modern period lead her to a central, striking conclusion. Since, she contends, 'at the "commonsense" level of our deepest philosophical and emotional assumptions, . . . the male–female dichotomy has damagingly translated itself into a conception of city culture as pertaining to men', women have become (and remain?) 'an irruption in the city, a symptom of disorder and a problem: the Sphinx in the city'.[10]

Given the complexity of the relationship between the female subject and the urban environment, it should come as no surprise that the city – whether taken 'as an actual place, as a symbol of culture, or as a nexus of concepts and values determining women's place in history and society' – occupies a unique position within women's writing.[11] As recent critical accounts of literary treatments of the urban suggest, women's reasons for 'writing the city' are multifarious. They do so because it is a cultural artefact, belonging to that broader cultural realm with which they enjoy an uneasy relationship; or because, while alienating in its androcentrism, the city provides release from domestic containment (even if it offers menial modes of labour in exchange); or because the urban space holds out, to women who penetrate it, new possibilities of female community – evidenced, for instance, by the lesbian literary subculture of Belle Epoque Paris.[12] Female-authored treatments of city life are also highly diverse. In her *Women Writers and the City*, Susan Merrill Squier notes contrasts between (i) the (relatively) upbeat accounts of urban possibilities offered by American women authors; (ii) the ambivalent responses to the city felt by Virginia Woolf and Katherine Mansfield, who are 'drawn to [its] opportunities for literary experimentation, anonymous wandering, and sexual freedom', while deploring 'the patriarchal tradition which they often see as its informing characteristic'; and (iii) the foregrounding, by French writers such as Marguerite Duras and Flora Tristan, of the city's hostility towards women's concerns.[13]

For all the variations in their individual depictions of the urban environment, women writers who take the city as a focus represent it, it seems, as a space that bears, unmistakably, the 'mark' of gender. This reflects a more general phenomenon whereby, argues Wilson, the city is regularly constructed, in the discourses of literature, film, social anthropology and history, as an entity which is in itself somehow (multi-) gendered: gendered 'masculine', for instance, 'in its triumphal scale, its towers and vistas and arid industrial regions', or 'feminine' in its 'enclosing embrace, its indeterminacy and labyrinthine uncentredness'.[14] In what follows in this essay, the notion of the 'sexed city' – that metropolis wherein 'male and female "principles" war with each other at the very heart of city life'[15] – will play a key role. With this in mind, it is time to narrow the scope of our investigation, and to address matters Parisian.

In the autobiographical *débuts* of the two women writers whose work is our particular focus here, the Paris that is textually mapped is the Paris of the early decades of the present century. Unquestionably, in these *récits de vie* (life stories), the city is framed, to borrow Wilson's term, as 'the city sexualised'.[16] This is less because Paris before the Second World War was a site of pleasure (although it was) than because both Simone de Beauvoir, in her *Mémoires d'une jeune fille rangée* (1958), and Violette Leduc, in *La Bâtarde* (1964),[17] present the engagement with the urban domain effected by their youthful autobiographical creations as part of a broader engagement with sexed subjectivity – an engagement in which Paris plays a vital formative role. The accounts of gendered experience within the urban environment, and of the gendered character of the city itself, which Leduc and Beauvoir offer the reader, are highly individual. They stand, even, as pendants. However, as this essay will reveal, both women writers 'genderize' the self and the city – the self *in* the city – in relation to a central female bond: the mother/daughter tie. We need, therefore, briefly to explore some contemporary accounts of the dynamics of that relationship before we can proceed to our examination of the ways in which, in the autobiographies of our two authors, Paris emerges not only as a sexualized entity but also as a key site of sexualization.

The mother/daughter bond is a significant focus of the writings of Luce Irigaray and Nancy Chodorow. Both women are feminists working in the field of psychoanalysis; however, their conceptual approaches are very different. Chodorow's standpoint is that of American object relations theory, and her work is empirical. Irigaray's theorizations of the status of the female subject under patriarchy, engaging as they do with Freudian and Lacanian thought, are speculative in the extreme. They reject the 'essentialist, quasi-biologist belief in fixed gender identities'; the 'failure to theorize the difficult [unconscious] construction of subjectivity and sexual difference' that, Toril Moi suggests, subtend the Chodorovian psychosociological perspective.[18] None the less, the visions of mother/daughter bonding offered by these theorists have much in common. Both women stress the phenomenon of non-differentiation, of interpersonal boundary-blurring, as a defining feature of the mother/daughter dynamic. Both isolate self/other mirroring, or specularity, as a key characteristic of it; a characteristic that can leave its participants with an insufficiently developed sense of singular selfhood. Both, above all, frame this central female relation as (potentially) stifling in its symbiotic fusionality, casting it as invasive and intensely problematic.[19]

What does any of this have to do with the autobiographical writings of Simone de Beauvoir and Violette Leduc? How, more particularly, do difficulties inherent in feminine intersubjectivity cast light on those representations of Paris, and of gendered interaction with Paris, offered by these women authors? The essential point of connection here, as later sections of this essay will demonstrate, is that Beauvoir and Leduc both reveal the self/city relation, the self/mother bond and the issues of non-differentiation intrinsic to that bond to be inextricably linked. Admittedly, they do so in ways that are patently dissimilar. In Beauvoir's *Memoirs*, Paris emerges as a 'masculine' space: as a space onto which the conventional, binary male/city : female/interiority gender divide is indubitably mapped, and as a space that Beauvoir's autobiographical heroine Simone seeks to exploit in order to liberate herself from the oppressive confines of the mother/daughter relation. In Leduc's *La Bâtarde*, on the other hand, the city is feminized and feminizing. It is marked by the maternal, constituting a realm in which mother/daughter mirroring is consolidated. That said, in the work of both writers, Paris functions as a stage on which the complexities of maternal/filial bonding are unmistakeably played out.

SIMONE DE BEAUVOIR'S 'PATERNAL' PARIS

In order to unravel the significance(s) accorded to Paris in Beauvoir's *Memoirs*, we need first of all to establish what the city is *not*. Clearly, Paris cannot be construed as the domain of Simone's mother, Françoise, who, transported by marriage from the provinces to the metropolis, found difficulty in adapting herself to it (p. 37). Paris lies beyond that (maternal) realm of 'inside' constituted by the family apartments the Beauvoirs inhabit (on the Boulevard Raspail and, subsequently, on the rue de Rennes) and the apartments belonging to Françoise's relatives. From the inception of Beauvoir's text, then, Paris is divorced from the domestic/motherly. It is represented as separate from that interior domain whose doors Françoise bolts against the city (p. 72): a domain cluttered with furniture and feminine trifles (pp. 7, 9–10), within which the childhood dramas engendered by Simone's identificatory tie with her mother (pp. 40–41) – her resistance to the invasiveness of the feeding process (p. 6);[20] the powerful rages inspired by her hatred of spatial constraint (p. 12) – take place.[21]

If Paris is not the province of Simone's mother, whose world is it? What kind of a space does it represent? Early in the *Memoirs*, we discover that the public realm of the city apparently possesses an emancipatory aspect, since it permits Simone's father to elude the confines of the home ('As for my father, I saw very little of him. He used to leave every day for the Law Courts, carrying a briefcase stuffed with untouchable things called dossiers under his arm' (p. 6).[†] This extract is highly premonitory. It signals to the reader that Paris will henceforth be constructed in the text not only, and in general, as a 'paternalized' realm but also, specifically, as an environment demarcated by a series of hallowed places and institutions incarnating the masculine mysteries of the exterior city space. As the narrative progresses, its predictions are confirmed. Paris proves to be the fiefdom of a number of the male individuals – chief among whom are Simone's father, Georges de Beauvoir, and her adored cousin Jacques – whose presence constellates the (cultivated, bourgeois) milieu in which her childhood and adolescence evolve. It emerges as a city of theatres and avant-garde cinemas to which Simone is introduced by Georges and Jacques (pp. 71, 202); as a world of bohemian bars and cafés where both men are at ease (Jacques 'frequented the brasseries of the Latin quarter, the bars in Montparnasse; he described the bars to me as fabulous places where something was always happening': p. 203);[‡] and – above all – as a

---

[†]*Quant à mon père, je le voyais peu. Il partait chaque jour pour le 'Palais', portant sous son bras une serviette pleine de choses intouchables qu'on appelait des dossiers. (Mémoires, p. 11)*

[‡]*[Jacques] fréquentait un peu les brasseries du Quartier Latin, les bars de Montparnasse; il me peignait les bars comme des endroits fabuleux où toujours il arrive quelque chose. (pp. 280–81)*

cultural and educational wonderland whose landmarks are prestigious establishments such as the *grands lycées*, the Sorbonne and the awe-inspiring Ecole Normale Supérieure in the rue d'Ulm: establishments in which girls are either absent or in the minority, afforded supernumary status (p. 295).

Unsurprisingly, Paris, as site of masculine privilege, obliges Simone to recognize the reality of sexual difference; a reality she strives in childhood to dismiss as insignificant (p. 55). In the second of the four sections of the *Memoirs*, the teenage Simone is introduced to the Collège Stanislas, a school attended by her father and her cousin. Faced with its inviolably male aspect, she is assailed by feelings of exclusion – and, significantly, by a sense of enstiflement that echoes the (food-related, 'female') difficulties evoked in Book One in connection with her infantile bond with her mother:

I tried to imagine the mystery that was being celebrated behind those walls, in a classroom full of boys, and I [felt] like an outcast. They had as teachers brilliantly clever men who imparted knowledge to them with all its pristine glory intact. My old schoolmarms only gave me an expurgated, insipid, faded version. I was being crammed with an ersatz concoction; and I felt I was imprisoned in a cage (pp. 121–2).†

In Book Three, Simone (now in late adolescence, and a student) must confront the fact that the urban, masculine, 'magical' bar-room world is less than easily accessible to persons of her sex:

Many young novelists – among them Philippe Soupault – declared that one could go on marvellous voyages without ever leaving Paris; they would describe the bewildering poetry of those bars in which Jacques spent his nights. [. . .] I, too, would have liked to try that 'hazardous and useless' existence whose attractions Jacques and the younger novelists were praising all the time. But how could I introduce the unexpected into my life? (pp. 263–4).‡

Simone's interaction with Paris is complex. In her childhood, its exteriority is so appealing that when her mother and her nursemaid deny

---

†[J]'évoquais le mystère qui se célébrait derrière ces murs: une classe de garçons, et je me sentais en exil. Ils avaient pour professeurs des hommes brillants d'intelligence qui leur livraient la connaissance dans son intacte splendeur. Mes vieilles institutrices ne me la communiquaient qu'expurgée, affadie, défraîchie. On me nourrissait d'ersatz et on me retenait en cage. (pp. 169–70)

‡[Q]uantité de jeunes romanciers – Soupault entre autres – affirmaient qu'on peut faire sans quitter Paris d'étonnants voyages; ils évoquaient la bouleversante poésie de ces bars où Jacques traînait ses nuits. [. . .] J'aurais bien aimé goûter moi aussi à cette existence 'hasardeuse et inutile' dont Jacques et les jeunes romanciers me vantaient les attraits. Mais comment introduire de l'imprévu dans mes journées? (pp. 365–6)

her access to the Luxembourg Gardens or to the Square Bourcicaut, fits of fury ensue (p. 11). Paris is a promised land, which the infant Simone spies on helplessly from the maternal enclave of the family home: 'In the afternoons I would sit out on the balcony outside the dining-room; there, level with the tops of the trees that shaded the Boulevard Raspail, I would watch the passers-by. [. . .] Already I was beginning to want to escape from the narrow circle in which I was confined' (pp. 54–5).[†] Later, after she has come into contact with certain of the privileged loci of the male city and has intimated their exclusionary character, Paris comes to be synonymous for Simone with a personal exile. Lying, apparently, out of her (female) reach, the city is resented, and rejected in favour of the ('feminine') antithetical sphere of the natural: 'I no longer held sway over the world: the facades of buildings and the indifferent glances of the passers-by exiled me from life. That is why about this time my love of the countryside took on an almost mystical fervour' (p. 124).[‡] Eventually, however, the magnetic power of the (male/cultural) urban environment reasserts itself, and Simone is driven back to it. In Books Three and Four of the *Memoirs*, we find her rushing off to cinemas and galleries, hurling herself into café culture, ranging across the streets and boulevards of a city that appears revivifying in its immensity (pp. 241, 259). Most importantly, we see her frequenting – as a student of literature, classics, mathematics and finally philosophy – the city's 'masculine' sites of learning and their environs. These include the Bibliothèque Saint-Geneviève; the Bibliothèque Nationale; the Sorbonne – her own school, chosen in preference to the all-female ENS at Sèvres ('I hardly wanted to shut myself up with a lot of women away from Paris': p. 159)[*] – and, lastly, the Ecole Normale Supérieure of the rue d'Ulm, that most elite of educational institutions, full student status at which was denied to women of her generation until 1927.[22]

How do we explain Simone's engagement with the urban environment – an environment whose mapping, in the *Memoirs*, is clearly extremely selective? What are the gendered processes in which it involves her? As indicated above, the key to her relationship with the public city space lies

---

[†]*L'Après-midi, je restais assise longtemps sur le balcon de la salle à manger, à la hauteur des feuillages qui ombrageaient le Boulevard Raspail, et je suivais des yeux les passants. [. . .] Déjà il m'arrivait de souhaiter transgresser le cercle où j'étais confinée. (pp. 75–6)*
[‡]*Je ne régnais plus sur le monde; les façades des immeubles, les regards indifférents des passants m'exilaient. C'est pourquoi mon amour pour la campagne prit des couleurs mystiques. (p. 173)*
[*]*[J]e ne tenais pas à m'enfermer, hors de Paris, avec des femmes. (pp. 221–2)*

in the emancipatory, non-maternal characteristics that are attributed to
Paris in this autobiography. Simone's 'irruptive' entry into the urban
realm may be interpreted, in other words, as a central facet of that
emergence from the maternal/domestic orbit and into life which is a
major thematic focus of the *Memoirs*. It intimates to the reader the
intensity of her desire to access autonomous, singular, maternally-
distinct selfhood; to 'untangle the strands of a double self, a continuous
multiple being [. . .] stretched across generations'.[23] We see this clearly in
Book Three. Here, the narrator frames her youthful embrace of Parisian
student life in terms of a break with her past, and, more especially, with
the maternal rules governing that past: 'When I read in the Luxembourg
Gardens and someone came and sat beside me and started a conversation, I eagerly entered into it. At one time I had been forbidden to play
with strange little girls, and now I took pleasure in trampling that old
taboo in the dust' (p. 197).[†] Later, it emerges that Simone enjoys being
able to work at the Sorbonne (an institution distrusted by Mme de
Beauvoir) and in the Bibliothèque Nationale because doing so permits her
to avoid the family mealtimes over which Françoise presides (p. 283), and
to elude that ritual of mother/daughter nurturance which, in the
Memoirs, emblematizes maternal/filial symbiosis. The connection
between Simone's insertion of herself into the city and her longed-for
individuation *vis-à-vis* Françoise is in evidence also in an episode during
which she penetrates, with Jacques, the illicit domain of Parisian bars and
night-clubs. Exulting at her initiation into the louche sanctums of the
nocturnal city environment, she senses that she is finally achieving
detachment from the closed world of mother/daughter interrelation
('Never would my mother have set her feet in such places': p. 273).[‡] What
is more, she seems to intuit the 'matricidal' character of her action, since
she perceives her embrace of bar and café culture to bind her to her cousin
in a profound complicity, as if they had committed a murder
(p. 269).[24]

Simone's entry into (public/male) Paris – specifically into those
Parisian spaces (Montparnasse, the Latin Quarter) qualified by Henri
Malric as the 'brain' of the city[25] – involves her on occasion in a sort of
gender metamorphosis. This phenomenon is the object of narrative
record in the text but is not, on the whole, explicitly analysed or

---

†*Quand je lisais au Luxembourg, si quelqu'un s'asseyait sur mon banc et engageait la
conversation, je m'empressais de répondre. On me défendait autrefois de jouer avec les
petites filles que je ne connaissais pas et je me plaisais à piétiner les vieux tabous.* (p. 273)
‡*Jamais ma mère n'aurait accepté d'y mettre les pieds [. . .].* (p. 379)

problematized.[26] It appears to be far from unwelcome to Simone. She may, in the bars of the Left Bank, enjoy a provisional flirtation with feminine display (p. 272). However, the real appeal of such establishments lies in the fact that within their confines she can be a 'regular'; one of the boys in an urban, male environment where fraternity reigns supreme (pp. 273, 283). As the *Memoirs* progress, Simone's Parisian incursions into the 'masculine' proliferate. In search of entertainment, with male friends from the Ecole Normale – friends whose privileged intellectual position affords them a privileged place in her affections – she enjoys for instance the pleasures of the miniature football tables and shooting galleries of the Porte d'Orléans funfair (p. 335). These pleasures, we suspect, become all the more pleasurable to her by virtue of their virile, virilizing character. A key dimension of the delights afforded her by Parisian student life derives from the fact that by attending the Sorbonne, by preparing for the philosophy *agrégation* (teaching certificate) there, and by achieving excellence in what was deemed to be an unfeminine subject,[27] Simone can not only access a male-oriented space but can herself become somehow (enjoyably) 'masculine' within it. This is suggested explicitly in Book Four. Here, an account of Simone's high-flying academic performance (a performance women students were not expected to pull off) and of the singular gender situation in which she finds herself as a consequence of it reveals the extent to which she is seduced by the possibility/prospect of masculine identification: 'One evening Pradelle [a fellow philosophy student] invited to his house his best friends and their sisters. [. . .] All the girls retired to Mademoiselle Pradelle's room; but I stayed with the young men. Yet I did not renounce my femininity': p. 295).[28][†]

We may choose to regard this last observation, which is endorsed by a report of the titivating preparations that preceded Pradelle's *soirée*, with a certain degree of suspicion. In fact, and in spite of her professed desire eventually to match the elegance of the *belles* she glimpses around Montparnasse (p. 295), it is hard not to view Simone's activities in the diverse sectors/institutions of the Parisian city space foregrounded in the *Memoirs* as indicative, precisely, of a kind of gender-disidentification. Her implicit privileging, in the context of her own gender-identity, of the masculine over the feminine can be related to her refusal of the mother/

[†]*Un soir Pradelle invita chez lui ses meilleurs amis et leurs soeurs. [. . .] Toutes les jeunes filles se retirèrent dans la chambre de la petite Pradelle; je demeurai avec les jeunes gens.* (pp. 412–13)

daughter bind. We may also – and it is important that this connection be
noted – explain it as a function of the conflicted position in which, as a
female intellectual caught up in 'a patriarchal system, surrounded by
male colleagues, friends and teachers', she comes to find herself.[29]
Whatever its basis, self-masculinization, within the urban geocultural
environment, is it seems a feature of Simone's textual trajectory. It
proves, however, to be impermanent. Beauvoir's autobiographical
heroine may penetrate ever further and, apparently, ever more successfully into Paris's masculine bastions (pp. 294–5). However, the
patriarchal city, in the end, returns her always and inevitably to the
feminine – a phenomenon that sits ill with Wilson's perception (based,
admittedly, on later volumes of Beauvoir's autobiography) that 'the
personal drama of [Beauvoir's] intellectual and sexual emancipation' is
inseparable from, and enabled by, her Parisian urban existence: an
existence which 'de-emphasizes' her femaleness.[30]

How does Simone's enforced *retour au féminin* manifest itself in the
Memoirs? Relatively early on, it is hinted at when she visits the Salle
Pleyel and a bookshop near Saint-Sulpice: symbols of Paris's status as
androcentric cultural fief. Here, she must submit to the (quintessentially)
female, humiliating experience of being sexually harrassed (p. 161). A
similar 'reinsertion' into femininity transpires when, having inaugurated
her student existence with a (phallic?) ascent of the stairs of the
Bibliothèque Saint-Geneviève, she finds that she is to sit in the section
reserved for ladies (p. 171). In *Street Noises*, Adrian Rifkin makes the
point that 'the ideal of Parisian pleasure as a paradigm of social freedom
[. . .] is an attractive and a cruel mythology'.[31] His comment meshes
pertinently with the downfalls that dog Simone's attempts at self/gender
transformation within the city space. These downfalls reach their climax
during an episode described by Toril Moi as the '*débâcle* in the
Luxembourg Gardens'.[32] The reader will recall that the Luxembourg
Gardens represent that key province of the city where, in Book Three,
Simone has sensed herself to be eluding the stifling, female taboos of her
past (p. 197), and has exulted in her victory. In Book Four, in the
company of Jean-Paul Sartre (urban male incarnate), Beauvoir's heroine
selects the Gardens as an ideal site in which to place on display her
conquest of masculine, intellectual authority. She does so by outlining to
Sartre the moral system her studies in philosophy have enabled her to
develop (p. 344). Her 'reward' is intellectual defeat: a defeat that, Moi
argues, ensures that henceforth she must embrace the female/secondary
role of 'helpmate or assistant to Sartre's philosophical project'.[33] Sartre's

demolition of Simone's system – a demolition that takes place in a particularly privileged locus of the Parisian cultural/academic map – may be interpreted, arguably, as the ultimate instance of the punishment Paris inflicts on Simone, and on the inappropriately gendered intervention she has been drawn to effect within the male city space.

Simone's 'disorderly' Parisian forays out of the feminine, like the 'corrective' reinsertions into it which befall her, may productively be read in tandem with Judith Butler's accounts of gender identity formation. These accounts suggest that gender is a kind of reiterated 'doing', produced 'through relations of power and normative constraints'.[34] Applying Butler's theories to Simone's urban *peripeteia* allows us to view these as so many gender performances: performances which, whether 'male' or 'female' in nature, are compelled by the patriarchal environment in which Simone finds herself. Analogously, a Butlerian 'take' on Beauvoir's Paris permits the reader to interpret it as a kind of forcefield, or formative arena of influence, in which gender identity is constantly being created and renegotiated anew.[35] A parallel reading may be made of the inter-war Parisian realm charted in Violette Leduc's *La Bâtarde*, even though the gender acts born in and regulated by that space are not identical to those manifested and pursued by Beauvoir's autobiographical heroine. With this in mind, we shall turn now to an exploration of Leduc's Paris, and to an investigation of the modes of gendered being into which that city, as 'inescapably female'[36] entity, impels Violette, Leduc's autobiographical self-creation.

THE CITY AS MOTHER: LEDUC'S *LA BÂTARDE*

In Leduc's first autobiographical volume, her heroine Violette moves to Paris from northern France in 1926. The move occurs during her adolescence, and follows her mother's (socially mobilizing) marriage to a man prepared to 'take on' a woman with an illegitimate daughter. Initially, Paris's impersonality alienates the schoolgirl Violette, who is accustomed to provincial living. Subsequently, however, she embraces the urban domain with a fervour resembling that manifested by Beauvoir's Simone, experiencing an almost epiphanic excitement in the face of its phenomena ('My powers fail me; I need comparisons if I am to celebrate the Place de la Concorde' (p. 148).[†] She pursues a Parisian voyage of discovery that brings her into contact with the city's streets and

---

†*Je suis impuissante, j'ai besoin de comparaisons si je veux célébrer la Place de la Concorde. (La Bâtarde, p. 148)*

gardens; its cinemas, bookshops, cafés and music-halls; its lovers and workers; its colourful blend of social and racial types (pp. 120–24). Within the confines of the city space she finishes her education and finds work in the cosmopolitan world of literary publishing; a world that fascinates her, and which eventually provides an impetus for her own writing career. She embarks on two domestic liaisons: a pseudo-marriage (with her lesbian lover Hermine), and an official one (with Gabriel Mercier, a man she meets shortly after her arrival in Paris, and with whom she enjoys a relationship of considerable complexity). The sections of Leduc's fifteen-part narrative in which Violette's engagement with the urban city space is at its most intense are sections six to ten (pp. 119–248). Consequently, these will provide the focus of the next part of this discussion.

In *La Bâtarde*, Paris emerges as many things. In the particular segments of the text on which we shall concentrate, echoing that cultural legacy proffered by those of her literary forefathers in whose 'heterosexual poetic economy' the city landscape becomes 'a seductive and mysterious woman',[37] Leduc imagines the Parisian realm to be female-gendered and nubile. Paris rustles in her *récit* as if it were clad in taffeta (p. 158), or fluffy with ostrich-feathers (p. 183). Perfumed with Mitsouko (p. 216), its streets are a 'forest of shapely calves' (p. 120). In addition, Paris is represented, increasingly, as a 'regulatory' space in which a squarely feminized gender performance is imposed on Leduc's (initially polymorphous, and highly unfeminine) autobiographical protagonist. That performance is desired for Violette both by her mother and by Hermine, who functions in the central part of Leduc's narrative as an ersatz husband/ provider and as a mother-substitute (p. 178). It is brought into being in Paris's female-oriented, consumerist zones; i.e., within those sectors of the city that are patently governed by a market mentality and in which it would be in no way an exaggeration to suggest that 'humans are duped and drugged into a spurious consumerly conformity and happiness which is most effective in relation to women'.[38]

Which specific elements of the Parisian environment depicted in the middle sections of *La Bâtarde* compel Violette towards an adherence to feminine gender norms, and what are the ways in which this adherence manifests itself? How, in other words, is Leduc's Paris mapped in these chapters, and how is her autobiographical persona influenced by those urban sectors foregrounded within them as centrally significant?[39] If Beauvoir's Paris is that Left Bank Paris of cafés and colleges – the Paris (*pace* Malric) of the mind – Leduc's metropolis is the Paris of the body beautiful. It is a city constellated by the famous fashion houses, beauty parlours and department stores of the *Rive droite*: stores that, argues Wilson, 'created an aesthetic demi-monde for the bourgeoisie in which beauty was for sale as a commodity'.[40] It is the Paris of the Boulevard Haussmann, the Place Vendôme, the rue de la Paix, and the rue Saint Honoré; the Paris of Hermès and Chanel. It is the Paris privileged in *Vogue*, *Fémina* and *La Jardin des modes*; fashion glossies in which gender difference is 'institutionalized and textually entrenched'.[41] It is that spectacular, fantasmagoric Paris wherein, in the late 1920s and '30s, *couturières* such as Elsa Schiaparelli could commission the likes of Cocteau to design their fabrics, so that the worlds of fine art and high fashion overlapped.[42] Within this highly particularized Paris – and because of its powerful effects – Violette is driven ever more urgently to transmogrify herself into the woman her mother and her lover wish her to become.

Violette's Parisian feminization is gradual. To begin with, she is spellbound by the spectacle of the city's feminine sanctums and sites of elegance, but remains personally detached from it, preferring to embrace a mannishness necessitated, she believes, by the curious companionship she enjoys with Gabriel (p. 167). She may be 'gnawed inwardly by a desire for frivolities', 'coveting Paris through a golden grill' (p. 150),[†] but she keeps right on wearing her suits and boots. Later, however, once she has moved with Hermine to suburban Vincennes, and, more importantly, has been forced by illness to abandon her job, becoming in consequence Hermine's 'little woman' (p. 187), she is seduced into embracing Parisian, feminine selfhood – a selfhood that is very much for sale. Thus we find her shopping in the fashion houses and big stores of the Boulevard Haussmann and the Place Vendôme. We witness her efforts, in the chic hairdressing and beauty salons of the capital, to reinvent herself aesthetically, so that she might attain the physical perfection of the female film-star (pp. 212–13). On one occasion, we see her stealing silk knickers, because, sensing that Paris is deriding her failure to ameliorate her 'defective' facial features ('Paris that year Paris inundated with feathers and down there goes Cyrano de Bergerac that's what they shout at you Violette the urchins of the capital': p. 177),[‡] she elects to purloin 'the things that make [other women] feminine' (p. 179).[*] On another, we

---

[†]*Je convoitais Paris à travers une grille d'or [. . .]. (p. 149)*
[‡]*Paris cette année-là Paris fut inondée avec des plumes et du duvet va donc Cyrano de Bergerac ils te le crient ma Violette ils s'esclaffent les mômes de la capitale [. . .]. (p. 177)*
[*]*Je volais [. . .] pour dérober aux femmes ce qui les féminise. (p. 179)*

follow her as, clad in a Schiaparelli costume and carefully cosmeticized, she parades around the elegant boulevards and squares of the Right Bank, in an attempt to dazzle the city and its denizens with her female charms:

Boulevard des Capucines at half-past four in the afternoon. Paris, be more transparent, I beg of you. I can't see myself in all the windows I have oil in my joints, thanks to my gymnastics. The policeman smiled as I went by, a lady in a car looked after me. Yes, she turned her head this way. Soon the river of cars will have frozen, the drivers will climb out on to their roofs to see me more clearly (p. 204).†

All of the episodes and extracts referred to above are infused, needless to say, with a good deal of self-directed narratorial irony. They do, however, in their accounts of Violette's hyperbolic forays into the ultra-feminine, confirm our sense that Paris – Violette's 'rival' in consummate femininity – is set up in *La Bâtarde* as a formative realm within which, to cite Butler, the 'regulatory apparatus' of the heterosexual order constantly calls up gender acts that constitute a 'compulsory appropriation and identification with [its] normative demands'.[43] For all that she exults in them, incessantly observing herself and her actions in mirrors and other reflective media, Violette's female performances intermittently provoke feelings of unease – hence the sensation that she is being turned into a mannequin destined to drown in a quagmire of femininity which assails her during a Schiaparelli sale (p. 196). Sometimes, Violette's antics become parodic (and are perceived as such by Leduc's heroine and her narrating persona alike), leaving the reader with the impression that she is less a 'real' woman than a female impersonator (pp. 202–4). Never the less, Violette is ill-equipped to elude Paris's powerful gender manipulations, in the central sections of her story at least. The objectifying feminine formation to which Leduc's heroine is made to submit in the inter-war, consumerist city space culminates in the 'theatrical' episode that takes place in a *maison particulière* (brothel) in the rue Godot-de-Mauroy. This episode follows an encounter on the Boulevard Males-herbes, during one of Violette's showy struts around Paris, and derives its impetus from her proclivity for luxury consumer durables (in this case an elegant lacquered table from *La Crémaillère*). It involves Violette – and

---

†*Boulevard des Capucines à 4 heures et demie de l'après-midi. Je t'en prie, Paris, sois plus transparente. Je ne me vois pas dans chaque vitrine. J'ai de l'huile dans les articulations, c'est ma gymnastique. L'agent a souri en me voyant, une dame dans son auto m'a regardée. Oui, elle a tourné la tête de mon côté. Bientôt le fleuve d'automobiles sera glacé, les conducteurs monteront sur le toit de leur voiture pour me détailler. (p. 203)*

the hapless Hermine – in a scene of feminine erotic display, staged for the benefit of a male voyeur who pays Leduc's venal heroine for the privilege of watching her parade her lesbian lovemaking (pp. 227–32). It constitutes a climactic moment in Violette's story: a moment at which she 'simultaneously apotheosises herself as female body and prostitutes herself'.[44] The rue Godot-de-Mauroy incident is highly reminiscent of the lesbian spectacles offered to male clients in the brothels of Belle Epoque Paris.[45] We may take it as the logical end-point of Violette's impulsion into performative Parisian feminine subjectivity. It cannot help but recall that city woman = prostitute stereotype present particularly in the literature of the nineteenth century, whose power to inflect modern women's real-life experience of urban existence (a power noted by Elizabeth Wilson) is clearly in evidence here.

How does Violette's urban gender trajectory, as delineated above, relate to that phenomenon of mother/daughter fusion evoked in the introduction to this essay? In order to see the connection at stake here, we need to bear in mind that Violette's mother, Berthe, is consistently framed in Leduc's narrative as a 'brushstroke of elegance' (p. 119), the very incarnation of (urban) femininity. Because Berthe is iconically feminine, the feminization into which Paris inserts her initially recalcitrant daughter (a feminization that recalls the 'corrections' imposed on the heroine of Beauvoir's *Memoirs*) concomitantly '(re)specularizes' the bond between the two women. It does so by transforming Violette into a (flawed) copy, or (imperfect) mirror-image, of her elegant mother ('We were both wearing Cendre de Roses powder and the same colour rouge [. . .] she was the more feminine, the more beautiful of the two' (pp. 134–5).[†] By making Violette 'female', in other words, the city blurs to a considerable degree the boundaries between herself and her maternal parent, and strengthens their relational connection. Paris functions, in consequence, as the vehicle whereby the mother/daughter dyadic bond – whose intensity, in Violette's fatherless childhood, was extreme (pp. 38, 40) – is reconsolidated, and reconsolidated in a way that must gratify the exigeant Berthe, whose constant demand is that Violette should, like herself, 'be a woman' (p. 178).

Leduc's Paris then – in contrast to Beauvoir's Paris – offers the means by which the mother/daughter tie may be reformed. Additionally, and more importantly perhaps, the city appears on occasion to be personified,

---

†[N]otre 'Cendre de roses', notre fard pour les joues étaient le même [. . .] de nous deux elle était la plus féminine, la plus belle. (pp. 133–4)

becoming a kind of maternal double. That Paris should emerge as somehow 'motherly' ought not to surprise us unduly. Its silky, ostrich-plumed, perfumed femininity mirrors, after all, that femininity manifested by Violette's mother (p. 20), who is presented early on in Leduc's narrative as 'a city person', utterly at home in the urban space (p. 54). However, the reader would be wrong to suppose that Paris's 'motherliness' is beneficent to Violette. In fact, the implicitly maternal nature of the city environment makes of it at times an engulfing entity, within which Violette's autonomy/singularity risks erasure. We see evidence of this on two occasions. Both of these focus also upon that engagement with the feminine which, as we saw above, serves to reconsolidate Violette's mirror-bond with her maternal parent. During the first episode – Violette's shoplifting spree in the department stores of the Chaussée-d'Antin – Paris is phantasmatically transformed into an oppressive wombspace in which Violette is first absorbed and then immolated (Paris is a killer Paris is killing me Paris is drowning me I am walking and dying in these stream of frenzied cars [. . .] my bed is waiting for me the sky will tuck itself around me' (p. 176).[†] During the second – a walk with Hermine that Violette embarks on in order to display the eel-coloured Schiaparelli suit she has acquired and in the course of which, as during her trip to the Boulevard Haussmann, she is plagued by halluci-natory visions – the city (specifically its river) flaunts its maternal, 'nurturing' charms, in an attempt to lure Violette into its motherly, deadly embrace:

Lights in the distance were making signs to me, a black bosom [gorge] was throbbing under an old tree: it was the river I loved. I am at your service, come in, come in, why don't you said the bosom under the vast sky. [. . .] No no, oh no, because my carnival nose will float on the water. The profound opportunity has been missed (p. 221).[46‡]

Early on in Beauvoir's *Memoirs*, which otherwise consistently 'paterna-lize' Paris, we find a single, and surprising, vision of an urban realm which is maternal – because ingestible – and which appears desirable by virtue of its (edible) motherliness (p. 7). In Leduc's *La Bâtarde* however –

---

†*Paris est tuant Paris me tue Paris me noie je me promène et je meurs dans ce fleuve d'autos forcenées [. . .] le lit m'attend le ciel borderait mon flanc [. . .]. (p. 176)*
‡*[D]es lumières au loin me faisaient des signes, une gorge noire palpitait sous un vieil arbre. C'était le fleuve que j'aimais. Je suis disponible, entre, mais entre donc dans l'eau, me dit cette gorge au-dessous du firmament. [. . .] Non non et non puisque mon nez de mi-carême s'en va sur l'eau. J'ai raté l'offre profonde. (p. 220)*

a text which intermittently 'maternalizes' Paris – the perils as well as the seductions of the maternal city space are powerfully intimated.

CONCLUSION

The women authors most consistently associated with Paris are, paradoxically, those American expatriates – Edith Wharton, Gertrude Stein, Nathalie Barney, Djuna Barnes – who discovered in the early decades of this century that life in the French capital permitted them to elude 'the patriarchal script of marriage and motherhood enforced in other cities of the world', and to substitute writing for constrictive domesticity.[47] Feminist accounts of the Parisian spaces inhabited by these women – Shari Benstock's *Women of the Left Bank*, for example – evoke a feminine-centred, private world; an empowering domain of artistic and erotic autonomy existing within and in spite of a broader, male-dominated urban realm which, ironically, had been 'feminized and sexualized by a masculine literary poetic'.[48]

Clearly, in the autobiographical writings of Beauvoir and Leduc we do not encounter that hermetic, 'intersticial' city space – that space of secret gardens and lesbian salons – illuminated in Shari Benstock's *Women of the Left Bank*. What we find instead, in Beauvoir's *Memoirs* and in *La Bâtarde*, are carefully demarcated, highly recognizable 'segments' of *public* Paris: segments whose textual evocations weave a kind of 'psychic map of our collective consciousness' of the city.[49] The public, urban sectors charted by Leduc and Beauvoir – Left Bank, intellectual Paris; Right Bank, fashionable Paris – constitute the sociospatial context wherein the pleasures and, more importantly, the discontents of their female protagonists' city existences are born. These discontents, although consistently gender-related, are by no means identical. In Beauvoir's autobiography, Simone's Parisian difficulties are a function of the fact that the androcentric, bohemian, academic city world – the world she has used as a vehicle for daughterly emancipation – refuses to let her 'perform' in 'masculine' mode with the consistency she apparently craves. In Leduc's narrative, on the other hand, Violette's problems derive primarily from the way in which Paris seems in the end – certainly in the central part of her story – to constitute a site of maternal supremacy, in which maternal dictates and desires prove hard to elude.

In the light of the latter observations, it is clearly not the case that either of the authors whose autobiographical *débuts* we have dissected offer their readers wholly positive accounts of Parisian life. This phenomenon meshes, up to a point, with Susan Merrill Squier's sense of the negativity

generally intrinsic in French woman's literary accounts of urban existence. Nevertheless, Parisian experience is, for all its ambiguities,
valorized in the work of Beauvoir and Leduc (both of whom were, very
definitely, writers of the city; writers whose literary trajectories were
intimately bound up with urban living). In consequence, their autobiographies may perhaps, when all is said and done, justifiably be added to
that corpus of female-authored texts that encourage us to conclude that
'in the end, urban life, however fraught with difficulty, has emancipated
women more than rural life or suburban domesticity'.[50]

7
The Poetics of Space Rewritten: From Renaud Camus to the Gay City Guide

ADRIAN RIFKIN

From the one to the other, from the elegant *littérateur* to the route map of sexual diversion; my title suggests a space rather than an evolution, a written space that I want to designate as specifically gay. A space densely and yet unevenly filled in with various representations of a sexual identity – representations that belong in quite different ways to the history of the city. Renaud Camus comes last in time, but first in our movements round this space. Novelist, inventor of a new genre of prose *élégie*, broadcaster and above all diarist, Camus could be thought of as a new Saint-Simon, chronicling gay Paris of the last fifteen years. Yet the complexity of his enterprise is such as to outshine the courtly records of his ducal predecessor. For one thing Camus writes his annual diary in order to be read. Each phrase is penned in the light of this stimulating compromise with reality. For another, the rounds of Versaillais social politics are of a radical, physical innocence when set aside the sexual episteme of gay Paris, its happy acknowledgement of the sex act itself and of the sexual *récit* as *the* essential sites for the cognition and narration of the city.[1] Of course the two diaries share a voice, curious and inquisitive, languid or contented and then abrupt, rebarbative and impossible by rapid turns, the more to underline their very strange comparability.

We have only to trace our passage through a few pages of Camus's 1988 diaries, *Aguets*, compacted with event and discourse, to realize the special dimensions of his project. The complexity of his contract with his social life and with his reader, to constantly engage and re-engage the one with the other in the very poetic structures of his text, is the source for an exponential explosion of endlessly overlapping and sometimes endless narrative, tales, moralities and observations. It was in *Tricks* (1979 and 1988) that Camus first systematically confounded the finalities of sex and text in his self-imposed task to narrate a succession of stories among which the one common element must be the ejaculation of some sperm. And if there experience was already wholly instrumentalized by the

demands of text, in *Aguets* the succession of his pages perfects a demand
or a strategy that Camus, following Barthes, names *bathmologie*; the
treating of each level as the strict equal of any other.[2] The effect, as we
will see, is miraculous in its discursive potential. None the less it must be
understood that Paris now is only one level among the many. True, it is
privileged; privileged as Camus's preferred ground for the true epiphany
of the merging of text and sex. But in its being merely preferred, as a place
of unproblematic enjoyment, to Rome, or Lisbon, or Tarbes or Clermont
Ferrand, Paris is already removed from the dark roster of exotic sites for
guilty pleasure that we know so well from a previous generation of
writers, be they gay or straight, be they Gérard Bauer or Pierre Mac
Orlan.[3] Turning up men of every nation, in baths and bars, into his bed,
men of every origin or colour, Camus's movements round the city realize
its hybridity not as the merely exotic, but as the very materiality of the
writer's subject. Paris, as a sign, is displaced from within and without, its
metropolitanism nothing more than the sum of its complexities.

In *Aguets*, then, for our example, the day in question is Saturday 21
May; writing begins at 11.00 hours. Camus first catches up with a few
days, his concordance. Rapidly, a performance of Massenet's *Werther*, a
visit to his editor, then collecting some cassettes of Robbe-Grillet's films
from the cultural service of the Foreign Office, two tricks at the baths
near the Opéra, a rapid dinner, *Othello* by Welles, another film, and this
morning a run in the Luxembourg. Right bank, Left bank, home, work,
pleasure, culture, food, sex in a few more lines than I have taken to
summarize them. Then two-and-a-half pages is devoted not to an account
of the performance of *Werther*, but to the abysmal state of public mores
represented in the noises made by the inattentive, uncultured public who
frequent the theatre. In particular there is a man, 'a guy with a
moustache, obviously *achrien*, who, despite his fine titles to my especial
indulgence, managed to plunge me into the most intense rage through the
stupefying festival or irritations that he was able to produce all by himself
and almost all at the same time' (p. 182).[†] The man and his companion
leave at the interval, so leaving Camus's text free to generalize its
reflection on ill manners; about one whole page is finally devoted to the
performance itself.

Then we are at yesterday, and if we have followed the grammar

---

† . . . *un moustachu, d'évidence achrien, qui, malgré ses beaux titres à ma relative*
indulgence, est arrivé à me plonger dans la plus intense fureur par le stupéfiant festival de
nuisances qu'il pouvait produire à lui seul, et presque tous à la fois.

carefully through this fictive Saturday that has not yet arrived at itself, carefully relating pronouns verbs and moments, 'this' man, with whom Camus now has an agreeable and simple orgasm in the sauna, is that self-same man, the noisemaker of the day, or possibly two days, before. And he remarks to Camus that having sex with him is just as he would have imagined from reading *Tricks*. Lives and the *récit* of life momentarily interleave. Camus diverges into brief reflection on the realism of this book, more or less accurate, he finds, save for some fantasies on penis size ('for which I don't have a good eye'). At last this leads us to Saturday itself, at 6.30 in the evening. New noisemakers now, outside his apartment, and sad meditations on the melancholy relation of writers with their correspondents. A brief Monday follows, 23 May; a lunch at the Dôme, where he does not take his Sunday trick, who displays enough of his lovely body through his fashionably shredded clothing to upset a *maître d'hotel*. Camus amusedly reproaches his own petit bourgeois mentality. Monday concludes in the Bar Quetzal with some quite intricate ruminations on the use of feminine pronouns by gay men, as well as on how the fetish for big penises allows him, Renaud, who does not share it, a freer access to all that which he does value. We are left in suspense as to whether this value is specifically physical or whether his phrase is the metaphor for another form of freedom.

Thus the city is written. Philosophy blurs its margins with sexual banalities, banal observation achieves as baroque a complexity in front of art as when watching two young men in the Quetzal. The free-floating subject of the gay man overturns the reader's expectations of the hierarchies of city space. The proper placing of work or sex or culture only through a grudging permission of access to a dominant discourse, the furtive stratagem of the Gidean description of the city, or the parodic voice of the 'man-woman' is now the once-upon-a-time of the Parisian *imaginaire*. Camus's presence imprints itself in the substance of the reader's loss of certainty, promiscuously sharing itself through the unfolding of the text.

Does this add up to something, or how should it be added up? The problem is simplicity itself. What might be the traces or signs of the vivacity of a city space that goes largely unseen and untrodden by the majority of its population? Clearly this is not without precedent. Certain shut in or isolated spaces impose themselves. The prison or the hospital, for example, both of which are classically *loci* of exception and at the same time banally present in the social imagination. But what of the bath-house, the bar and the backroom, the gay spaces in the modern city, spaces of an utterly different enclosure? How do they line up with these other institutions as sources for, or as sites of, a common urban *imaginaire*? Would we need to start counting heads to decide if the question is worth the asking? For instance, if there are less gay men in Paris than there are prisoners and their visitors, do their spaces matter less than the prison, especially if a very large number of these gay men might themselves rarely or never frequent them? Are there more or less readily available representations of prisons than of bars, and what is their relative value in the literary imagination? If I pose these questions it is not just to ridicule them, but to shuffle off any responsibility for me either to answer them or to suggest the sociological apparatus that might be needed so to do.

This essay is rather in the nature of a message – not, I hope, from too far away. It is about something that might be happening not just *in* the city but also, following historical precedent, *to* the city, to the systems of its representation. It is just as well to be prepared, ready to take account of these changes among a number of insecurely related yet inseparable forms of social behaviour, those of gay and straight people, and their poetics. You may do this either through looking out for the ways in which such changes might be inscribed in a general consciousness; or through a non-sovereign indifference, a state of mind surpassing that of shallow toleration, merely in noting that all of this is part of your and the City's *I*.

Anyway, I do not want to represent myself as unreasonably heroic in my undertaking, which is simply to trace some of the current borderlines between the ethnography and poetics of the city. But I do think that it is a difficult task. In one sense it is too obviously an oxymoron. Ethnography, after all, has a poetic of its own dissembled in its attention to an apparently irreducible materiality of human relations. And it is the work of ethnologists, such as Marc Augé, who have had the courage to desert their traditional responsibilities, that has helped to reveal the poetics of material life.[4] So we are probably concerned more with foldings of discourses into one another rather than borderlines, relations of discourses that are already brought into being as effects of urban complexities. Probably this delineation is best left neither to sociologists nor to ethnologists, but to poets and writers like Italo Calvino or Renaud Camus. Cultures so rich in repetitions, fetishisms or elaborate rituals of self-realization, as are certain elements of gay society, may, quite casually, be able to generate an imagery in which something of Calvino's interweaving of space, building and body is transformed into a practice of the quotidian. In spite of their (in)visibility they can come to be exemplary.

For the reproduction of gay society – I should say societies, but for reason of tactics I will stick with the optimistic singular – is necessarily elaborate, and never more so than in our own day. Ironically, the more open it becomes, the more matters get complicated. For the more assertive it is of a right to recognition and then to one of indifference, the more closely it passes into new modes of interaction with the main streams of urban culture, interactions that go beyond occlusion or mutual disdain which themselves often partially remain in place. And this is crucial, for it is at the very point of interaction, through magazines, shopping, discothèques, bars, the evolution of a gay business circuit, the movement around city spaces as well as academic writing – gay studies – that the precise registers of difference, from the subtlest of nuances to the most definitive of ruptural gestures, are established. It is here, amidst these interferences, that a gay society renews itself, finds a terrain for a semblance of exogamy of which the purpose is to sustain its fundamentally endogamous system of comportments. For it is here too that men may begin to join this society and learn its mores, on a cusp with the current and desirable discourses of 'normality', sifting through those signs to remain in common, to be adapted or to be left behind. It is also here that gay society leaves an imprint in general mores through widespread imitations of its diverse models of comportment, from codes of dress to modes of human feeling or new forms of sexual relationship.[5]

But perhaps I am too sentimental, and nothing much will come of the last two-and-a-half decades of city life. The twin machines of literary and sociological representation will run on, entropically reproducing the same old urban tropologies under the guise of describing a societal dynamic for which their descriptive apparatus is in fact sorely lacking. The comparison of a passage from Anne Cauquelin's interesting and imaginative *La ville – la nuit* of 1977, with a passage from Renaud Camus' *Tricks*, dated 1978, may fascinate in the perfection of the miss! In Cauquelin, the homosexuals or cross-dressers (*travestis*) – she makes no distinction – are listed with *dériveurs* (drifters), *casseurs* (rowdies), marginals and drug addicts. They 'fall' into a tightly limited space, from which they rarely stray: 'A certain precisely limited section of the pavement; turn the corner, and it's finished. For a heterosexual the field is more vast . . .'.[†] And, despite the number of one-night stands, Cauquelin laments, 'one is finally alone, very alone' (pp. 114–15). In Camus,

---

†*Tel bout de trottoir dont la limite est précise; passé l'angle c'est fini. Hétérosexual le champ est plus vaste; . . .*

It was in the Square Jean-XXIII, it was a little after one in the morning (of the 23rd), it was good weather and there were plenty of people. I was looking for someone I might take back home, where Tony was waiting for me. I followed the kind of alley, narrow, uneven and sinuous which there end up tracing, with their pacings and explorations, behind the cathedral, along the railing which separates the square from the clergy's garden, those who take their adventure amongst the bushes.' (1988 edn, p. 188)[†]

The misrecognition between the perception of emptiness, the unconscious assumption of a dominant 'normality' over and above an abject
liminality in Cauquelin's text, and the social density in Camus is so
satisfying that one is forced to ask oneself, 'who feels alone?' Is it
Cauquelin, with her impoverished and worn-thin, nineteenth-century
vocabulary of Parisian types, the sense that there is nothing to be felt
beyond her observation? Or Camus with his sense of both a social and
grammatical abundance – the exquisitely witheld subject of the sentence
that pulls us through his *drague*, wandering by his side, and then the
waiting Tony in his apartment? Today still, in the cheap sophistication,
the bemused tone, in the wide-eyed yet patronizing prose of certain recent
reportages such as that of Monique Gehler in her journalistic enquiry
Adam et Yves, this mismatch persists. It is the replayed drama of a
normative identity that unconsciously projects its own crisis into the
representation of its other, that cannot imagine this other when it
declines to be furtive, to play the underside.[6]

It makes for a pressure, a desire to maintain the imaginary morphology
of the city in the face of the ensemble of social, demographic and
architectural transformations. Pyramids may rise, whole *quartiers* fall
and rise again, social classes vanish from the streets, but across the
matrices of the city's perception such writers reproduce the gay man's
abjection, even when, as with Gehler, he is 'one of my best friends', when
she knows so many of 'them'. Again, this undercurrent of powerful
regression undermines my utopian *imaginaire*. A political or economic
disaster, a moral backlash, could yet overtake the gay Paris that is the
subject of this essay, conveniently turning a new style of comportment
back over to the exclusive grasp of the abject, catholic poetic of a Saint
Genet or the autocratic social privileges of a Jean Cocteau – those
antinomic figures of an *ancien régime*, of an outmoded, guilty world, so

---

[†]*C'était au square Jean-XXIII, il était à peu près une heure du matin (le 23), il faisait très
bon et il y avait beaucoup de monde. Je cherchais quelqu'un que je puisse ramener à la
maison, où m'attendait Tony. Je suivais l'espèce d'allée, étroite, inégale et sinueuse, qu'ont
fini par tracer, de leurs pas et de leurs explorations, derrière la cathédrale, le long de la
grille qui sépare la square du jardin de la cure, ceux qui s'aventurent parmi les buissons.*

readily assimilated as literary, whether in the cinema or in the uniform of the Académie Française.

I recall that when Nico Papatakis turned Genet's *Les Bonnes* into his film *Les Abysses* (1962), André Breton and Simone de Beauvoir wept tears of gold and diamonds to make it glitter with their prestige. According to a cultural habit of that time, it was with their glory that they set about redeeming the other's abjection as profundity, emblazoned on the publicity outside the cinema. These accolades of Breton and Beauvoir made the matter of Genet's existence above all their own, made that most visible of homosexual writers little more than an epiphenomenon of their power to name him. A spectacle that took place, then, almost a decade before a militant of the Front Homosexuel de l'Action Révolutionnaire (FHAR) was to write and, despite Genet, needed to write, of homosexual oppression in these terms:

Our loves? Let's insist on the matter; a stinking urinal, shit and bottles full of piss, dusty crusts of bread expressly thrown there as if to say to us 'there is what you are, a turd, nothing more.[7†]

Let us make no mistake here: the partition of the city space between class and sexual oppression shares nothing of Genet's glorious damnation in the ecstatic combination of the sexually and socially *maudit*. The elaborate and romantically imaged sexual cross-cultures of the pre-war world, from which he came, now have their threads severed by the long-term brutality of the Vichy and Gaullist states and their literary accompaniment in the overblown, hollow rhetorics of a Roger Peyrefitte or a Marcel Jouhandeau, the patronizing publicity for Papatakis's art-movie version of Genet.

FHAR's representation of the Parisian space of sexuality comes closer to Julien Green's carefully deliberated corrective to Genet that was his novel *Le Malfaiteur* (1954).[8] For while Green was clearly anxious to counter-act Genet's transcendantly evil *jouissance*, it was in favour of delineating the structures of a certain profound difficulty of *being*, and their importance for an ensemble of social relations of which the homosexual narrator is not himself the principal victim. Rather than counter Genet with a coyly winking or self-tormented abjection, Green developed something that may be yet more radical than either, a dense argument for the urgency of a politics of 'homosexual social realism'. If Green's hero

---

†*Nos amours? répétons-le: Une vespasienne qui pue, de la merde et des bouteilles pleines d'urine, des croûtons de pains poussiéreux disposé là exprès, comme pour nous dire: voilà ce que tu es: une merde, rien de plus.*

and the provincial schoolmaster both end up moving from the shady
quais of Lyon to the dark squares of Paris, the movement is both one of a
relative liberation and an enslavement. For Paris plays its historic role as
the site of an ambivalent redemption, accomplished through the violent
occlusion that is the making visible or enfolding of its margins. The still
inexperienced narrator, Jean, new to the city, chances on his sometime
teacher, M. Pâris, and tries to help him find a fleeting lover:

Try to remember at least which places he frequents.
   He frequents . . . the street, as I do.
   But which street?
   All streets.
   And with his right arm he outlined a sort of windmill motion which set his hat
flying onto the road. Anger boiled up in my heart, and with it a similar feeling,
and one that I felt for the first time with its entire strength; desire. (1973 edn,
p. 171)[†]

These gloomy encounters are the reverse space of the cinema hoardings
that publicize the Saint. At the same time Green seems to be less on the
side of literature and more on that of his characters. Far removed from,
but strangely belonging to Renaud Camus's pondering on his Paris, to his
displacement of desire into the unmeasurable frisson of pleasure that is
the embracing of public space. It is 5 in the morning on the point of the Ile
Saint-Louis, and his diary has just dwelled for a few paragraphs on the
beauties of the night-time city – to think that one might live in the
provinces! Renaud is satisfied from a recent encounter and content to
watch other men seeking out their pleasure:

I was thus without any urgent desire, free, detached, in some way absent to these
shadows, these trackings, these rare troths between the two waters. And yet I felt
once more, with all my strength, that there indeed was my universe, that these
stubborn strollers were my brothers, that I was for ever on their side of the
barricade, against the sleepers, the virtuous and the indifferent; that this garden
was my camp, this river my friend, this beauty my sleep and this watch my joy.
(*Aguets*, p. 300)[‡]

†-*Essayez de vous rappeler au moins quels endroits il fréquente.*
   -*Il fréquente . . . la rue, comme moi.*
   -*Mais quelle rue?*
   -*Toutes les rues.*
   *Et il esquissa du bras droit une sorte de moulinet qui fit voler son chapeau sur la
chaussée. Le colère bouillonait dans mon coeur et avec elle un sentiment qui lui ressemblait
et que j'éprouvai dans toute sa force pour la première fois: le désir.*
‡*J'étais donc sans désir immédiat, libre, détaché, absent en quelque sorte à ces ombres, ces
quêtes, ces rares accordailles entre deux eaux. Et pourtant je sentais une fois de plus, de
toutes mes forces, que là était bien mon univers, que ces marcheurs obstinés étaient mes
frères, que j'étais pour toujours de leur côté de la barrière, contre les dormeurs, les*

And is there not also an ironic if distant echo of that nineteenth-century text which, in 1937, Roger Caillois read as the founding moment of Parisian modernity: Sir William's invocation of the city of crime in the Rocambole story *Le Club des Valets de Coeur*? Camus in his turn invokes the spaces and sociability of the sexual outlaw as the condensation of the city's pleasure, the modernity of pleasure as, incidentally, gay.[9]

But given the disparate character of all these elements, it is far from evident that we may set up any simple dia- or synchronology of representations. The discrepancies and dispersions of social transformations and institutional dynamics ensure that the relations of sexualities and their imagery are intractibly uneven and complicated. For 1971, the date of FHAR's *Rapport contre la normalité*, one can hardly imagine a sexual politics that did not have to pass through a certain puritanism, distinct from Cauquelin's, precisely in order to achieve an autonomous as well as a hedonistic visibility. Not, I think, a puritanism that seeks to reject the historic, sexual 'gestuelle' with its very real pleasures, but at least to refuse the social and political conditions of its enforcement, the traditional spaces of its coming into sight, with their ready made décors of oppression, caricature, toleration and abjection. Indeed, after 1968, the confluence of different social and identity politics in the city has been such that the making of a connection between them can only be at the expense of the old poetic of Paris that was structured precisely by its profound sentimentality on matters of class and sexuality.

As it happens, this is at the risk of jettisoning some apparently desirable ideas of a homosexual 'community'. Not only those that imagined a society of secret connections and hardly mentioned networks, but, ironically, the newer more open and relatively militant visions of the 1950s. The FHAR seems to turn its back as much on the achievements of the homophile review *Arcadie*, which had pioneered an active and positive representation of homosexuality since 1954, as on the regressive general mores of the early 1970s. In 1959 *Arcadie* celebrated its fifth anniversary with a geographical sketch of its distribution in what was an affirmation of an essentially sexual solidarity. The countrywide distribution was something to be proud of, one dominated as a matter of course by all-seeing and consuming Paris, but including a wide range of social classes and professions, a stronger base in the industrial cities than

vertueux et les indifférents; que ce jardin c'était mon camp, ce fleuve mon ami, cette beauté mon sommeil, et cette veille ma joie. (Aguets, p. 300).

in the countryside, the whole wrapped up in the common cause of homophilia. And as if to confirm this community, the fictions in *Arcadie* often play across precisely the Parisian spaces that FHAR is to deject from its politics. These are the luxurious *mondanité* of an urban cultural community of artists, dealers, crooks or writers, stories that play the special, marginal knowledges of the sophisticated 'pédéraste' with and against the conventions of light literature. Yet, in uncritically embracing social difference as punctum in their adventures, they more often than not inadvertently fissure the very idea of community to which they make their appeal. Class remains a Parisian game, crossing it with an imagined privilege of homosexuality's abjection and furtive secrets. The FHAR writer continues in a very different vein:

> Let us remind ourselves: here I am not interested in those who have an apartment with a lovely view over the Bois, nor in those who pet a toy-boy, bought in Saint-Germain or the rue du Colisée, in a luxurious bed in the bedroom of their private house in Neuilly. I speak of others: of workers who crash out in a damp hut at Saint-Ouen (or elsewhere), of low-grade office workers, Spanish domestic servants, all of whom are devoted not to the marvel but to the horror of the streets. (*Rapport*, p. 42).[†]

The conclusion is obvious enough. Or, in retrospect two conclusions should have been obvious. Either there will be an end to class oppression, and the liberation of all will be achieved with social liberation. The formulation stands beyond the older, Communist one of a prior downfall of class society, and has seized something Gramscian about the leading role of culture and of sexuality as a construct belonging to culture. Or, as it turned out (a Gramscian or a Debordian might well have forseen this), there will be an unprecedented access to a specialized sexual consumer culture for all who will live in a big city. Everyone will have his Facel Véga and his rent-boy, and this will take place neither on the rues Sainte-Anne, nor at the Place Clichy nor behind the Drugstore Saint-Germain. In the spirit of the movements of modern capital it will be in the old, Jewish, working-class Marais, the memory of which it will come to occlude – just for a change. Let us admit that, though this has come to pass, it is true only for Paris, now, in the relatively liberal days of post-1981. But in either outcome, the one hoped-for or the one that has come to pass, there

---

†*Rappelons-le: je ne m'intéresse pas ici à ceux qui possèdent appartement avec belle vue sur la bois, à ceux qui caressent un minet, acheté à Saint-Germain ou Rue du Colisée, sur un lit luxueux dans la chambre de leur hôtel particulier à Neuilly. Je parle des autres: ouvriers qui crèchent dans une taule humide à Saint-Ouen (ou ailleurs), petits employés de bureau, domestiques espagnols, tous voués – non à la merveille – mais à l'horreur des rues.*

remains a common objective. It is common in all senses, yet utterly radical. This is not to be able simply to name something: to name oneself. To name oneself without connoting the whole poetic of homophobia, from the Prefect Carlier to Frédéric Hoffet, from Jean Lorrain to Jean Genet, a poetic that happens to be a crucial part of the name of Paris.[10]

I can think of no better metaphor for this process that of Yves Bonnefoy's notion, developed in the *Notes sur la couleur*, of a *dénomination abusive* (abusive naming), single words that substitute monolithic fixity for all the names a thing might be were one to name them as they appear. At the beginning of this essay Bonnefoy encounters a people who use several colours to name each single colour, differentially in a perpetual motion of language, of multiplicity, deep currents, foam, and light. 'Do you know a better path towards joy?', asks his imaginary interlocutor;

To undo abusive naming, to lift by this lever the infinite, the arbitrary sadness of the sign, it's to wash the face of the world, my friend, it's to rediscover yourself, breathing in the silent breath of all. We have invented the second degree of speech! (*Récits en rêve*, Paris, 1987, p. 145)[†]

I like this formulation. Its subtle grammatical construction throws into relief the problem of *dénomination abusive* as an ordering of signs as well as of their fixing; as a belonging in an order where inversion, more than a rule broken for effect, is a half-occluded principle of difference, the very principle of meaning. And it suggests how Renaud Camus, incidentally an admirer of Bonnefoy, is able to achieve this effect of cleaning with the invention of a *single* new word, 'achrien', for those who love their own sex and 'hinarce' as its inversion. A word that connotes nothing in particular, an utterly free denoter. And this reminds me that what concerns me most is the timeless story of narrativity itself, of denotation and connotation, metaphor and metonym, formed by the experience of the city and retold against a décor of changing sexual mores. The mores of the movements for sexual liberation in general, and gay liberation in particular during its evolution in the 1980s and '90s. That is to say of a decade after Stonewall in the USA, GLF in England or the FHAR in France, a decade of consolidation into a new consumer culture of urban gentrification in the East Village in New York, in London's Soho or in the Parisian Marais.

---

†*Défaire la dénomination abusive, lever par ce levier, l'infini, l'arbitraire triste du signe, mais c'est laver la face du monde, mon ami, c'est se retrouver respirant dans la respiration de tout, silencieuse. Nous avons inventé le second degré de la parole!*

The difficulty of approaching this rupture is ever present within new representations themselves, especially when they emerge within forms of mass entertainment – where, more than anywhere, a dominant culture requires the preservation of its tropic rights. For example, in André Téchiné's two most recent and utterly liberal films, *J'Embrasse pas* (1993) and *Les Roseaux sauvages* (1994), which respectively concern the arrival of a young provincial on the Parisian streets and the life of a rent-boy and a difficult if essentially happy provincial coming to self-awareness as gay, the general structure of traditional topologies stands firm. In *J'Embrasse pas* the couplet of lurid abjection and abjection in luxury is systematic in the representation of Parisian homosexuality, setting the hard but spontaneous sociability of the streets in a heartaching opposition to the desiring, needy search for affection of the middle-aged television personality. The spaces of '90s Paris are still those constructed for the confrontation of predatory maturity and its hungry, if none the less streetwise and well adapted, victim, which is the immigrant, provincial youth. An intense sympathy or even empathy with the protagonists, the investment of a real emotional charge across the frontier between pavement and luxury automobile, do little more than rework these structures in the modes of a current sensibility that simply allows us to see more of styles of personal comportment. Less parodically than tradition, perhaps allowing a certain autonomy of being, but no more than that.

Meanwhile the emergence of innocent and optimistic self-realization is the affective memory-work of a small town provincial idyll in *Les Roseaux sauvages*, a natural space for the fulfilment of a nature – ahead of which will lie the Paris of *J'Embrasse pas*. Indeed it may be argued that Téchiné, in all his fundamental good will, elides precisely those new tropes of Parisian being-gay that may sometimes arouse the resentment of provincials, but which paradigmatically represent a genuinely new mode of being. After all, this last decade is the first in which it has been possible for a young man to come to Paris and work openly in a gay enterprise, drink in a gay bar and visit festivals of gay cinema without there being a break, a space or abjection and occlusion sundering him in guilt, through difficult transitions. Camus writes eloquently on the matter in his ironic rebuttal of those young provincials who find Parisians hard, and their ineluctable and usually contented adaptation to the freedom that this signifies is a recurrent theme of his texts. Significantly, the chain is not even broken in such an acclaimed work of attempted 'out' realism as Cyrille Collard's film *Les Nuits fauves* (1993), with its purely contingent claim of autobiographical veracity. Collard's antiphonic montage of the 'drague' under the expressway at Bercy with the artist's studio and then with a bourgeois apartment reasserts the normality of the latter, a normality put under a stress by homosexuality but ultimately able to recuperate both itself and homosexuality through redemptive, heterosexual love. And homosexuality, divided by social class, pushes the artist to martyrdom and the working-class boyfriend to fascism in a series of narrative gestures that restitute the urban underside, the concrete jungle and the 'voyou' to the abject as their only viable articulation. Paris for Collard is not too far removed from Paris for Francis Carco. For his troping of sexual space it is as if time had stood still, certainly as if the FHAR's utopian hopes had never been written.

Even as this imagery proves so difficult to shift, it becomes the imagery for a gay public too, who take it on as their culture, yet as one that is dissonant with its comportments. For the *presence* of this public in the cinema queue, clearly defined by dress and style and sociability, changes the way the city looks more radically than do the films themselves. It is a presence that undoes the 'horror of the streets'. Yet it is precisely this 'horror' that is constantly reinvented, in a new form, far from the screens of art cinema. In the underground spaces of a whole new generation of bars, baths, cinemas and sex clubs that currently characterize the commercial cultures of gay Paris, and which, in the age of AIDS provide the space for an educated culture of safer sex, it is here that *vieux Paris* survives. Deep, low lighting of blue or orange, sparsely distributed to create great pools of dark such as once lay outside the limit of a *réverbère* (street-lamp); rough walls of concrete or sometimes the vaulted stones of truly ancient cellars beneath the inner city buildings; complex morphologies of pathways and alleys with lacquered doorways, cabins, or 'recoins', flickering colours of video screens that bleach and tarnish flesh; tension, expectation, anxiety, involvement and distance, rapid decisions and long moments of patient waiting, all are the attributes of the long-lost *flâneur*; the vertiginous slippage from the polished gymnasium to the *pluie fine* of the steam-room, perhaps up a twisting staircase. Such are the spaces of sexual 'drague' that now replicate the old atmospheres of Paris more than any of its daily streets – or than traditional trysting places such as the square Jean-XXIII, these days shut off by splendid railings to keep it neat for tourists. But they accomplish this through a complex sexual democracy. One that is far from free of the day to day neuroses of the average city dweller, but is at least as free from the traditional heterosexual exchanges of either power or money as it is from the heterocratic parody; and where – for this democracy is a utopian space – abjection is only one mode of desire among many, one chosen and assumed.

This evolution has been one of a delicate interplay of imagined or sedimented marginalities: those of the broad infiltration of consumer avant-gardes into once decaying areas of the city, and those of sexualities that require marginality both as representation of a historical position (that is to say, a relation to the dominant) and as a phantasy for the space of enjoyment – conserving the 'horror of the street'. Endlessly a borderline is crossed and kept in play, one that articulates or registers the social *frisson* of vacillating between the occupation of a marginal space as one imposed and as one desired, as well as constantly and ineluctably disclosed and redisclosed in the details of the everyday.

At the same time, the learning to be gay through these codings ensures on the one hand a *durée* of abjection that must always be shed on 'coming out' – which is identically a 'going-in' to this culture, and also the delicate folding of the abject back into subject as a pleasure in itself. The abject now figures not as other but as a technology of pleasure, a naming of parts, of things, of bodies, of spaces. It goes without saying that not everyone is out or happy, nor belongs to the same generation, nor to their own generation, in the same way, nor to the unfolding of the city centre that is contingent with the evolution of gay mores, but not identical to it. In gay writing from Daniel Guérin in the 1970s to Guy Hocquenghem's recent, posthumous *Mémoires anticipées*, writing, that is, of the militants of liberation, the longing to retrieve a lost invisibility emerges as a trope, for to be liberated and part of a social body is also to succumb, to yield up one of the great romantic spaces of the modern city, the liminal space of criminality.[11] But unlike the boundaries of an older form of class slumming, this is a division within the subject, both within the individual and the social subject that is a given sexuality in our days, like 'gay'. As for the narrative form of the city, this vacillation, as the fluctuation of visibility and its loss, of invisibility and its loss, becomes an unreliable and only pointer to certain profound processes of its structures and overdetermination. How might this be written anew, as a new kind of game, across and in which texts?

The gay guide of our own day represents the degree zero of poetic language, and this is not without its importance. For the sideways look, knowing, winking, evading, half-truthing, is no longer an element of the very ontology of being gay. Rather, its specific practice is one of open recognitions and exchanges, and since Barthes's later writings at least, we have come to recognize the ways in which sexual cruising is a paradigm for other processes of cognition where the subject recognizes itself in an object, whether this be a paper in the archives or the punctum in a photograph. Even in a decade, guides have made real advances in their capacity to denote and characterize a space or a place. Then a swimming-pool might, in the *Gai Pied* guide, be described in these rather elaborate terms: 'and on the vast lawns you will see some obvious possibilities (possibilités évidentes) . . .'. While today, with the more summary 'drague', 'drague a.y.o.r.' (at your own risk) or 'r.t.' (rough types), the guide, in its sexual specificity, names what spaces promise. And what they have in common, in the city or in the provinces, on the beaches of West Africa or the public places of Hong Kong, is a 'bathmologie' of unimpeded denotations. The importance of this language lies in its being a register of the hard-won shrugging off of the either guilty or boastful traditions that extend from the *Cythères parisiennes* (1864) of Alfred Delvau in the last century to the *Ces Petits Messieurs* (1925) of a Francis de Miomandre in the Belle Epoque or the old pink pages of the mainstream guide 25 years ago. Paris, along with so many other cities, is stripped of its mystery only to be mapped with a plenitude of expec-tations.

In doing this the guide brings off a radical inversion of the Old Paris style of *flânerie*, exemplified in writings such as Georges Cain's *Le Long des rues* (1913) or Georges Hillairet's *Dictionnaire historique des rues de Paris* (1963). These anecdotal guides, fawning on an aristocratic past, will often construct a fantasy of erotic gallantry or intrigue to turn even the most insignificant remains of a building or unimportant street into a sign for the loss of presence that is historical nostalgia. With the humble namings of the gay guide, the street is left empty of its promise to be fulfilled by the reader's own narrative of pleasure. When the tomb of Héloïse and Abelard in the cemetery of Père-Lachaise marks only the limits of a cruising ground, then it is the normalizing, sentimental narratives of the nineteenth century that are effaced. The episteme of Paris is turned upside down.

I have argued elsewhere that the historical identity of the city, of this city perhaps more than any other, has depended both on the repression- and construction-as-abject of what we now call gay sexuality, and that heterosexuality has needed the gay-abject as an other-metaphor of its own, unacknowledged abjection.[12] The 'radical' intellectual mode of this subjection, the mode of Bataille and Klossowski, made for itself heroes of Sade and Genet, while its populist mode has made homosexuality speak in hidden, veiled or parodic voices of abjection and sentimentality – Jean

Lorrain, Edith Piaf and sundry 'copains'.[13] If this city, capital *par excellence* of heterocracy, has made the gay man symbol of a dis-ease projected from its unconscious, then the emergence of such man as non-abject, it may be supposed, will put the whole structure of the urban poetic under stress. Indeed the general mayhem of liberations, of which that of gay men is but one and women is, of course, another, risks turning over all poetics to the language of the guide, and it is here that we must return to Renaud Camus.

We have seen how his diaries are written to imitate an everyday in which the visibility and invisibility of the *achrien* is precisely the reader's problem rather than the writer's. For even when he goes outside straight society, Camus remains fully present. The integrity and the consistency of his voice yields nothing to the old requirements to modulate either vocabulary or tone, respecting only the aesthetics of pleasure, delectation or irritation, as the case might be. The finer points of a small, provincial painting of the seventeenth century seen in a private gallery, the technical and aesthetic aporetic of Schoenberg's serial romanticism, the behaviour of a young man pushing past him on the narrow staircase of the baths, the quantity of sperm spilled in an encounter, the casual conversations on and of sex and passion, the waiting for a 'phone to ring, or the minitel to turn up an interesting proposition, all these are framed by and with each other and together imagine a morphology of Paris. Their super- and juxtaposition themselves become narrative form for an urban comedy with many beginnings, but few ends, sometimes elegaic and sometimes farcical. In the end his language, this spun-out analogy for experience, is no more representational than that of the guide. But, inscribed on the space–time of a specific sexual identity, an identity like that embodied in the guide (which is always at his hand), it is rich with a plenitude of cultural complexities. And this identity in the text is the space–time of the non-abject gay: filling space rather than passively or grudgingly accepting its seclusion; refusing to expend its entire energies either in self-repression or rebellion. Now it distends so that a sudden incident or its pleasures, sexual or aesthetic, may turn a single moment into a major digression on their meanings and affects. Now it compacts so that days on end are nothing more than a few meetings with publishers, spaces covered, trajectories, but each one liable to interfere with another to demand a discourse. These are the poetics of an equal value and weighting of spaces and their experience, specific to this historic configuration that is the sexual episteme of gay Paris.

Should we venture quite so far into a radically separate sector of the city, even if to do so holds out a new understanding of its future in representation, as of its history? Renaud Camus preserves for us an exquisite irony:

In effect I believe that the truth of discourse, but also of sexual activity, the truth of the subject face to face with his desire, implies and involves a truth of one's relation to the world a thousand times greater, a thousand times more precise but also, because it is a thousand times more exciting, a thousand times more *poetic*. (*Aguets*, p. 299)[†]

Where sex is put in brackets, he explains, all social exchange is tiring for him. In effect he feels closer to heterosexuals, 'who are passionate for pleasure and who love to speak of it', than to homosexuals – and *here* he does use the word – who are 'puritans, discreet, decorous, or who think that all that is nothing but a matter for the intimate, of mystery, of secrecy'. Not for them the great trajectories of the beautiful city, the night-time river, the island at five in the morning. The homosexual cannot enjoy the freedom of the *achrien* any more than the *hinarce*, because he orders experience according to the rules of decency. It is not so much that the poetic is driven by sex as the manner in which the poetic embraces it: it is the endlessly elaborate forms of sexed city that the poetic engrosses, nourishes and then discloses to reproduce itself. Renaud seems almost to turn back to the histories of urban writing. But his is not so much a version of this tradition as its complete, rhetorical inversion. And it is in this transformation of the rhetoric of the city that he subtly yet radically refuses the very sexual terms within which Genet had worked, to reveal a new identity as the city's text.

[†]*Je crois en effet que la vérité du discours mais aussi de l'activité sexuels, (sic) la vérité du sujet face à son désir, implique et entraine une vérité mille fois plus grande du rapport au monde, mille fois plus précise mais aussi, parce que mille fois plus excitante, mille fois plus poétique.*

8

'Mirages de Paris': Paris in Francophone Writing

BELINDA JACK

Given the sheer quantity of writing that has emerged in the francophone world, which has accelerated during the last thirty-five years, it is
probable that any attempt at comprehensiveness in terms of the treatment of my topic would require volumes. Even to consider Paris solely
as a city of exile – and this would be to reduce the complexities of
many texts that treat Paris in this way yet do much more – within
francophone writing in any sense globally, would be a massive undertaking. In any case, excellent short studies of Paris within particular
francophone literatures were included in the two-volume *Paris et le
phénomène des capitales littéraires* (*Paris and the Phenomenon of
Literary Capitals*), published by the Centre de la Recherche en Littérature Comparée.

Within this collection is Jaqueline Arnaud's 'Le Paris des Maghrébins' ('North Africans' Paris'). Arnaud notes the areas of Paris most
frequently referred to by North African novelists: the Gare de Lyon,
and less often the Gare d'Austerlitz, points of entry to, of first
encounter with, Paris, arriving from Marseille, point of entry to, of first
encounter with, France. The cafés and hotels around these stations are
also significant *loci* for meetings with compatriots and other immigrants. Less obvious are the numerous evocations of the world of the
Métro. In Rachid Boudjedra's *Topographie idéale pour une agression
caractérisée*, the Métro becomes a labyrinthine space in which the hero
is lost in a three-dimensional maze, trapped physically, and psychologically wholly disorientated. The experience is a preface to death. As
Arnaud writes:

At the end of the labyrinth which the man, caught like a rat, like a ballbearing in a
pinball machine, will only find his way out of after a day of anxiety, of wandering
[. . .]. He will meet his death [. . .]. The underground space of the métro is the
symbol of a futuristic universe wholly different from the natural space in which
the immigrant lived. In contrast with the ordered spaces on the surface, it is

totally strange, the tragic *locus* of a failed journey of initiation which emerges at the point of death.[1†]

Arnaud concludes her analysis of Paris as a place of exile thus:

Rare are the places outside the ghetto where the immigrant worker can attain and taste a degree of calm, not to say happiness: it is thanks to a woman that Lakhdar (in Kateb's [Yacine] *The Starry Polygon*) takes walks along the banks of the Seine, or frequents Montparnasse. She is a Bretonne exiled in Paris, and he comes to the conclusion, in the union of their loneliness, that: 'It is not the same thing, but it is nevertheless similar.' (p. 197)[‡]

Arnaud's concluding remarks depend on certain antitheses: between the artificial (Métro) landscape and a 'natural' home landscape, between surface order, and subterranean chaos. Lakhdar's analysis depends on a careful consideration of the antithesis same/different and the differences between sameness and similarity. Consideration, elaboration, and something akin to deconstruction, of these antitheses lies at the centre of the francophone project. This is an area to which the discussion will return later.

In the same volume as Arnaud's article on North African writing is Robert Jouanny's 'Des Nègres à Paris' ('Negroes in Paris'), which considers Paris in francophone African novels beginning with Bernard Dadié's *Un Nègre à Paris* (1959). He concludes:

In all the novels that we have examined, the voyage of initiation to Paris has been at once fervent and disappointing. In each case, it ends in a cruel stalemate: suicide, murder, imprisonment, break up of the couple, rupture with a rediscovered Africa, uneasy solitude, melancholy distancing [. . .].[2*]

By and large the 'fields' proposed in the *Paris* volumes are national: 'L'Image de Paris dans la littérature tunisienne' by Tahar Bekri and 'Paris

---

†*Au sortir du labyrinthe dont l'homme, pris comme un rat, comme une bille de flipper, ne se dégagera qu'après toute une journée d'angoisse, d'errance [. . .] Il rencontrera la mort. [. . .] L'espace souterrain du métro est le symbole d'un univers futuriste totalement différent de l'espace naturel où vivait l'immigré. Par rapport aux lieux aménagés de la surface, il est la totale étrangeté, le lieu tragique d'un parcours initiatique manqué qui débouche sur la mort.*

‡*Rares sont les lieux hors ghetto où le travailleur immigré peut accéder et goûter un peu de calme, voire de bonheur: c'est grâce à une femme que Lakhdar (dans Le Polygone étoilé de Kateb) se promène sur les bords de la Seine, ou fréquente Montparnasse. C'est une bretonne exilée à Paris, et il en conclut à la conjonction de leurs solitudes: 'Ce n'est pas la même chose, mais c'est toujours pareil.'*

**Dans tous les romans que nous avons examinés, le voyage initiatique vers Paris a été à la fois fervent et décevant. Dans tous les cas, il s'achève par un cruel échec: suicide, meurtre, emprisonnement, rupture du couple, rupture avec l'Afrique retrouvée, inquiétante solitude, distanciation mélancolique . . .*

et la description des villes d'identité par quelques romans algériens' by Charles Bonn; regional: 'Le Paris des Maghrébins' by Jacqueline Arnaud; or racial, crudely defined: 'Des Nègres à Paris' by Robert Jouanny. The definition of a text rather as 'francophone', on the other hand, needs careful consideration. The Algerian writer Nabil Farès includes the following writers within his definition of 'francophone writer':

Beckett, Ionesco, Jabès, Todorov, Kristeva [. . .] Sarraute, Cixous, [. . .] Mme de Staël, Supervielle, and [. . .] not to close, but to open even wider the field of language and internationalism: yes, Saussure, the Swiss linguist. You know?[3†]

These writers, he argues, and many more whom he cites, 'by their practice of active communication have moved *la francophonie* to a place other than that where it was originally, a miserable doctrine of colonial segregation.'[‡] Farès opens wide the definition of what *now* constitutes the francophone and emphasizes its historicity.

The term 'francophone' was first coined by the geographer Réclus in his book *La France, Algérie et colonies* (1880) to describe both a linguistic, and geo-political, French-speaking bloc. Farès, on the other hand, emphasizes a subversive 'strangeness' as central to the development of the francophone:

It is to a space of strangeness in the language and of the language that *la francophonie* owes its development: so-called francophone literature surpasses in its movement, multiple reductive narrownesses. (p. 24)[*]

To assume a trans-historical definition of the francophone is thus to suggest a spurious fixity. This *caveat* needs to be borne in mind when considering the place of Paris within so-called 'francophone' writing particularly because the move from stability and closure of meaning (with regard to the notion of the francophone) to openness and defiance of easy definition (often dependent on references to apparently all-embracing antithetical pairs such as those mentioned by Arnaud above) is one in which Paris itself plays a part. This needs brief preliminary

†*Beckett, Ionesco, Jabès, Todorov, Kristeva [. . .] Sarraute, Cixous, [. . .] Mme de Staël, Supervielle, et [. . .] non pour clore, mais ouvrir encore plus grand le champ de la langue et de l'internationalité: oui, Saussure, le linguiste suisse. Vous connaissez?*
‡*Par leur pratique de la communication active ont installé la francophonie dans un autre lieu que celui où elle fut à l'origine, pauvre doctrine de la ségrégation coloniale.*
**C'est à un espace de l'étrangeté dans la langue et de la langue que la francophonie doit son développement: la littérature dite francophone dépasse en son mouvement les multiples étroitesses réductrices.*

illustration. In the first case, Paris, in parallel with early formulations of *la francophonie* imposes an identity which must be wholly assimilated: 'Ah! palpitating Paris! Ah! vibrating Paris! Oh! trembling Paris! You who know how to make others' hearts beat *in unison with yours*'.[4†] More recently, on the other hand, the West Indian writer Edouard Glissant's first-person narrator arrives within a 'landscape of the mind' in which he is no longer the islander arriving at the centre. Of Paris he reflects: 'Suddenly I know her secret: and that's that Paris is an island which receives from every direction and then transmits.'[5‡] Glissant's *Soleil de la conscience* will be described in greater detail below. The purpose of its mention here is to demonstrate the parallel historical shifts in formulations of the concept of the francophone on the one hand, and treatment of Paris in francophone writing on the other. The relationship between Imperial capital, in one instance, and linguistic capital, in the other, is a complex one.

During the last decades of the colonial period, the relationship between Paris and the French Empire was supposedly embodied in the Exposition Coloniale of 1931. In the opening address (to which Jon Kear refers), Jean de Castellane succinctly – and somewhat lyrically – expressed the idea of the exhibition:

Motivated by a sense of patriotic solidarity and fraternal union, the peoples will come to Paris to examine, to appreciate and to love, in the laughing decor of this verdant wood, the true image of France, the France of the five continents.[6*]

It is the reduction of the multiple ('five continents') to the singular ('*the* image of France' (in the singular) which is remarkable here. And this is sanctioned, made apparently reasonable by the worldwide use of a *single* language, *Francien*, originally, crudely speaking, the language of Paris. Assimilation, a notion central to French colonial policy, was first and foremost linguistic, and even 'body language' was considered, as the following Preface to Paul Hazoumé's *Doguicimi* (1937) by Georges Hardy bears witness. He wrote, telling us nothing whatsoever about the text:

†*Ah! palpitant Paris! Ah! vibrant Paris! Oh! trépidant Paris! Toi qui sait faire battre le coeur des autres* à l'unisson du tien. [*my emphasis; D. Oussou-Essui, La Souche calcinée, 1973*].

‡*Je sais soudain son secret: et c'est que Paris est une île, qui capte de partout et diffracte aussitôt.*

**Dans une pensée de solidarité patriotique et d'union fraternelle, les peuples viendront à Paris examiner, apprécier et aimer dans le riant décor de ce bois verdoyant, l'image véritable de la France, la France de cinq parties du monde.*

If his skin colour did not betray his origins you would take him for a Frenchman of France; everything in his free and easy manner of expression, in his courteous manner, in his gestures [. . .] is like one of us.[7†]

What numerous prefaces to early texts in French by Africans written by Frenchmen emphasize is the degree to which the text testifies to the success of linguistic and cultural assimilation. This in turn leads to political assimilation. Hardy's preface continues: 'as a French citizen he can imagine no other homeland than ours'. The relationship between acquisition of language and culture – and loyalty to 'the homeland' – is explicit. As the North American critic Christopher Miller put it so well in a recent essay: 'Francophone literacy arrived in colonial Africa like a Trojan Horse, bearing an ideology of collaboration and assimilation.'[8] And this is true not only of French in colonial Africa but throughout the French Empire.

It is equally – and perhaps more surprisingly – to a single, monolithic 'universal civilization' that the Senegalese poet and politician Léopold Sédar Senghor, who was soon to become the most vociferous spokesman of Negritude as an ideology, then only a Député at the Assemblée Nationale Constituante, repeatedly referred from the mid-1940s onwards: 'It is thus that we will together create a new civilization of which the *centre* will be Paris, a new humanism.'[9‡] More recently, in his essay 'Qu'est-ce qu'une capitale littéraire', which forms the introduction to *Paris et le phénomène des capitales littéraires* mentioned earlier, he considers a number of objections that might be made to the idea of Paris as a 'literary capital'. He describes his third possible objection thus: 'Between the country and the world there exists a linguistic field over which the metropolis transmits' ('Entre le pays et le monde, il existe une domaine linguistique sur lequel rayonne la métropole').[10] This relationship between geographical space and language he sees as problematic, but he nevertheless continues: '*Aside from all political considerations* I would like to see in this francophonia, a sort of ideal and moving literary state' (p. 5; my italics). [*] To leave aside 'political considerations' is to deny the colonial origins of the francophone. It is to deny all sorts of complex entanglements. As Edward Saïd argues in the 1984 preface to *Beginnings*:

†*Si son teint ne trahissait son origine, vous le prendriez pour un Français de France; tout sans sa façon libre et gaie de s'exprimer, dans son allure courtoise, dans ses gestes [. . .] est d'un homme de chez nous.*
‡*C'est ainsi qu'ensemble nous créerons une nouvelle civilisation dont le centre sera Paris, un humanisme nouveau.*
*En dehors de toute considération politique, je voudrais voir dans cette Francophonie, une sort d'Etat littéraire idéal et mouvant.

Literature, history, philosophy, and social discourse and indeed most modes of
writing about men and women in history are, in fact, tangled up together. [. . .]
They are often separated on professional, even epistemological grounds in order
to accomplish social goals of one sort or another. [. . .]
  Criticism [Saïd claims] if it is to be criticism and not only the celebration of
masterpieces, deals with the separations, the entanglements.[11]

To juxtapose passages from Senghor's speeches, such as those quoted
earlier in which Paris is proposed as the 'centre' of a new 'civilization',
with passages of his poetry is to reveal fundamental tensions if not
contradictions between his socio-political and poetic discourses. 'In
Memoriam' (written in memory of the Senegalese soldiers who died in
Europe fighting for France during the Second World War) was published
in 1945 in his collection *Chants d'ombre*:

> O shades of the Dead, who have always
> refused to die, and always known resistance
> to Death
> Even at the Sine, at the Seine, and in my
> delicate veins, my unconquered blood,
> Protect my dreams as you have guarded your
> sons, the wanderers with delicate feet.[12]†

Senghor's apostrophic utterances are spoken in Paris; the poem continues:

> O Dead! Watch over the rooftops of Paris in
> the dominical fog.‡

The antithetical relationship between here (Paris, place of exile) and the
Serer kingdom (home) is the central structuring element of the poem,
supported by the notion of migration and above all by the juxtaposition
of two rivers: the Sine and the Seine. The Sine is a river in the Serer
kingdom in Senegal where Senghor grew up. Why the juxtaposition is so
striking is because of the similarity of the two names. As readers we move
– because of one letter – between two worlds. A single letter transports us
across the globe, across seas, from one climate to another, from one race
to another (the last lines of the text refer to 'mes frères aux yeux bleus')
and more. Here Senghor's poetics do not seem to be the corollary of his
political discourse where what is stressed are the ideas of an undifferenti-

---

†O Morts, qui avez toujours refusé de mourir, qui / avez su résister à la mort / Jusqu'en Sine
jusqu'en Seine, et dans mes veines / fragiles, mon sang irréductible / Protéger mes rêves
comme vous avez fait vos fils, les / migrateurs aux jambes minces.
‡O Morts! défendez les toits de Paris dans la brume dominicale.

ated, singular 'civilisation universelle' or 'humanisme nouveau', for which Paris is proposed as the origin, the centre. What the poetics elaborate most persistently is a poetics full of paradox, of anxious shifts to and fro, from belonging to non-belonging. Here is evidence to support Saïd's claim that discourses are muddled up together and that the entanglements need to be explored.

The alienation that results from the experience of not belonging to a single culture or of belonging (if that is the right word) to two cultures or more, is the generative *donné* of much francophone writing. The most famous articulation of an alienation which is at once geographic, cultural and linguistic is the Haitian Léon Laleau's, in his early poem 'Treachery' ('Trahison'), published in Senghor's *Anthologie de la nouvelle poésie nègre et malgache de langue française* (1948):

> Do you feel this suffering
> And this unequalled despair
> To express with the words of France
> this heart which comes from Senegal.[13][†]

This is not the experience of belonging to a privileged 'humanisme universelle' (to use Senghor's term), but perhaps closer to the experience described, for example, by the Congolese poet Tchicaya U Tam'si:

Every civilization is a syncretic encounter between two worlds, barbarous for one and other, barbarous one and the other. And this produces, according to all evidence, a new barbarism, so turned against itself that it is necessarily a tragic beast, fatal, because it is inhabited by two deaths, that of the two worlds which raised it.[14][‡]

The tragedy described by Tchicaya U Tam'si is a tragedy lived out by many of the first generation of francophone African writers.

On the one hand there is the experience of non-belonging:

Fara felt that the white crowd assimilated him poorly. It succeeded in tolerating him only out of kindness [. . .]. In the street he found again in the smiles of passers-by that same protective irony which rained arrows on him.[15][*]

[†]*Sentez-vous cette souffrance | Et ce désespoir à nul autre égal | D'apprivoiser avec les mots de France | Ce coeur qui m'est venu de Sénégal.*
[‡]*Toute civilisation est une rencontre syncrétique de deux mondes, barbares l'un pour l'autre, barbares l'un et l'autre. Et cela produit de toute évidence un nouveau barbare si controversé en lui-même que c'est forcément un être tragique, fatal, parce qu'habité par deux morts, celle de deux mondes qui l'ont enfanté.*
[*]*Fara sentait que cette foule blanche l'assimilait mal. Elle n'arrivait à le tolérer qu'à force de bienveillance [. . .]. Dans la rue il retrouvait sur le sourire des passants cette même ironie protectrice qui le criblait de flèches.*

The experience of alienation in Paris – variously encoded – is frequently combined with a growing sense of alienation from the home culture:

He no longer had faith in the existence of the souls of his ancestors; he renounced his father, he denied all that he had respected.[16†]

Jouanny, in his article 'Des Nègres à Paris', in the volumes mentioned earlier, exploring a range of novels published between 1953 (Dadié's *Climbié*) and 1984, concludes:

In all the novels which we have examined, the voyage of initiation to Paris has been both fervent and disappointing [. . .]. Marked with the sign of the Other, the initiate will never be anything other than a hybrid. (pp. 338–9)[‡]

The linguistic corollary of 'hybridity' is, of course, bi- or multi-lingualism. An obvious but much neglected *donné* of the francophone is that it exists – out there beyond the metropolis, and indeed in microcosm within its urban suburbs – in bilingual or more often multilingual spaces. The consequences of this are multiple and complex for the individual psyche – and, of course, for writing. The quotations from Senghor's 'In Memoriam', Laleau's 'Trahison' and from Tchicaya U Tam'si suggest and imply the psychological corollaries of belonging to two cultures, speaking two languages; others are more systematically explored in a fascinating collection of essays, *Du bilinguisme*, presented by the Moroccan writer and critic Abdelkebir Khatibi. Tzvetan Todorov's essay 'Bilinguisme, dialogisme et schizophrénie' offers what is in part a historical analysis:

In the not too distant past, everything which approached what today we call dialogism was seen as a blemish. There is no point calling to mind Gobineau's invectives against mixed races or those of Barrès against uprooted people. I will cite, rather as a curiosity, this more recent phrase of Malraux which rests on another authority: 'Colonel Lawrence said from experience that any man who truly belonged to two cultures [. . .] would lose his soul.' If I do not dwell on this kind of affirmation it is not that they no longer exist, nor that the positions from which they emanate are not powerful ones; but because I do not share with them any common ground, to the point where I am unable to embark on any dialogue; [. . .]. These attitudes seem to me to belong, historically, to the past; they are consonant with the great patriotic moment of the bourgeois States.[17*]

---

†*Il n'avait plus foi dans l'existence des mânes de ses ancêtres; il abjurait son père, il reniait tout ce qu'il avait respecté. [Jouanny, p. 335]*

‡*Dans tous les romans que nous avons examinés, le voyage initiatique vers Paris a été à la fois fervent et décevant [. . .]. Marqué du signe de l'Autre, l'initié ne sera jamais qu'un hybride.*

Dans un passé pas très éloigné, tout ce qui pouvait se rapprocher de ce que nous appelons aujourd'hui le dialogisme, était perçu come une tare. Inutile de rappeler ici les invectives de Gobineau contre les races mixtes, ou celles de Barrès contre les déracinés. Je citerai, plutôt comme une curiosité, cette phrase plus récente de Malraux qui s'appuie, sur une autre

What Hazoumé's early writings suggest – and Hardy's preface makes explicit (quoted above) – is the relative success of linguistic and thus cultural assimilation. Senghor's poetics – and they can be proposed as a transitional moment – suggest psychological, even epistemological paradoxes. The transitional moment is transcended, however, by a deconstructive move, such as that taken by a number of North African theorists and West Indian writers. In his text *Maghreb pluriel*, for example, Khatibi proposes deconstruction as a philosophical equivalent of decolonization. Contesting the idea of an absolute legitimizing origin which authenticates meaning and truth, Khatibi deconstructs Frantz Fanon's famous call to abandon Europe and instead declares: 'We are always in the process of asking ourselves: which West are we talking about? Which West opposed to us?' ('Nous sommes toujours en train de demander: de quel Occident s'agit-il? De quel Occident opposé à nous-mêmes?')[18] Khatibi (and Bounfour) elaborate instead a new epistemological approach, an 'orphan reason' ('raison orpheline'):

What is orphan reason if it is not the practical refusal of ethnocide, of glottophagia and ethnocentrism. Vigilance in the face of all 'original' legitimacy?'[19†]

Similarly, Alain Baudot has argued:

Turning back against all that would like to see the triumph of the Identical (the Same) and thus of domination, francophonia manifests itself as a strategy of alterity, and truly makes itself (in Adorno's terms) a better aesthetic and social practice.[20‡]

So we've moved from francophonie in terms of 'civilization universelle', of coincidence between what happens at the *centre* and *beyond*, to a 'strategy of alterity' ('stratégie de l'altérité'). In fictional terms the former frequently – even necessarily – leads to tragedy. Where does the

---

autorité: 'Le colonel Lawrence disait par expérience qui toute homme qui appartient réellement à deux cultures . . . perdait son âme.' Si je ne m'attarde pas sur ce genre d'affirmations, ce n'est pas parce qu'elles n'existent plus, ni parce que les positions dont elles procèdent ne sont pas puissantes; mais parce que je ne partage avec elles aucun territoire, de sorte que je puis non plus engager aucun dialogue; [. . .] ces attitudes me parraissent appartenir, historiquement, au passé; elles sont consonantes au grand moment patriotique des Etats bourgeois.

†Qu'est-ce que la raison orpheline sinon le refus pratiqué de l'ethnocide, de la glottophagie et de l'ethnocentrisme. Vigilance donc à toute légitimité 'originelle'.

‡Se retournant contre ceux-là mêmes qui aimeraient y voir le triomphe de l'Identique (du Même) et donc de la domination, la francophonie se manifeste comme une stratégie de l'alterité, et se fait véritablement (pour parler comme Adorno) d'une meilleure pratique esthétique et sociale.

new aesthetic and social practice manifest itself as francophone writing, and what part has Paris played within it?

One of the most outstanding examples and one which moves in a sense from an early position to a radically new one in its 71 pages is Edouard Glissant's *Soleil de la conscience* (1956):

Having come from Martinique (which is an island in the Caribbean belt) and living in Paris, here I've been, for the last eight years, committed to a French solution: I mean to say that I am no longer so committed because it is so decided on the first page of my passport, but because I find more and more necessary, a reality from which I am unable to absent myself.[21]†

It could be read as a highly poetic essay made up of fragments relating to a young Martinican's stay in Paris in the 1950s:

Thus, on the woolly noise, some object of silence rises up, but so vast. It is, for example, the signal of morning which comes and goes on the milkman's cart. It is the bus which doesn't stop at this hour, and which I follow on its way: a shooting star whose sound decreases like the light of a comet [. . .]. (p. 55)‡

It could be read as a work in the manner of Aragon's *Le Paysan de Paris*: both texts are nourished by the experience of a Parisian landscape. The topography of Glissant's *Soleil de la conscience* is one of initiation which passes from loss of self to self-discovery. Winter in Paris is experienced as an 'inverted exoticism' ('exotisme à rebours'):

With the winter [. . .] the snow arrives, crystallized reality of difference, of whiteness. [. . .] The snow of (and in) Paris, a revealing metonym, more than matter with tangible repercussions for sight and touch, is above all the symbolic image of an opening up towards illumination, an illumination other than that of the sun, and thus, the image of the experience (felt, lived) of the different, the Other.[22]*

---

†*Venu de la Martinique (qui est une île de la ceinture caraïbe) et vivant à Paris, me voici depuis huit ans engagé à une solution française: je veux dire que je ne le suis plus seulement parce qu'il en est ainsi décidé sur la première page d'un passeport, ni parce qu'il se trouve qu'on m'enseigna cette langue et cette culture, mais encore parce que j'éprove de plus en plus nécessaire une réalité dont je ne peux pas m'abstenir.*
‡*Ainsi, sur la laine du bruit, quelque objet de silence s'élève, mais si vaste. C'est par exemple le signal du matin, qui vient et va sur la charrette du laitier. C'est l'autobus qui ne s'arrête pas à cette heure, et que je suis dans sa course: étoile filante dont le bruit décroit comme la lumière d'une comète [. . .].*
**Avec l'hiver [. . .] arrive la neige, réalité cristallisée de la différence, du blanc, tout court.*
La neige de (et à) Paris, métonymie révélatrice, plus qu'une matière aux répercussions tangibles sur la vue et le toucher, est avant tout l'image symbolique de l'ouverture vers une luminosité autre que celle du soleil et, par là, l'image de l'expérience (sentie, vécue) du différent, de l'Autre.

Glissant's Paris is above all a witness that watches and encourages not a physical or geographical encounter but the subject's acquisition of language. As Glissant himself described it in 1981: 'The intellectual trajectory is committed to a geographical itinerary, by means of which the thinking of Discourse explores its space and binds itself in.'[23]†

Soleil de la conscience is an account of the islander's experience of arrival at the centre, a centre known hitherto only on paper. It is an experience of nearness and farness, legitimacy and bastardy, of being himself and other. 'Paris, France, [. . .] a reality from which I cannot absent myself' ('Paris, France, [. . .] une réalité dont je ne peux m'abstenir': p. 11), but a reality that eludes:

Thus Paris, at the heart of our times, receives, uproots, confuses, then illuminates and reassures. I realise, suddenly, her secret: and it is that Paris is an island which receives from everywhere and which then diffracts. (p. 68)‡

Paris thus emerges from Glissant's writing as a *mirage* in a very different sense from that of Ousmane Socé. In the latter's *Mirages de Paris*, expectations are not fulfilled and the city is thus no more than 'an illusion' (as far as the hero is concerned). For Glissant, Paris is a reflection, a refraction which has no absolute original base reality but which is there constantly to be deconstructed and reconstructed. In this respect Paris, it might be argued, is no different for the francophone writer than for other post-modern artists. Yet the creative freedom to re-create and re-present the (former) colonial capital is both post-colonial and inherently post-modern. The title of a recent two-volume publication of *Yale French Studies*, 'Post/Colonial Conditions: Exiles, Migrations and Nomadisms', celebrates francophone writing and the coincidences that render francophone writing among the most exciting of contemporary literatures.[24] Paris frequently remains, for myriad historical, linguistic, political and literary reasons, the *locus* that orientates those exiles, migrations and nomadisms. As an international meeting-place – like Montreal, Dakar and other French-speaking metropolitan centres – Paris brings people into contact with each other, and thus with themselves. As Farès writes:

†*Le trajet intellectuel en est voué à un itinéraire géographique, par quoi la pensée du Discours explore son espace et s'y tresse.*
‡*Paris ainsi au coeur de notre temps, reçoit, déracine, brouille, puis éclaircit et rassure. Je sais soudain son secret: et c'est que Paris est une île, qui capte de partout et diffracte aussitôt.*

From now on francophonia, despite racist attitudes which are still present, is that space in works where different domains of the cultural and human pluralism enter into communication.[25]†

†*Désormais la francophonie, en dépit d'attitudes encore 'racistement' présentes, est cet espace des oeuvres où entrent en communication différents domaines de la pluralité culturelle et humaine.*

9

Electronic Paris: From Place of Election to Place of Ejection

VERENA ANDERMATT CONLEY

A recent article in *The New York Times* (22 December 1994) announced that the 'bistros in Paris are dying in droves'. The text was accompanied by a shot of two workers dressed in their *salopettes*, arched over two glasses of wine on a zinc bar, smoking and conversing almost loudly enough to shatter the photographic silence in which they were frozen. The demise of the bistro is attributed to transformations in society and to changing habits: the disappearance of the working class; acceleration of daily life through technologies, the doing away with the extended lunch-hour, and the increasing preference for fast foods, la cuisine *lite*; reduced alcohol intake (in France, the annual consumption has dropped from 60 to 18 litres per person); the erosion of public life in favour of 'le cocooning'; and the advent of the static audio-visual vehicle. The French capital is opting for a healthier, but also a more material and faster life-style at the cost of traditional routines of everyday life, such as cooking, walking and talking, elements of the myth of Paris that now are increasingly rare.

I posted the article in evidence on the side of my refrigerator by means of a magnetic holder distributed by a fast food chain (Bruegger's Bagel Bakery), set back and relaxed in anticipation of the comments of my holiday visitors. The most immediate reaction was: 'Oh! That's so sad!' Thereupon, contemplating the theme of *Parisian Fields*, I decided to begin some utterly passive fieldwork as I sat, as was my wont, in the Scandinavian-style 'breakfast nook' next to the refrigerator. Numerous francophiles, French citizens, Midwestern American neighbours (genre Mr and Mrs Francesca Johnson à la *Bridges of Madison County*), colleagues, students and handypersons were studied 'reacting' to the signpost depicting the end of a Parisian institution 'as we know it'. The results were as I had predicted: rock-solid American citizens praised the new French abstemiousness and sobriety ('It's high time! They used to drink like fish! They still smoke like chimneys!'). Younger francophiles had no real bearing on the business, some having admitted, to my chagrin, that they found no glaring social contradiction in the sight of a McDonald's arch opposite the east entrance to the Jardin du Luxembourg ('I should tell you, Professor Conley, French coffee isn't that great at, oh, where is it? The Rostand? And there it's too damned dear! But a cup of java from McDonald's really hits the Parisian spot! And there are none of those snotty waiters . . .'). Older friends, many of French extraction, sighed in the style of Pierre Fresnay (in *La Grande Illusion*, in dialogue with Eric von Stroheim, 'Yes, it's true, the world is democratizing itself . . .').[†] For the people of my generation the transformation of the Parisian space was felt as a 'loss'.

Whence I concluded that Americans' affective investment in the French capital seems to be in a certain Paris arrested in time, that of bistro culture demarcating the convivial spaces of good food and conversation, of streets and boulevards built for a peculiarly neo-Benjaminian *flâneur*, able to browse with credit cards and travellers' cheques, to come and go according to the airline schedules, and imbibe the Paris of collective dreams. Ironically, of the older people who sauntered through the kitchen, most wanted Paris to stay the way it is engraved in our hearts or inscribed in our memories based on films of the 1950s (the first third of *The Sun Also Rises*, all of *The Last Time I Saw Paris*), through images of a bygone culture that lives on (or *sur-vit*) as an artefact promoted by advertisements intended to lure tourists and sell products. In North America the contradictions grounding that 'bygone' culture of Elysian Parisian fields are especially enthralling, even fascinating. It can be noted in two paradoxes that I would like to invoke at the beginning of this essay, that the arrested Paris, the Paris *hors temps* marketed in travel brochures and in film revivals, is a Paris whose non-history is staunchly historical. It smacks of the post-War years (1950–60) and is designed to perpetuate the marvel, intrigue and adolescent wonder of the kind we see Jean Seberg experiencing way back in *Breathless*.

It has returned to North America with a vengence. It takes place in pullulating coffee-shops that use Parisian décor (parasols, round tables on which are posed sparse but elegant bouquets coded to match the wood or marble of the tops) and atmosphere to promote a lazy stimulation of caffeine in place of that fatal glass of red with all of its communist, socialist or governmental innuendo of 'un coup de rouge'. The second paradox is that in the United States, bistro culture is sold in the form of

†*Oui, c'est vrai, le monde se démocratise . . .*

blue-and-white checkered bistro napkins made in Hungary; or latticed folding chairs and tables, sold through upscale catalogue businesses and often standardized in the décor of international hotel chains, fabricated in Taiwan. In the acceleration to increase productivity, to step up material gain and consumption, enjoy the ease of travel and of instant communication, the consumer of neo-Parisian culture wishes that the other space, the Parisian space of an imaginary pre-War condition, would remain 'the same', the way it was represented when the first massive economic invasion of France took place in the 1950s, following its liberation by the Allied armies.

But Paris, in fact, has long lost its authenticity and status of auratic object – first, in the age of mechanical reproduction and later, of teletopia. I wonder if the disappearance of Parisian bistro culture is marketed to be understood as a loss. If so, must it be remembered nostalgically or simply taken to be a transformation?[1] Is it linked to the disappearance of an 'art of the eco', that is, an ecological relation that every subject establishes with the world in everyday activities, and to new problems of habitability that result from global acceleration and techno-logization?[2] Problems of habitability are the very stuff of the Parisian visions of two culture critics, Michel de Certeau and Paul Virilio, whose work I shall use to establish two points of reference in this essay: the compression through technologization and loss of an 'art of the eco'; and what is needed to reintroduce such an art by reorienting technologies in view of persisting ways of thinking and living the world.

In L'Invention du quotidien (The practice of everyday life), Certeau distinguishes between 'arts de faire' (arts of doing) and technologies of application that make Paris a rational construct of bourgeois Enlighten-ment that flattens and grids space. In the rational view, urban space expands from a geometrically established centre to a periphery that continually extends outward. Logical control eliminates all that concerns relief, shadow, contour or, in subjective terms, whatever is unknown, dark, irrational or unconscious. Rationalized urban space replaces words and stories with numbers and toponyms reflecting current ideology. The division is familiar. It is drawn between a static, centralized power symbolized by the controlling gaze that surveils and immobilizes and an unruly, non-productive citizen who tries to escape it.[3] Writing in dialogue with Michel Foucault, Certeau calls 'arts de faire' those ways we use not to subvert, but to ruse, or to play, with a centralized power. The practitioners are Certeau's 'hommes ordinaires', avatars of Musil's 'hommes sans qualités', his Wandersmänner, far from remaining subjected individuals suffering from Durkheimian *anomie* or agoraphobia in urban space, individuals who reintroduce movement in stasis, who fold time into space. He or she recovers physical and psychic mobility and escapes the status of subjected subject through walking and talking – but also in eating, drinking and cooking.[4] Through talking, through storytelling (with the mouth full or empty, drinking wine or coffee, no matter) and in both 'walking acts' and 'speech acts', Certeau's subject restores at another level, often through the powers of the false, the haptic experience that had been lost.[5] Use of everyday language recovers a simple but aromatic savour. Utterances such as 'here lived la mère Dupuis', or, let's imagine, to a stranger who is looking for a bakery that is open on Tuesday, 'first you'll turn right and go by the store of la mère Dupuis', are chosen as examples. They come from the *quartiers populaires*, from the ordinary people's sections of the city. They carry with them ways of living that introduce an unproductive wedge in order to ruse with, even temporarily 'undo', dominant power and give ordinary men and women a sense of habitability. Certeau pre-empts criticism by proposing his writings as a little 'white pebble', in what he sees as the progressive enslavement by technologies. The demarcation that Certeau draws cuts a line between a pervasive bourgeois state, one that uses corporate and consumerist strategies to subjugate growing populations, and *le peuple*, which reacts with tactical means to loosen the web of control that bourgeois economy everywhere imposes, decompressing both physical and mental states. The ordinary man, or human being, far from being simply enslaved, 'fabricates actively' something with the images or the products he or she receives. They create their living spaces with words charged with affect and memories that slow down, or sidetrack, a technocratic system of power.[6]

It can be asked if, on the one hand, there holds such a simple division between fixity and immobility? Is there such a thing as a centralized power in an era that laments – or celebrates – being 'out of control' and continually asks how we can 'regain control'.[7] On the other, does *le peuple* of such a heartwarming, slightly archaic and folkloric vision still exist? Did it ever exist? In Paris, *les quartiers populaires* around Les Halles, the Bastille or Montmartre, have long been taken over by cultural enterprises, the fashion industry, fast food conglomerates and hotel chains. An international clientele has infiltrated the major cities of the world, effectively detaching them from the regions or nations to which they had belonged. New York has little to do with the state of that name; Los Angeles is perched on the other side of many American fault-lines;

the centre of Paris has become an eerily unreal city that materializes postcard images of its fabled monuments and vistas. 'Pray, tell me in what land is Lutetia [Paris]?'[†] Now, the common people of Villon's ballads or the proletarians of Zola's world may not simply have moved. They have, according to the article on the bistros, at least in part, virtually disappeared. Indeed, Paris would follow the model that can be found in most contemporary Western societies that have been transformed during a lengthy and quiet revolution into Knowledge Societies.[8] With the advent of electronic equipment, technicians have replaced proletarians who either retrained or became marginalized. If unskilled, they have joined the ranks of a growing Fourth World. The nation-state is undergoing massive transformations, and contrary to Marx's theses, the new citizens of the Knowledge Society usually are wired into their own means of production, and they dictate the ebb and flow of the international economy. For both – the symbolic analyst and the unemployed – the opposition between State and immobilized citizen from which Certeau's analyses are constructed has been complicated. Both sets appear to have their shares of mobility and immobility that have been redistributed in pernicious ways.

The relation between movement and stasis elaborated by Certeau, while an attractive vision at the basis of much feminist fiction and film, thus no longer quite holds.[9] As a second step (following the predicament that seems to capture Certeau's wily subjects) toward the formulation of a hypothesis about an 'art of the eco', I now wish to turn to the futuristic vision of Paris as seen in the texts of Paul Virilio.

The right to move is one of the claims to freedom, Virilio has noted, that broke with feudal practices around the time of the French Revolution. The new bourgeois citizen of 1793 was granted mobility but also the right to be. He or she was free to choose a place of 'election' and not simply be assigned to one of 'ejection'. In one of his early studies, *Vitesse et politique*, Virilio shows how the bourgeois request for a right to a place, to fixity emblematized by the word and fact of *immobilier*, did not necessarily extend to other classes. Workers, be they soldiers, proletarians or factory workers, were the ground on which the bourgeoisie trod in its ascendency before and after 1789.

Transforming Certeau's familiar view of Paris into an abstractly energetic powerboard, Virilio points to the early perception by the bourgeoisie of the power of mobility, less of the friendly *marcheurs* than

[†]*Dictes moy ou, n'en quel pays est Lutèce . . .*

of a *foule* transformed into a mob that the ruling class proposed to harness and control for its own purposes.[10] Virilio cites Engels, writing in the aftermath of the Revolution of 1848 in Paris: 'The first public gatherings take place on the wide boulevards, where Parisian life circulates most intensely.[11]† Virilio astutely operates the transformation of *foule* into *mob* and *mass* with its dynamic, its potential and its loss of centre or direction: 'The mass is no longer a populace, a social group, but the multitude of passers-by, the revolutionary contingent, that does not achieve its ideal form in the place of production but in the street, when for a moment it ceases to be a cog in a machine and becomes itself a motor (an assault machine), in other words a generator of speed' (*Vitesse et politique*, p. 13).‡ Though coming from opposite political ends, Virilio joins Goebbels to remark that 'he who owns the street, owns the state'. The people in the street are not the unproductive *flâneurs*, they are not Aragon's fabulous *paysans de Paris*, but they comprise a dynamic mob. The immobile bourgeois takes advantage of the animal body of this mob, mass or *meute* whose energies he wants to channel and control. Far from simply restraining the crowd, he uses it *and* condemns it to movement. The opposition is now between the bourgeois fixed by their *immobilier* and the people who are condemned to controlled movement, hence immobile in another way. In other words, bourgeois power condemns the people from a chosen to a forced mobility and migration – residues of which may linger in the daily shuttling forth and back between the *banlieue* and the city.

Virilio had anticipated the relay of thermodynamics by information theory. In *Bunker Archaeology* (1975) he had shown how the (thermo) dynamic engine transforms the geophysical space of a country (or a city) by invalidating the distinction between inclusion and exclusion, or inside and outside. Once planes fly over the walls, there are no more walls or doors to keep the enemy out. The expression 'open city' is thus, in a sense, invalidated. This is brought to completion with the teleport, which renders borders seemingly useless. The physical territory in general has become less visible. It seems that it has been forgotten with the advent of the electronic city, though it has not disappeared.[12] Several ecological

†*Les premiers rassemblements ont lieu sur les grands boulevards, là où la vie de Paris circule le plus intensément.*

‡*La masse n'est plus un peuple, une société, mais la multitude des passants, le contingent révolutionnaire n'atteint pas à sa forme idéale sur les lieux de la production mais dans la rue, quand il cesse pour un temps d'être relais technique de la machine et devient lui-même moteur (machine d'assaut), c'est-à-dire producteur de vitesse.*

speeds coexist from which new types of citizens' mobility and immobility result and intersect. First, there is the mobility of those with access to the data highway and their progressive immobility that Virilio so decries. Indeed, teleterminal citizens have delegated all their natural movements and senses to the machine. Their position can be contrasted with those who are in the zone, in the *banlieue* and who, often forced to migrate, remain none the less immobile in their mobility. Virilio cites from Balzac: 'Neutral spaces, indeterminate spaces, where all the vices and misfortunes of Paris have their seat' (*Vitesse et politique*, p. 18).[†] A quotation from Geoffroy Saint-Hilaire on the domestication of animals serves as an analogy with the bourgeois treatment of proletarians: 'To tame an animal is to make it accustomed to living and reproducing itself in the midst of human dwellings' (p. 18).[‡] From which Virilio concludes:

The 'right to accommodation' is not, as has been claimed, the 'right to the city'. Like the inorganic pack of animals in the wild, the proletarian horde harbours a threat, the explosive charge of a potentially ferocious unknown quantity. As a 'pet' it is allowed to group together and reproduce where humans dwell, under their surveillance. The problems of the genuine human *habitat* are totally different from those of the proletarian herd. Ever since its accommodation in the castle farmyard or on the outskirts of the fortified stronghold, as if in the stable or agricultural enclosure, the provisional lodging of the migrating masses implies relative isolation from human dwellings, in other words, from the city.[*]

And Virilio points out that the bourgeoisie did not derive its initial power from money and industries, since it shared the latter with the feudal society, but from its strategic implantation of the fixed domicile as monetary and social value. The right to live behind the city walls gave it security and assured it – at least temporarily, that is, until the invention of new techniques – survival against migrating hordes of soldiers and vagrants now replaced by immigrants.

[†]*Espaces neutres, espaces sans genre où tous les vices, tous les malheurs de Paris on leur asile.*

[‡]*Domestiquer un animal, c'est l'habituer à vivre et à se reproduire auprès de la demeure des hommes.*

[*]*Le 'droit au logement' n'est pas comme on a prétendu le 'droit à la ville,' comme celle inorganique des animaux sauvages, la meute prolétaire porte en elle une menace, une charge d'inconnu et de férocité, elle est admise en tant que 'domestique' à se regrouper et à se reproduire auprès de la demeure des hommes, sous leur regard – les problèmes de l'habitat humain proprement dit sont absolument différenciés de ceux du cheptel prolétaire, dès son logement dans la basse-cour du château fort, dans les faubourgs de la place forte, à la manière de l'étable ou de l'enclosure, le logement provisoire des masses migrantes implique leur relatif éloignement de la demeure des hommes, c'est-à-dire de la cité.*

But since 1977 this thermodynamic vision has been increasingly relayed or complemented by theories of information. The French bourgeoisie itself has shifted some of its power from the *immobilier* to the mobility of speculation afforded by electronic equipment. It has acceded to great mobility in the new Knowledge Society, if memory of the bistro is recalled, and it can be imagined thriving on coffee while speculating on wine futures by e-mail and fax with dealers in Saint-Estèphe and Pauillac. The post-revolutionary nation-state is disappearing in favour of multi-national or transnational companies relying on speed for competition and whose invisible networks of fibre-optic cables expand far beyond the nation-state. Thus, the urbanization of space is followed by that of time: Paris–Tokyo–Los Angeles! In her celebrated book, *The Global City*, Saskia Sassen exposes how the mobility of the global electronic city less immobilizes people physically than it lends them another type of forced 'mobility'. Henceforth, the difference circulates between different types of mobility and immobility. Within the electronic or information revolution that follows the thermodynamic one, on which Virilio bases his early analyses in *Vitesse et politique*, are distinguished several types of mobility and immobility. Thermodynamics are related to the advent of mass transportation. The latter already had less to do with travel than it did with employment agencies. The control of city space by virtue of the factory and public modes of transport is inflected differently in the age of information. What was 'He who owns the street, owns the state' in the mechanical era can be rewritten now into 'Who owns the data highway owns the business'. Those who have access to the data highway are nourished not by food (unless it is 'fast'), but by 'speed' and have to be mobile, both on the highway and professionally. Yet they are more and more immobilized, both physically and mentally. Immobilized in present time through teletopia, they are also being programmed mentally. They cannot be separated from a mass of which they are, more and more, a part. That mass is now a mass of consumers that cannot be distinguished from a centralized power. They *are* that power that circulates every-where. By contrast, it is those who do not have access to teletopia, that is, those who are still walking and talking, who are forced to migrate physically and are immobile in their mobility, mostly invisible. In both cases, for the professional and the unemployed, there are new articu-lations between mobility and immobility, in physical but also in mental terms. Those on the data highway, mobile in their immobility, having transferred all physical functions to sensors and cathodes, keep others out. Those who are still in the streets and whose experience is not denatured, are immobile in their mobility since they do not have access to teleports.

In Virilio's analyses several ecological speeds converge. The speed of those who link thermodynamics with invisible networks uses the speed of light, and truly actualizes that other name of Paris as *Ville-Lumière*. Those who, made invisible, continue to live in a mental space of agrarian measurements and for whom the city of Paris is like a medieval fortress that keeps undesirable social elements out by keeping roads and doors closed. The dilemma of Paris becomes a tale – or rather a vision – of two cities, that of citizens whose measurement is calibrated by the speed of light and that of those who live in a Euclidean space that goes by centimetres and decilitres. It is less, as Certeau would have it, between the controlling gazer and the *marcheurs*, than between those who do and who do not have access to the teleport that now replaces the protected maritime port of the Seine (at a distance from Viking marauders on the coast) that was the centre of the city for many centuries. The latter, like the bistro, has become another artefact where barges shuttle tourists and serve as stages for theatrical productions.

Both Certeau and Virilio deal with time/space compression and technologization. Certeau inserts his analysis at the level of the *peuple* that ruses with, and subverts, imposed immobility. By contrast, Virilio's new teleterminal citizens are immobilized outside of time (−) and space (+), in present time, in a new critical space measured by the speed of light (o). This new measurement, by abolishing time and space, by appealing to 'present time', immobilizes. Such a state of things is lived as a loss, as a kind of dehumanization through *techné* that reduces humans to valid invalids. The loss of senses and the exteriorization of knowledge are denounced as denaturalization. Virilio contrasts the immobility of these citizens with the forced movement of those who are kept outside of the city, a mixture of Third and Fourth Worlds, who can still be described in Balzac's words, as those invisible people kept in the *banlieue* and who only become visible when we take the RER, at the cost of an extra ticket, that leads us from Roissy airport to the heart of Paris.

Virilio's fascination is with technology and the immobilized, 'valid invalid'. He rightly shows how to a physical immobility there corresponds a progressive mental enslavement in a regime that controls and mass-produces subjectivities even at the primary level. By trying to master, one kills life. Both critics discussed here warn of the destructive forces of technologies. But while Certeau opens a space for rusing and musing, Virilio condemns technologies of speed while spinning on their wheels. Only in his most recent work does he urge for a *sortie*. Virilio also retraces the crowd, less the poetic, inventive *marcheurs* than the dynamic, revolutionary mob of the nineteenth century, propelled, with no centre, by its own kinetic force, and whose energy was harnessed, in Virilio's opinion, by the bourgeois regime for its own profit.[13] In times of peace, that mob paraded in orderly fashion on the newly created Champs-Elysées, in an order whose primary unruliness is always ready to erupt again. Perhaps, one of the last of these parades was what Virilio called 'l'apothéose sportive' of May 1968. Derealization has reached even movements in the streets.

While teletopia has done away with the streets, the latter have not quite disappeared. In May 1994 the orderly parade of members of the future Knowledge Society, who contested Balladur's proposed reduction of salary that would serve to assure employment for post-*baccaleuréat* students, was disrupted by a new, unruly force from the suburbs – those youth of Saint-Denis and Yvelines, usually kept out in their *banlieue*, who entered the city through the gates of the Métro. Stores and cars were randomly trashed. Several cultural speeds were colliding inside the city – namely that of the physical space of those in forced migration with that of those whose physical immobility is countered by real mobility on the data highway. Truly, if for the former, Paris, the miasma of flexible capitalism, has become a place of ejection, for the latter it is still one of election, though any notion of 'place' may have become largely irrelevant to their everyday lives.[14] The question is, can poor youth from the *ban-lieue*, who operate according to a different code of speed, use civil disobedience productively to disrupt the electronic city? Are they, in fact, precursors of Jean Raspail's novel of 1973, *Camp of the Saints*, now suddenly being unburied?[15] Or are they but the last spasms of physical archaisms? In any case, they invite us to take another look at the relation between the Knowledge Society and what can still be called its repressed.

It is now time to come back to our bistro story. Both Certeau's and Virilio's vision come together in their noting of time/space compression, of progressive immobilization and loss of words. Both critics insist on a return to words as a way of reintroducing an 'art of the eco', to open a space, to reintroduce time, memory, the body, affect, as well as some agency through storytelling.[16] As we have seen, Certeau's popular *marcheurs*, rusing with and outsmarting a distant and surveilling bourgeois gaze, have been replaced. Now it is between forced migrants and teleterminal citizens, themselves physically immobile, yet mobile on data highways, who belong to a cultural elite that is both tuned in and logged on and that owns, through stock and sophisticated retirement plans, the very studios, presses and TV networks it criticizes. And if, with Certeau and Virilio, we can say that words disappear under the general equivalence of *money = cultural goods = natural sites*, spacing, walking and talking reintroduce healthy non-productivity, establish a territory that is also a *non-lieu*, that contributes to, and reorients, technologies that have led to new and invisible types of colonialism. It is those on the data highway, *us*, who browse in cyberspace and fly about in aircraft, who lament the disappearance of old-style Parisian bistros.

We saw that for Certeau, it was a question of technologies of application that discipline the body and of *marcheurs* who reintroduce arts of doing. Virilio's vision transforms Certeau's through information theory. Electronics that move at the speed of light are seen to be completely altering our notions of time and space, hence also those of subjectivity. Technologies work hand in hand with increased massification and problematic conditions of subjectivity. Compression and forced consumption gag citizens and make them blind to the world around them. Virilio chooses to link information theory to one strand only that stands for reduction and compression rather than for transmission of differences.[17] Information theory in Virilio's vision is linked to the loss of an art of the eco, in which, as a consequence, habitat is eroded. To such an *art du moteur*, in a book with the same title, he opposes the art of writing.[18] Now, for Certeau, writing was one with the flattening of the world and the elimination of voice.[19] But Virilio wants to return to a writing that he opposes to present-day images – or imaging – and voice. Yet, it can be shown that writing – or *techné* – is also part of information. There is no life possible without writing, without an inscription – or information – as *techné*.[20] Writing precedes and makes life possible. A certain *techné* is at the basis of biology. In addition, reversing a trend, today, technological models borrow more and more from biology. Biological metaphors infiltrate technology. So, for example, that of the beehive, of the swarm, that is, of a network of beings, without a centre, always far from equilibrium and in movement. Earlier we saw that the mob is also a swarm – energetic, ultimately unpredictable, and out of control. Yet *swarm* with its biological resonance is less threatening than *mob*. Perhaps we can use this term to displace older binary divisions between subject and object with echoes of resolution of opposites and control and replace them with a lexicon of feedback, pressure relations and conditions of disequilibrium that are both local and global. It has been said that the atom is the figure of the twentieth century and the network (the beehive or the swarm) will be that of the twenty-first.[21] Indeed, the network has displaced simple binaries of subject and object, of self and other, of city and country, but also oppositions between circulation and stasis. In a network, concepts of self and other are linked to pressure relations and feedback. Local interventions as well as decisions to reorient a situation seemingly 'out of control' are not in vain. The figure of the network, with local and global implications, replaces the more linear image of a road and invites us to think in existential terms of territory, more specifically of deterritorializing and reterritorializing that have to do with mental more than physical territories.[22] We now see that the art of ecology and habitat, both urban and rural, are an ongoing reinvention, a mental precondition to any kind of physical change.

Let us have a last *coup de rouge* in our bistro. Yes, Paris will 'never be the same again', we mutter over our glasses, worrying about the influx of McDonald's and syndicated restaurants that pepper the Boulevard Saint-Michel. The loss of the old bar and tavern can be no cause for nostalgia. For, in our most unguarded moments as pedagogues of French civilization and culture, the vanishing tavern will allow us to extrapolate freely on the 'function of the bistro in New Wave cinema', 'Belleville and the working-class bar in Communist Paris', 'Zinc and its relation to everyday life', 'The telephone, the toilet, and the tavern in France in the 1950s', 'The incidence of throat and pancreatic cancer among tavern-goers', 'The cultural meaning of *tabagie*', or 'Lévi-Strauss and the anthropology of the *gargot*'. . . In the newspaper the dying bistro was in essence the beginning of a new myth, of the raw material for tales of old Paris that greying and grizzling post-War children, yuppies and francophiles in general will be able to share with children and students born after 1970. The general point, and we know it well, is that we cannot return to a previous state of the city, such as that of the 1950s that was purveyed to be timeless, communitarian, of a rosy-cheeked aura that the TV show 'Cheers' would be hard put to duplicate. We have to take off from where we are. A certain bistro culture, seen retrospectively as plenitude, can remain only as a parody of Paris. In view of what we have seen in our comparison of Certeau and Virilio, the City of Light's elysian fields have been transformed into electromagnetic fields, but none the less, the *populus*, no matter what its origins may be, will create or, if a neologism can be fashioned from the opening pages of *La Pensée Sauvage* and their gloss and application in *L'Invention du quotidien*, will *bricolate*. Despite all strategic efforts that are made to create a controlled and controlling city, a site of ejection, in Paris there will always remain a creative activity that makes the city other than what it is known to be. Creation may not need the *bistro* as its site of activity, its atelier or its meeting-place, for the politics of bricolage to take place.

The city's present dynamics may come from its pressure relations with its contiguous and distant *bans-lieux*. Of importance for making a *lieu d'élection* in a *lieu d'éjection* is a mental mobility, an opening of passage, the introduction of a wedge in current compressions. In that space we can realize the interrelation between subjective, social and natural registers. I would like to argue that the elective activities have much to do with a cultural ecology – a sense of tact, of economy, and of xenophilia – that draws much from what we know and see in the biological domain, both in the way it works and in what we know about what threatens it, from increasing compressions of time and space (as David Harvey has shown in his classic *The Condition of Postmodernity*) in the economy of geography and in the degradation of the physical world (seen in the obvious facts of loss of species, acidification of rainfall, resumption of nuclear testing, relaxation of environmental laws, and the like). The remarks that pertain to Paris could, perhaps, be applied to any one of a number of cities. Yet there remains in the conundrum of the dying tavern two specific implications. One is that of the American vision of Paris that sees in the city a mythic place of circulation of affect and words. It is far from the politics that inhere *in situ*, where the French, whether Certeau or Virilio, or others, such as those intellectuals who contributed a recent special section on technologies to *Le Monde diplomatique* (July 1994), who speak in terms of dehumanization through *techné*, of loss, where Americans, while mourning the disappearance of bistros or other Parisian cultural icons that produce space, still see progress and the equivalence of *new = better*. The myth that Americans have made of 'Parisian' ideas tend not to relate the elaboration of concepts with their politics.[23] The Parisian psyche appears to resist a simple takeover by strategies of production.[24] Parisian bistro culture may be disappearing, along with its popular life in the streets. It can, however, be lived as a mental condition that, when turned to the future rather than to the past, can continue to cultivate an art of the eco that encourages practices that assure spaces of circulation, of affect, and of words. The bistro remains, therefore, to be begun again, but in terms other than those that turned it from a site of election to one of ejection.

10

Paris and the Ethnography of the Contemporary World

MARC AUGÉ

In a number of essays published over the past few years I have focused on my walks through Paris, attempting to produce a kind of 'ethno-analysis' that could also be understood as a self-analysis. In a way, I was asking myself questions I had previously been asking others, mainly in Africa; I was testing those questions, to see whether they really made sense for the only native at hand (myself, as it happened) and for others who shared the same environment.

Surprisingly, it turned out that I always answered these sociological questions in 'spatial' terms. Without actually intending it, I described a number of Parisian scenes, such as the open space of a garden (the Luxembourg) which my narrator traversed, paying attention to both personal concerns (his memories and fears, his health, his work) and the more or less aggressive incidents that took place around him.[1] Another 'space' was that of the Paris Métro, an underground and occasionally above-ground space, where the most private memories combine with those of a more general history, that is, history as it had been experienced by the more elderly passengers in the carriage (the German occupation, the Liberation, May '68), or history as commemorated by the names of the stations, which faithfully echo the streets and monuments above (Solférino, Opéra, Bastille).[2] Finally, I examined a partly imaginary space (a space, at least, always reinvented and recreated) of a photographer, Mounicq, who, in *Paris retrouvé* went through the looking-glass to show us the courtyards and gardens that facades and gateways usually steal from view, favouring the uncommon, uncanny, unreal aspect of objects or places that, at first sight, would not seem arresting to a lazy or pressed passer-by: a public clock, a fountain, a street-corner, a wet pavement.[3]

That intimate Paris is not entirely subjective; nor has it totally vanished from view. It still exists. It should not be reduced to the more or less distorted arrangements of imagination, memory and nostalgia. One can

still sense, in the various districts of Paris, a local patriotism that imparts
to the word 'Parisian' a kind of metonymic quality. The 'true' Parisian
belongs to a particular neighbourhood. Such a kinship is more or less
ancient; it may be fostered by more or less artificial references to
literature, or even be related to a class or status snobbery, but it does
exist. You cannot feel and call yourself a Parisian if you do not feel, first,
that you belong to Montparnasse, to the 13th or 16th arrondissements.
Let me tell you a little secret, which, I grant, is no proof at all: a child of
the 5th arrondissement from my early years, I have always considered my
later years in the 15th as a kind of exile – a feeling I have never
experienced elsewhere, even in Africa. Léo Malet might have been of
some comfort if I had had to live in the 14th, and I cannot but think of
Proust whenever I walk by the gardens that stretch from the Concorde to
the Rond-Point des Champs-Elysées.

   This 'village' quality can probably be found elsewhere, but it is
particularly marked in Paris, and I am pretty sure that some of my
American friends living in Paris, and faithful to the 6th arrondissement,
would find an exile on the right bank as painful as I would. Its village
quality makes Paris a *place*, or rather an agglomeration of places. I call a
'place' a space where individual and collective identities, as well as the
relationship between people and the history they share, are so perceptible
that anyone could read or decipher them. The ideal place, for an
ethnologist, is naturally an island, or at least a village where tradition is
so deeply rooted that each and every individual plays his or her own part;
such is the ideal place for an ethnologist, who may think he will analyse
culture from space and society from culture. Needless to say, this
supposed coherence between space, culture and society is quite illusory,
even if one thinks of the remotest groups on earth. In other terms, it
would be too vague and generalized a statement, psychologically as well
as sociologically, to speak of the *typical* Parisian or the *typical* Londoner.
Yet an ethnologist is like every other man, he has and keeps his fantasies,
even if it be consciously. He knows they exist at least as fantasies, and
that, as such, they have a kind of reality. Those very same fantasies
require that many Europeans (not only French) buy country houses (the
richest of them buy 'historic' mansions) in French provinces where they
were not born (such as the Dordogne or Brittany), but which they haunt
long and lovingly enough to establish a mock-kinship with them.[4]

   Yet the Parisian (including the Parisian ethnologist) does not live
exclusively in his neighbourhood, with his memories and the illusion of
village life. On the contrary, he is confronted day after day with the most

spectacular aspects of modernity. Parisian modernity could be defined as that active coexistence of various temporalities which Baudelaire described in a number of his *Tableaux Parisiens*.[5] Nineteenth-century Paris combined smoke-stacks and old steeples; the Carrousel was (already!) a large building site, and Haussmann's rebuilding programme painfully worked its way through a city that wanted to secure both its past and its future. The glass and stone architecture of the Paris arcades seemed to Walter Benjamin a foretaste of the century to come; Jules Verne expressed a very similar view in *Paris in the XXth Century*.[6]

The ideal of modernity is still at work in Paris, by virtue of the same strategy, namely the introduction of a new element, at the core of an ancient pattern, which forces one to re-read and redefine the new whole thus assembled. The Louvre Pyramid seems to me, in this respect, quite modern, as was the Centre Pompidou in its day. The idea that different aesthetics can be brought together without annihilating one another, and that such a juxtaposition will create a new place, is in complicity with the ideal of modernity – which remains a social ideal. In the modern place people of various ages and origins meet and find a kind of aesthetic alibi for their presence together in the clash or juxtaposition of styles. In that respect, modernity is the contrary of segregation: in spatial terms, we might say both that it does not preclude the combination of genres and that it allows for every possible itinerary (including walking, as an expression of the freedom of wanderers and of what Michel de Certeau called 'pedestrian rhetorics'). However, I shall make two complementary remarks concerning this point. The combination of genres is not a patchwork, for it reasserts the historicity of each and every element it brings together, as well as implying the establishment of a meaning that transcends this connection. The modern place is still a social, distinctive and historical place; it is not a post-modern space. As for the circuits and the freedom of improvisation so beautifully expressed by the *flâneur*, in the modern place they mesh perfectly with both technique and technology. On the other hand, the *dissociation* between the means of transportation and the ways of communication (highways on the one hand, pedestrian streets on the other) brings about a new aesthetics and another logic, which are not those of modernity.

Let me say a word about the definitions I suggested in my book *Non-lieux* (Non-places) for the terms 'supermodernity' and 'non-place'.[7] Supermodernity is characterized by the acceleration or enhancement of the determining constituents of modernity, and by a triple excess (of information, images and individuality), which, in the technologically most advanced areas of modernity, creates the practical conditions for immediacy and ubiquity mentioned by Paul Virilio. Non-places are the contemporary spaces where supermodernity can be found, in conflict with identity, relationship and history. They are the spaces of circulation, communication and consumption, where solitudes coexist without creating any social bond or even a social emotion: one simply cannot analyse a waiting lounge in Roissy–Charles de Gaulle airport in Durkheimian terms.

Paris of course, like any other city, is affected by supermodernity – which can be of some interest for the sociologist, but may well alarm the *flâneur* and Parisian in him. First, Paris tends to stretch out in every direction, and in those remote suburbs (usually called the Parisian 'region') you will find supermarkets and shopping malls surrounded by highways. This space can also be defined by the style of its dwelling places (large apartment blocks on the one hand; detached houses on the other). More and more, we hear about the suburban districts and their problems, about 'suburban youths' and immigrants; here the social language and the spatial language seem to match perfectly, as they both tell of what looks like an exclusion or a segregation. Suburban districts are not non-places for those who live there, especially for the youths who claim they belong there because it is a place they cannot escape from, fostering playful and aggressive relationships with other districts, and more aggressive than playful ones with the police. Yet it is also in these zones, so poorly structured from an architectural point of view, that cheap hotels (such as 'Formule 1') will rise, next to huge warehouses or shopping malls, with no staff on the premises, where travelling salesmen or star-crossed lovers, provided they own a credit card, will find a functional and anonymous shelter.

Highways lead from the *Périphérique* to large airports, and at Roissy airport the RER (suburban railway), the TGV (high-speed train) and long-haul planes meet every day, while Paris becomes a mere destination or starting-point of a journey. Every morning, highways A1 and A6 are packed with cars, traffic comes to a standstill, bringing together, for minutes on end, people who have nothing to share: there, you will see profiles side by side, strained faces, eyes hypnotized by the more or less dazzling lights of the facing car. In this respect, the Défense area is an ambiguous place. On the one hand, circled as it is by highways running among the offices, shops and pedestrians streets, it is typically a 'non-place'. On the other hand, the Arch of Brotherhood reveals and extends the 'axis' which, from the Louvre to the Etoile and beyond, crosses the history of France and the space of Paris: it asserts itself right away as a significant place, as the expression of a myth.

The non-place is not only a space: it is virtually present in the gaze, which, too accustomed as it is to images, cannot see reality any more. The whole world is nowadays transformed into images and shows. This is particularly true in big cities: renovated housefronts, floodlit monuments, protected areas inexorably turn the city into a life-size stage set. Every night thousands of tourists, most of them foreigners, embark on huge steamers that, ironically enough, are called 'bateaux-mouches' (fly-boats); they cast a white light on the banks of the Seine, irradiating them with a somewhat obscene glare. Notre-Dame, the Ile Saint-Louis, the Louvre, the Zouave under the Alma bridge, and the smaller statue of Liberty are offered for a while, bit by bit, to the curiosity of onlookers. Paris coincides with its stereotype. We come full circle.

With a little optimism, we might consider it quite normal that the big cities of today should look like the rest of the world; their rapid spread also allows us to think that the world looks like a large city. And yet neither the city nor the world can be reduced to their most supermodern or stereotypal aspects; the city is, *par excellence*, a place of sociological diversity. Metonymic Paris (for instance, Saint-Germain des Prés, Montmartre or Pigalle) was always easily translated into images and songs; modern Paris allows for the most common commentaries ('What do you think of the Pei Pyramid?'). Supermodern Paris might well frighten, tire, or even annoy us. Yet all of them manage to keep the particular magic of a word, of a name. I love Paris.

References

Introduction

1 For the script see *Deux ou trois choses que je sais d'elle* (Paris, 1984). The film was made in 1967.
2 See note 5 below.
3 The *Physiologie* evolved in the 1830s as a genre offering typological knowledge about specific trades, categories of individual, institutions or spaces in a confident and colourful form. See Richard Sieburth, 'Une idéologie du visible: le phénomène des Physiologies', *Romantisme*, 47 (1985).
4 Jean-Christophe Bailly, *La Ville à l'œuvre* (Paris, 1992), p. 139.
5 Walter Benjamin, *Paris, capitale du dix-neuvième siècle*, 2nd edn (Paris, 1993).
6 Roger Caillois, 'Paris, mythe moderne', *Nouvelle Revue française*, xxv/284 (May 1937).

1 Roger Clark: Threading the Maze

1 References in the text are to the World's Classics translation of *Le Père Goriot* (Oxford, 1991), by A. J. Krailsheimer.
2 References in the text are to the World's Classics translation of *L'Assommoir* (Oxford, 1995) by Margaret Mauldon.
3 One wonders here, in choosing the name 'Lantier', whether Zola was playing with the homonym *lente*, louse egg: given his frequent quest for onomastic symbolism it seems unlikely that this is mere coincidence.
4 Barnes uses the *Méduse* story as the basis for one of the chapters in his *A History of the World in 10½ Chapters*. Yet in Barnes's recent Syrens edition of Flaubert's *Dictionary of Received Ideas* (Harmondsworth, 1994), the 'radeau' entry is mysteriously omitted . . .
5 Thus the entry under 'Englishwomen' in Flaubert's famous dictionary: 'Express surprise that they have pretty children.'
6 Page numbers given in the text are to the eleventh edition of 1819, the year in which Balzac's *Le Père Goriot* is set.
7 Page numbers given in the text are to the eleventh edition of 1894.
8 James Buzard, *The Beaten Track* (Oxford, 1993), p. 287.
9 The reference will be toned down and become the 'Communard rebellion' in the 1900 edition before disappearing completely with the 1904 edition. Evolving patterns of taste may thus be charted through a study of the alterations the Baedeker team introduced to the successive editions of their guides.
10 See, among many others, Jonathan Culler's 'The Semiotics of Tourism' in his *Framing the Sign* (Oxford, 1988) and Buzard's *The Beaten Track*.

11 References in the text are to the Penguin Classics translation: *Against Nature* (Harmondsworth, 1959) by Robert Baldick.

12 Jacques Réda, *Premier livre des reconnaissances* (Paris, 1985), p. 7 (translation mine).

2 *Nicholas Hewitt: Shifting Cultural Centres in Twentieth-century Paris*

1 See Herbert Lottman, *La Rive Gauche* (Paris, 1981).

2 See Louis Chevalier, *Classes laborieuses, classes dangereuses* (Paris, 1958).

3 See, for example, Paul Lesourd, *Montmartre* (Paris, 1973).

4 *Guide secret de l'étranger célibataire à Paris* (Paris, n.d.).

5 *Guide général dans Paris pour 1855, suivi d'une Visite à l'Exposition* (Paris, 1855), p. 128.

6 Louis Chevalier, *Montmartre du plaisir et du crime* (Paris, 1980).

7 Ibid., p. 95.

8 See: *Guide de Poche 1900. Paris la nuit* (Paris, n.d.).

9 See Francis Carco, *De Montmartre au Quartier Latin* (Paris, 1927).

10 Jean Cocteau, 'Le Boeuf sur le toit ou the nothing doing bar', *Oeuvres complètes* (Paris 1948), VII, p. 309.

11 François Mauriac, *Nouveaux mémoires intérieurs* (Paris, 1965), p. 153.

12 Ernest Hemingway, *A Moveable Feast* (London, 1964), p. 72.

13 Clive Holland, *Things seen in Paris* (London, 1926), p. 108.

14 See, for example, Jacques Hillairet, *Evocation du Vieux Paris*, III: *Les Villages* (Paris, 1954), p. 9.

15 Albert Demangeon, *Paris. La Ville et sa banlieue* (Paris, 1933), p. 42.

16 Ibid., p. 42.

17 See Louis Chevalier, *Montmartre du plaisir et du crime*.

18 See P.-H. Chombart de Lauwe, *Paris et l'agglomération parisienne* (Paris, 1952), p. 164.

19 See Bernard Rouleau, *Mémoires et documents*, 5: *Le Trace des rues de Paris. Formation, Typologie, Fonctions* (Paris, 1967), 'Legende de la Carte XIII'.

20 P.-H. Chombart de Lauwe, *Paris et l'agglomération parisienne*, p. 43.

21 Ibid., p. 167.

22 See, for example, P. Joanne, *Paris-Diamant* (Paris, 1908).

23 William Wiser, *The Crazy Years: Paris in the Twenties* (New York, 1983), p. 85.

24 Ibid., p. 95.

25 Francis Carco, *De Montmartre au Quartier Latin* (Paris, 1927), p. 97.

26 Ibid., p. 108.

27 Ibid., p. 190.

28 See: *Paris. Guide Bleu* (Paris, 1992), p. 386.

29 Wiser, *The Crazy Years*, p. 99.

30 Ernest Hemingway, *A Moveable Feast*, p. 89.

31 Ibid., p. 72.

32 Clive Holland, *Things seen in Paris*, p. 109.

33 Wiser, *The Crazy Years*, p. 207.

34 Ibid., p. 207.

35 For a full account of right-wing intellectual activity at this period, see Jacques Laurent, *Histoire égoiste* (Paris, 1976).

3 *Jon Kear: Vénus noire*

1 On Josephine Baker's origins see L. Haney, *Naked at the Feast: A Biography of Josephine Baker* (New York, 1981); P. Rose, *Jazz Cleopatra* (London, 1990); P.

O'Connor, *Josephine Baker* (London, 1988); and M. Sauvage, *Les Mémoires de Joséphine Baker* (Paris, 1927). The importance of these origins was to become inextricably woven into accounts of Baker. It formed a crucial component of the 'passage of rights' of her biography and came to be an integral part of the spectacle of Baker. When 'Jorama', a wax museum of the career of Baker was opened, there were reconstructions of her family home in St Louis.

2 On Sissle and Blake see R. Kimball and W. Bolcom, *Reminiscing with Sissle and Blake* (New York, 1973). A. Rose, *Eubie Blake* (New York, 1979). See also H. T. Sampson, *Blacks in Blackface: A Sourcebook on Early Black Musical Shows* (London, 1980).

3 Baker's dancing at this time was largely derived from that of 'Bert and Bennie' from the Cotton Club.

4 Baker was recruited by Carol Dudley, who was acting as an agent for Rolf de Maré, the manager of the Ballet Suédois, who had recently taken over the running of the revamped Théâtre Champs-Élysées.

5 See Rose, op. cit., p. 5.

6 On Primitivism see J.-C. Blanchère, *Le Modèle Nègre: Aspects littéraires du mythe primitiviste au XX e siècle chez Apollinaire, Cendrars, Tzara* (Dakar, 1981); W. Rubin, ed., *'Primitivism' in Twentieth-century Art*, 2 vols, (New York: Museum of Modern Art, 1984).

7 See Rose, op. cit., p. 45.

8 One feature of the selection of the 25 black Americans appears to have been that their skin colour should be fairly light, and it is a significant feature of the Baker performance that her skin was lightened and a yellowish foundation applied to her body. Commentators often allude to this 'banana' colour of her pigmentation. See for instance Pierre de Regnier, 'La Revue Nègre', *Candide* (12 November 1925). Referring to her performance at the Folies-Bergère, e.e. cummings spoke of her as 'a wand of golden flesh' in his 'Vive la Folie! An analysis of the Revue in General and the Parisian Revue in particular', *Vanity Fair* (September 1926), p. 55.

9 On the initial planning for *La Revue Nègre* see J. Charles, *De Gaby Deslys à Mistinguett* (Paris, n.d.).

10 P. Colin and M. Sauvage, *Le Tumulte Noir* (Paris, 1927). For a detailed analysis of Colin's imagery, see P. Archer-Straw, *'Nègrophilia, Paris 1925: A Study in the Artistic interest in and Appropriation of 'Negro Cultural forms in that period'*, PhD diss., London, Courtauld Institute, 1994, pp. 177–8, 186–200.

11 In this regard it is interesting to note that the company of *La Revue Nègre* was to be invited to perform at the *Soirée Adieu*, which closed the International Arts Décoratifs exhibition on 7 November 1925. Accompanying them on the bill were Georgette Leblanc, the opera singer, and Pavlova.

12 André Daven, 'Bonjour Joséphine', *Les Nouvelles Littéraires* (Paris, 1959), pp. 1–10.

13 Jacques-Émile Blanche, *De Gauguin à La Revue Nègre* (Paris, 1925), pp. 8–9. For other comments on *La Revue Nègre*, see Rose, op. cit., ch. 12, and Bibliothèque de l'Arsenal Pressbook (RO 15.702), vols I and II.

14 P. Achard, 'Trout en Noir ou la "Revue Nègre" ', *Paris-Midi* (27 September 1925); Bibliothèque de l'Arsenal Pressbook (RO 15.702), vols I and II.

15 André Levinson, 'Danses Négres', *L'Art Vivant* [Paris] (February 1925), pp. 115–16. See also André Levinson, *La Danse Aujourd'hui* (Paris, 1929).

16 Pierre de Régnier wrote: 'Is it a man? Is it a woman? Its lips are painted black, its skin the colour of bananas, its hair cut very short and pasted on the head like caviar, its voice is shrill, and its body is in a perpetual state of tremor, twisting like a serpent . . . it grimaces and contorts, it squints, it inflates its cheeks, its movements are disarticulate, making great leaps and landing on all fours, its legs stiff and behind raised higher than its head like a young giraffe . . . this is not a woman, this is not a dancer, it is some

extravagant thing as fugitive as the music . . . for the finale there is a dance of exceptional impropriety, it is the triumph of lubricity, the return to the morals of the dark ages . . .'. See P. de Regnier, 'La Revue Nègre', *Candide* (12 November 1925).

17 G. Bauer, 'Le Théâtre: Une Revue Nègre', *Annales* (18 October 1925).

18 See Rose, op. cit., pp. 19–40.

19 R. de Flers, 'La Semaine Dramatique', *Le Figaro* (16 November 1925).

20 See, for instance, Clément Vantel, *Journal* (17 November 1925). See also M. Grant, *The Passing of a Great Race, or the Racial Basis of European History* (New York, 1916). L. Stoddard, *The Rising Tide of Color against White World-Supremacy* (New York, 1920).

21 Archer-Straw, op. cit., pp. 169–74.

22 A. Levinson, 'The Negro Dance under European Eyes', *Theatre Arts Monthly* [New York] (April 1927), pp. 282–93. See also A. Levinson, 'Danses Nègre', op. cit., pp. 115–16, and 'Le Danse Aujourd'hui', op. cit.

23 On Baker's stay in Berlin, see Rose, op. cit., pp. 83–90.

24 On the Parisian music-hall see J. Damase, *Les Folies du Music-Hall: Histoire du Music-Hall à Paris de 1914 à nos jours* (Paris, 1960). On the Folies-Bergère see P. Derval, *Folies-Bergère*, trans. L. Hill (New York, 1955); Charles Castle, *The 'Folies-Bergère'* (London, 1984); Jacques Feschotte, *Histoire du Music-Hall* (Paris, 1965); Colette, 'Backstage at the Music-hall', in *The Collected Stories of Colette*, ed. R. Phelps, trans. M. Ward (New York, 1983).

25 In 1881 Sari, in a curious move, attempted to go upmarket. Sari sacked his entire staff, employing a choir of classical singers under the patronage of a committee that included Massenet, Gonoud and Saint-Saëns. The result was by all accounts a fiasco. On the history of the Folies-Bergère see C. Castle, *The 'Folies-Bergère'* (London, 1984).

26 Cummings, op. cit., p. 55. On the relation of Modernism to the music-hall, see T. J. Clark, *The Painting of Modern Life: Paris in the Art of Manet and his Followers* (London and New York, 1985), ch. 4; R. Barthes, 'Au Music-Hall', *Mythologies* (Paris, 1957), pp. 199–201; J. Weiss, 'Picasso, Collage, and the Music Hall', in K. Varnedoe and A. Gopnik, eds, *Modern Art and Popular Culture: Readings in High and Low* (New York, 1990).

27 L. Léon-Martin, *Le Music-hall et ses Figures* (Paris, 1928). See also his article on the Folies-Bergère: L. Léon-Martin, 'La Revue des Folies-Bergère', *Paris Midi* (1 May 1926), where he describes Baker's performance as 'genuinely cubist'.

28 Derval exploited the nude revue in the service of a redefinition of the glamour spectacles within the Folies. One of the first revues under his direction, *Coeurs en Folie*, featured nude swimmers in a glass pool onstage. Derval also pioneered the use of the famous 'folie titles', whereby each revue had to consist of thirteen letters and have the word folie in it. P. Derval, 'Folies-Bergère', trans. L. Hill (New York, 1955).

29 This tradition of the 'half-caste' negro star at the Folies-Bergère has included Lisette Molidor, Laurence Darpy and, most recently, Latoya Jackson.

30 This scene was one of the couple of performances that were captured on film.

31 See Léon-François Hoffman, *Le Nègre romantique: Personnage littéraire et obsession collective* (Paris, 1973), pp. 114–15.

32 Pablo Picasso, *Olympia*, 1901 (untraced).

33 On fetishization and the Hottentot Venus see Sander Gilman, 'Black Bodies White Bodies', *Critical Inquiry* (Autumn 1985). For Baker's own account of this accent on the rear see Sauvage, op. cit., p. 89.

34 A. Rifkin, *Street Noises* (Manchester, 1992), p. 70.

35 Cummings, 'Vive la Folie! An analysis of the Revue in General and the Parisian Revue in particular', *Vanity Fair* (September 1926), p. 55.

36 Rifkin, op. cit., ch. 2.

37 Gustave Fréjaville, 'La Folie du Jour', *Comoedia* (30 April 1926), cited Rose, op. cit., p. 99. See also 'A Furious Attack: Bulletin d'informations Anti-Pornographiques' (July 1926), Arsenal Pressbook (Ro 18.757), p. 39.

38 For a discussion of this connection see Archer-Straw, op. cit., p. 194.

39 Colin and Sauvage, preface to *Le Tumulte Noir*.

40 Ibid. See also André Coeuroy, 'Le Jazz', *L'Art Vivant* [Paris] (February 1927).

41 See M. Sauvage, *Voyages et aventures de Joséphine Baker* (Paris, 1931), p. 130ff.

42 See Rifkin, op. cit., ch. 2.

43 On Berlin in the Twenties see P. Gay, *Weimar Culture: The Outsider as Insider* (New York, 1968), and J. Willett, *The Weimar Years: A Culture Cut Short* (New York, 1984).

44 On Baker's European tour, see Rose, op. cit., pp. 123–4. See also Sauvage, op. cit., pp. 66–8.

45 On this issue see D. Van Arkel, 'Racism in Europe', in *Racism and Colonialism*, ed. R. Ross (The Hague, 1982), p. 12.

46 G. Schmitt, 'Joséphine Baker', *Volonté* (9 April 1929). P. Lazareff, 'Joséphine Baker sage est revenue à Paris', *Paris-Midi* (20 April 1929). In another interview shortly afterwards again with Lazareff, she stated 'Your country is the only place where one can live in peace': 'Joséphine en bourgeoisie', *Canard* (30 May 1929), p. 17.

47 A. Rivollet, *Gringoire* (13 February 1931).

48 Homi K. Bhabha, 'Of Mimicry and Man: The Ambivalence of Colonial Discourse', *October*, 28 (Spring 1984), p. 126.

49 To a degree the recognition of contradiction had always been a part of the writing about Baker. In 1926 cummings had written: 'She enters through a dense electric twighlight, walking backwards on hands and feet, legs and arms stiff, . . . a creature neither infrahuman nor superhuman but somehow both: a mysteriously unkillable something, equally nonprimitive and uncivilized, or beyond time in the sense that emotion is beyond arithmetic.' See cummings, op. cit., p. 55.

50 This sense of divided belonging is well captured in Baker's remark in an interview with Pierre Lazareff, 'But I am French, I am *une Française noir*': Lazareff, 'Joséphine Baker sage est revenue à Paris', *Paris-Midi* (20 April 1929). See on this Rose, op. cit., pp. 147–8.

51 On this question of black Americans in Paris, see J. Rogers, 'The American Negro in Europe', *The American Mercury*, xx/77 (May 1930), pp. 1–10. Langston Hughes, *The Big Sea: An Autobiography* (New York, 1940); F. Berry, *Langston Hughes: Before and Beyond Harlem* (Westport, CT, 1983); S. Bechet, *Treat it Gentle* (New York, 1960). Bechet had been a member of the musical troupe for *La Revue Nègre*. For black American writers in Paris see M. Fabre, *La Rive Noire: De Harlem à la Seine* (Paris, 1985).

52 Luce Irigaray, *Speculum of the Other Woman* (New York, 1985), pp. 142–3. On the question of 'mimicry' and race see Homi K. Bhabha, 'Of Mimicry and Man: The Ambivalence of Colonial Discourse', op. cit., and 'The Other Question: The Stereotype and Colonial Discourse', *Screen*, 24 (November/December 1983).

4 *Tom Conley: 'Le Cinéaste de la vie moderne'*

1 Richard Terdiman, *Present Past: Modernity and the Memory Crisis* (Ithaca, NY, and London, 1993), p. 119.

2 See, for example, Roger Clark's essay in this volume. The 'neutral' style of the Baedeker's guide, observes Clark, is used to enhance an ideology of the city through the *accessibility* it offers to the tourist. The camera records what anyone on foot would also be able to see, offering a miraculous impression of economy.

3 Gilles Deleuze, 'Un Nouveau Cartographe?', in *Foucault* (Paris, 1985), pp. 49–51.

4 In cinema the icon of Parisian 'fields' under the Eiffel Tower, it shall be argued, replaces Baudelaire's emblem of the new Carrousel with the advent of René Clair's *Paris qui dort* (1924), a film devoted to the modernity of the city. It is part of the *Querelle des anciens et modernes* that resurfaces in the tracking shots of the Tower beneath the credits of François Truffaut's *Les 400 coups* (Four-hundred blows, 1959). If memory of Truffaut's virulent attack on the 'anciens', of directors working under the illusion of the *tradition de qualité*, in 'Une certaine tendance du cinéma français' (1954) was still fresh, the views of the metal tower would be thus associated with the 'modernes', both Apollinaire's *esprit nouveau* and, thanks to the mobilization of the Tower by means of the moving camera, a *caméra-stylo* of the kind recently emblazoned by Alexandre Astruc. In Truffaut's vision, the Tower is not just an icon of the modern: it is in its most literal sense a writing instrument. Apropos Astruc and Truffaut's polemical style, see Peter Graham, *The New Wave* (London, 1959). Recently, Priscilla Parkhurst Ferguson has argued that the erection of the Eiffel Tower foreclosed the historical relation that Parisians had kept with the idea of perpetual revolution since 1789. With it came not the celebration of the festive violence of an origin but the timelessly monumental condition of 'progress'; see her *Paris as Revolution: Writing the Nineteenth-century City* (Berkeley, 1994), p. 221.

5 'Thus these old cities that in the beginning were only small towns that have, over time, become great cities, have usually been so ill-conceived and poorly planned in comparison with those symmetrical ones that an engineer dreams of building on a plain . . .', *Discours de la méthode* (1637), §2.

6 Samuel Edgerton, Jr, 'From Mental Matrix to "Mappamundi" to Christian Empire: The Heritage of Ptolemaic Cartography in the Renaissance', in *Art and Cartography: Six Historical Essays*, ed. David Woodward (Chicago, 1987), pp. 10–12. But Clair *flattens* the illusion of perspectival depth through his appeal to the maze of the Eiffel Tower. Deleuze remarks that he 'gives life to geometrical abstractions in a homogenous space, luminous and grey, that lacks depth' (*Image-mouvement*, p. 63). Elsewhere he notes that in *Paris qui dort* Clair 'reunites a human world with the absence of humans. . . . The deserted city, the city absent from itself, endlessly haunts cinema, as if it concealed a secret' (p. 120). For Deleuze, the secret is the notion of an *interval* where movement stops, and in stopping can be inverted, or caused to accelerate or decelerate. But the secret is also that of the controlling agency of geography.

7 As Guy Rosolato defines it in 'L'object de perspective dans ses assises visuelles', in *Pour une psychanalyse exploratrice de la culture* (Paris, 1993), pp. 29–52, especially p. 39.

8 Jean Salès-Gomez, *Jean Vigo* (Los Angeles and Berkeley, 1972).

9 See Josef W. Konvitz, 'Remplir la carte', in *Cartes et figures de la terre* (Paris, 1980), pp. 304–14; Konvitz, *Mapping in France, 1660–1848* (Chicago, 1988), ch. 4.

10 In 'Vigo Van Gogh', *New York Literary Forum*, V (1983), pp. 153–66, I attempted to establish parallel compositions of objects, décor, and characters between the Dutch painter's work and Vigo's film.

11 The continual passage between hearth–home–cosmos is taken up in Gilles Deleuze and Félix Guattari, *Qu'est-ce que la philosophie* (Paris, 1991), pp. 175–7. Yi-Fu Tuan studies its filiations in *From Hearth to Cosmos* (Minneapolis, 1995). Furthermore, if Marc Augé's remarks about the overriding effect of centralization in the history of French administrative process are heeded, then Vigo's film can be seen as vaporizing Paris, turning it into a non-site in a world of sempiternal labour and oppression that are everywhere depressing and decentralized. France remains centralized, Augé notes, 'dans l'esprit des Français, du fait, notamment, de l'organisation de son réseau routier et de son réseau ferré, conçus l'un et l'autre, au moins au départ, comme deux toiles

d'araignée dont Paris occuperait le centre': *Non-lieux: introduction à une anthropologie de la surmodernité* (Paris, 1992), p. 84.

5 *Michael Sheringham: City Space, Mental Space, Poetic Space*

1 Baudelaire, *Oeuvres complètes*, ed. Claude Pichois, 2 vols (Paris, 1975–76), II, p. 496.
2 Ibid., II, p. 692.
3 Ibid., I, p. 291.
4 Ibid., I, p. 91.
5 Guillaume Apollinaire, *Oeuvres en prose complètes*, ed. P. Caizergues and M. Décaudin, 3 vols (Paris, 1989–93), III, pp. 3–10.
6 For a useful general survey see Marie-Claire Banquart, *Paris des surréalistes* (Paris, 1972). On Aragon see Yvette Gindine, *Aragon prosateur surréaliste* (Geneva, 1966). On Breton see Jean Gaulmier, 'Remarques sur le thème de Paris chez André Breton' in *Les Critiques de notre temps et Breton*, ed. Marguerite Bonnet (Paris, 1974).
7 André Breton, *La Clé des champs* (Paris, 1967), p. 280.
8 Ibid., p. 276.
9 André Breton, *Oeuvres complètes*, ed. Marguerite Bonnet, 2 vols (Paris, 1988–92), I, p. 196.
10 Ibid., I, p. 380.
11 Ibid., I, pp. 352 and 372.
12 Ibid., I, p. 380.
13 Ibid., I, pp. 681–3.
14 Ibid., I, p. 716.
15 Ibid., II, p. 177.
16 Ibid., II, p. 179.
17 Ibid., II, p. 205.
18 Ibid., II, pp. 710–35.
19 Ibid., II, pp. 697–709.
20 Walter Benjamin, *Paris: Capitale du dix-neuvième siècle*, ed. Rolf Tiedemann, trans. Jean Lacoste, 2nd edn (Paris, 1993), pp. 555–6.
21 Walter Benjamin, 'Surrealism' in *One-way Street and Other Writings* (London, 1979), pp. 227 and 229.
22 Margaret Cohen, *Profane Illumination: Walter Benjamin and the Paris of Surrealist Revolution* (Berkeley, CA, 1993).
23 Benjamin, *Paris*, pp. 14–16.
24 Ibid., p. 842.
25 Ibid., p. 447.
26 Ibid., p. 449.
27 Ibid., p. 434.
28 Ibid., p. 459.
29 Ibid.
30 Ibid.
31 Ibid., p. 470.
32 Prendergast, *Paris in the Nineteenth Century* (Oxford, 1992), pp. 134–5.
33 Ibid., pp. 876–7.
34 Ibid., p. 337.
35 Ibid., p. 384.
36 Ibid., p. 385.
37 Ibid., p. 439.
38 Ibid., p. 831.
39 See also Susan Buck-Morss, *The Dialectics of Seeing: Walter Benjamin and the*

Arcades Project (Cambridge, MA 1991), Gary Smith, ed., *Benjamin – Philosophy, Aesthetics, History* (Chicago, 1989), Heinz Wissman, ed., *Walter Benjamin et Paris* (Paris, 1986).

40 See *Les Ruines de Paris* (Paris, 1977), *Hors les murs* (Paris, 1987), *Le Sens de la marche* (Paris, 1992). For an interesting treatment of the relation between Réda and Benjamin see Catherine Coquio, 'Le Retour éternel du flâneur', *Approches de Jacques Réda* (Pau, 1994), pp. 45–64.

41 *Châteaux des courants d'air*, back cover.

42 On this aspect of Réda see my article, 'Jacques Réda and the Commitments of Poetry', *L'Esprit créateur* (Summer 1992), pp. 77–88.

43 *Châteaux*, p. 13.

44 Ibid.

45 Ibid.

46 Ibid., p. 14.

47 Ibid., p. 84.

48 Ibid., p. 89.

49 Ibid., p. 95.

50 Ibid.

51 Ibid., p. 96.

52 Baudelaire, op. cit., I, p. 192.

53 Ibid., pp. 275–6.

54 Benjamin, *Paris*, especially pp. 797–804.

55 Ibid., p. 799.

56 Bailly, *La Ville à l'œuvre* (Paris, 1992), p. 175.

57 Ibid., p. 26.

58 Ibid., p. 10.

59 Ibid., pp. 23–42.

60 Ibid., p. 57.

61 Ibid., p. 34.

6 *Alex Hughes: The City and the Female Autograph*

1 See for example, J. Little, L. Peake and R. Richardson, eds, *Women in Cities*, (Basingstoke, 1988) and G. Rose, *Feminism and Geography* (Cambridge, 1993).

2 G. Rose, op. cit., p. 122.

3 Ibid., p. 125.

4 S. Seagert, 'Masculine Cities and Feminine Suburbs: Polarized Ideas, Contradictory Realities' in *Women and the American City*, ed. C. R. Stimpson (London, 1981), pp. 93–108 (108), cited in Rose, op. cit., p. 125.

5 E. Wilson, *The Sphinx in the City: Urban Life, the Control of Disorder, and Women* (London, 1991).

6 Ibid., p. 9.

7 Ibid., p. 59.

8 Ibid., p. 157.

9 Ibid., p. 8.

10 Ibid., p. 9.

11 S. M. Squier, ed., *Women Writers and the City* (Knoxville, 1984), p. 4.

12 See ibid., pp. 4–5. For an illustration of my last reference, see S. Benstock's *Women of the Left Bank* (Austin, TX, 1986).

13 See ibid., p. 7.

14 Wilson, op. cit., p. 7.

15 Ibid.

16 Wilson, op. cit., p. 47. Wilson's sense of Paris's sexualized status derives from the fact that the city was, in the last century especially, the pleasure capital of Europe.

17 Various translated editions of these texts exist. Those referred to here are *Memoirs of a Dutiful Daughter* trans. J. Kirkup (Harmondsworth, 1963), and *La Bâtarde*, trans. Derek Colman (London, 1965). Henceforth, the English version of Beauvoir's autobiography will be used. *La Bâtarde* has no neat equivalent in English, and Leduc's translator retained the original French title. Page numbers to the French edition of *La Bâtarde* (Paris: Gallimard (NRF), 1964) are appended to the extracts supplied.

18 See Toril Moi, 'Patriarchal Thought and the Drive for Knowledge' in *Between Feminism and Psychoanalysis*, ed. T. Brennan (London and New York, 1989), pp. 189–205 (191). For a detailed account of the differences between the two theorists, see Margaret Whitford's essay 'Rereading Irigaray' in the same volume, pp. 106–26.

19 See, for example, N. Chodorow, *The Reproduction of Mothering: Psychoanalysis and the Sociology of Gender* (Berkeley and Los Angeles, 1978) and L. Irigaray, *Et l'une ne bouge pas sans l'autre* (Paris, 1979).

20 As Irigaray's *Et l'une ne bouge pas sans l'autre* suggests, the process of mother/child nurturing may be taken as symbolic of the problems of mother/daughter indistinction (see ibid., p. 9). It is illuminating to compare Irigaray's text with Beauvoir's account of the revulsion Françoise's insipid milk puddings, porridges etc. inspired in her childhood self (p. 6).

21 For an account of the problems of the symbiotic mother/daughter bond as chronicles in Beauvoir's autobiography, see my 'Murdering the Mother: Simone de Beauvoir's *Mémoires d'une jeune fille rangée*', French Studies, XLVIII (1994), pp. 174–83.

22 For an account of the Ecole Normale Supérieure of the rue d'Ulm and its relationship with women students in the early decades of this century, see T. Moi, *Simone de Beauvoir: The Making of an Intellectual Woman* (Oxford, 1994), pp. 48–9. Moi's book charts Beauvoir's academic *péripéties* in a way which helps the reader of the *Memoirs* to follow the text's account of these.

23 Marianne Hirsch, 'A Mother's Discourse: Incorporation and Repetition in *La Princesse de Clèves*', Yale French Studies, 62 (1981), pp. 67–87 (69).

24 Irigaray suggests that the (Oedipal) break with the mother that Freud and Lacan posit as the basis of subjectivity and the precondition for entry into the cultural/sexual domain must be read as 'murderous': 'Freud says our culture is built on a parricide. More fundamentally, our culture is built on a matricide: the matricide of the mother/ lover'. Irigaray, 'Interview', *Women Writers Talking*, ed. J. Todd (New York, 1983), pp. 232–45 (238).

25 H. Malric, *Paris 1943, arts et lettres* (Paris, 1943), p. 95, cited in A. Rifkin, *Street Noises: Parisian Pleasure, 1900–1940* (Manchester and New York, 1993), p. 45.

26 As Leah Hewitt remarks, because Beauvoir's 'adult [narrator] rarely intervenes with an explicit commentary in the present', the reader of the *Memoirs* 'is never sure if the narrator reads the importance of gender differently from her character': L. Hewitt, *Autobiographical Tightropes* (Lincoln, NB, and London, 1990), p. 29.

27 Moi discusses the scarcity, in 1920s France, of women students of philosophy and especially of philosophy *agrégées* – Beauvoir eventually joins their number – in her *Simone de Beauvoir: The Making of an Intellectual Woman*.

28 Pradelle is the fictional name Beauvoir gives to the philosopher Maurice Merleau-Ponty.

29 Moi, op. cit., p. 66. For Moi, Beauvoir's youthful, 'privileged' status as an intellectual woman in a masculine elitist space ensured that for much of her creative and philosophical life, she thought, wrote and lived in an identical way to those male individuals, specifically her *normalien* friends, who were the 'legitimate heir[s] to French intellectual prestige' (ibid., p. 66).

30 See Wilson, op. cit., p. 63.

31 Rifkin, op. cit., p. 11.

32 Moi, op. cit., p. 22.

33 Ibid., p. 22.

34 See J. Butler, *Gender Trouble* (London and New York, 1990), p. 25; idem, *Bodies that Matter* (London and New York, 1993), p. x.

35 It is worth noting that if we read Beauvoir's Paris as a space in which gender-identity can shift performatively, we do not need to view the Luxembourg Gardens episode as the definitive/cataclysmic 'fall' into the feminine that Moi suggests it to be.

36 Wilson, op. cit., p. 47. Wilson bases her sense of Paris's femininity on literary, artistic and intellectual representations of the city thrown up predominantly in the nineteenth century; a period when 'poets sometimes likened Paris to a prostitute, but more often sang her praises as a queen'.

37 Benstock, op. cit., p. 447. Benstock notes here the misogyny inherent in the feminizing representations of Paris produced by French and non-French male authors of the modern period.

38 R. Bowlby, *Shopping with Freud* (London and New York, 1993), p. 2. The consumer society Bowlby refers to here is that urban distopia evoked in Huxley's *Brave New World*.

39 Elements of the following section of my argument are indebted to insights into the representation of the body in Leduc's autobiographical writings offered by Shirley Neuman in the reading of *La Bâtarde* contained in her ' "An appearance walking in a forest the sexes burn": Autobiography and the Construction of the Feminine Body', *Signature*, II (1989), pp. 1–26. Neuman's focus is the constructive effect on the anatomy/behaviour of Leduc's heroine by patriarchy's 'cultural script of femininity', a script dictated and determined by the masculine gaze (Neuman, op. cit., p. 15).

40 Wilson, op. cit., p. 59.

41 R. Ballaster *et al.*, eds, *Women's Worlds: Ideology, Femininity and the Women's Magazine* (Basingstoke, 1991), p. 5.

42 See J. Nunn, *Fashion Costume, 1200–1980* (London, 1984), p. 174.

43 Butler, *Bodies that Matter*, p. 12.

44 Neuman, op. cit., p. 17.

45 'Lesbian roles [. . .] enforced by nineteenth-century literature (especially in writings by Balzac, Zola, Louys, Gautier and Baudelaire) [. . .] were exploited by the more exotic Paris brothels where the lesbian couple was a *pièce de résistance*, a form of harem lesbianism': Benstock, op. cit., p. 51.

46 I have modified Derek Coltman's translation here because, prosaically and inappropriately, he renders 'gorge' as 'throat'.

47 Benstock, op. cit., p. 448.

48 Ibid.

49 Susan J. Rosowski uses this evocative phrase to describe Cather's representation of London in *Alexander's Bridge*. See Rosowski, 'Willa Cather as City Novelist', in *Writing the City: Eden, Babylon and the New Jerusalem*, ed. P. Preston and P. Simpson-Housley (London and New York, 1994), pp. 149–170 (153).

50 Wilson, op. cit., p. 10.

7 Adrian Rifkin: The Poetics of Space Rewritten

1 For a cross-section of his work, not including either novels or 'collaborations', see, for example, Renaud Camus, *Notes Achriennes* (Paris, 1982); *Chroniques Achriennes* (Paris, 1984); *Tricks* (Paris, 1979) and its *Edition définitive* (Paris, 1988); *Vigiles (Journal 1987)* (Paris, 1989); *Aguets (Journal 1988)* (Paris, 1990); *FENDRE L'AIR*

(Journal 1989) (Paris, 1991); *Élégies pours quelques-uns* (Paris, 1988) and *L'Élégie de Chamalières* (Pin-Balma, 1989).

2 Camus explains his application of this theory as well as his relation to Barthes in his contribution to the regular series of literary radio conversations, *À voix nue*, France Culture, September 1992.

   Since completing this essay, an important new work on French gay writing has been published – this is Christopher Robinson's *Scandal in the Ink: Male and Female Homosexuality in Twentieth-century French Literature* (London, 1995). There are some striking parallels between his approach to Camus and my own. On pp. 99–100 Robinson also takes a random selection of six passages, from the *Notes Achriennes*, and writes of 'sexual and textual experience'. There are some obvious divergences in our interpretation of Camus's fragmentations and what they mean for the writing and the reading 'subject', and our analyses of Julien Green are very different. His discussion of the 'otherness' of homosexuality, p. 12ff, may be compared to my own in *Street Noises; Parisian Pleasure 1900–1940* (Manchester, 1993), ch. 4. Robinson's book is the most comprehensive general work on its subject and likely to remain the best.

3 See Gérard Bauër, *Recensement de l'amour à Paris* (Paris, 1922) or Pierre Mac Orlan, *Filles d'amour et ports d'Europe* (Paris, 1932).

4 See, for example, Marc Augé, *Non-Lieux, introduction à une anthropologie de la surmodernité* (Paris, 1992).

5 In using the word 'comportment' I am conscious of my subscribing to Michel Foucault's discussions of gay life, now collected in *Dits et Écrits, 1954–1988, édition établie sous la direction de Daniel Defert et François Ewald* (Paris, 1994). Three interviews collected in volume IV deal with the question of comportment. They are 'Entretien avec Gilles Barbedette, le triomphe social du plaisir sexuel' (p. 308), 'Choix sexuel, acte sexuel, entretien avec J. O'Higgins' (p. 320) and 'An Exchange with Michel Foucault' (p. 458). They were published in *Christopher Street* (1982), *Salmagundi* (no. 58/59) and *The New York Review of Books* (March 1983) respectively. At the same time I am anxious that these texts of Foucault should not be treated as a canonical authority on these matters, something of which the materials of this essay should be a constant reminder.

6 See Anne Cauquelin, *La Ville la nuit* (Paris, 1977) and Monique Gehler, *Adam et Yves, enquête sur les garçons* (Paris, 1994). The recurrence of words like 'tristesse' and 'fascination' is indicative of the mood of Gehler's text, and it is worth looking at chapter 1 of Robinson, op. cit., as a corrective.

7 For a good account of modern militancy see Jacques Girard, *Le Mouvement homosexuel en France, 1945–1980* (Paris, 1981). This from FHAR, *Rapport contre la normalité* (Paris 1971, 2nd edn 1976). By contrast see Camus cited in Robinson, op. cit., pp. 238–9, or an account of clean sensuality in Camus, clean body surfaces, fresh smells. While conscious of '68 politics, Camus is a writer for whom class is a social category rather than a figure for sexual experience.

8 For an especially interesting account of the publishing history of *Le Malfaiteur* (Paris, 1955 and 1973) see Robinson, op. cit., pp. 87–91. Robinson also makes an interesting comparison between Camus and Green (see his p. 238).

9 In Roger Callois, *Le Mythe et l'homme* (Paris, 1989), p. 158.

10 See, for example, François Carlier, *Les Deux prostitutions, étude de pathologie sociale* (Paris, 1887) and Frédéric Hoffet, *Psychanalyse de Paris* (Paris, 1953). Robinson, op. cit., p. 8ff discusses Carlier.

11 See Daniel Guérin, *Autobiographie de jeunesse* (Paris, 1972) and, more recently, a posthumously published interview with him in *3 Keller*, the review of the Centre Gai et Lesbien de Paris, no. 13 (June 1995). Guy Hocquenghem, *L'Amphithéâtre des morts, mémoires anticipiées* (Paris, 1994).

12 In my *Street Noises*.

13 See Pierre Klossowski, *Sade mon prochain* (Paris, 1947 and 1967).

8 *Belinda Jack: 'Mirages de Paris'*

1 Jacqueline Arnaud, 'Le Paris des Maghrébins', *Paris et le phénomène des capitales littéraires*, 2 vols (Paris, 1984), 1, pp. 194–202 (196).

2 Robert Jouanny, 'Des Nègres à Paris', *Paris et le phénomène des capitales littéraires*, 2 vols (Paris, 1984), 1, pp. 327–41 (338–9).

3 Nabil Farès, 'En d'autres lieux', *La Quinzaine Littéraire*, special number on 'Salon du Livre' (1985), p. 24.

4 D. Ossou-Essui, *La Souche calcinée* (1973), p. 38, cited by Jouanny, op. cit., p. 330.

5 Edouard Glissant, *Soleil de la conscience* (Paris, 1956), p. 68.

6 M. Jean de Castellane, 'L'Inauguration de l'Exposition coloniale', *Le Figaro* (7 May 1931).

7 Georges Hardy, Preface to Paul Hazoumé, *Doguicimi* (Paris, 1937), p. 10.

8 Christopher Miller, 'Nationalism as Resistance and Resistance to Nationalism in the Literature of Francophone Africa', *Yale French Studies*, 82 (1995), p. 64.

9 Léopold Sédar Senghor, quoted by Pierre Brunel, op. cit., p. 5.

10 Pierre Brunel, 'Qu'est-ce qu'une capitale littéraire', *Paris et le phénomène des capitales littéraires*, 1, pp. 1–11 (5).

11 Edward Saïd, *Beginnings* (1985; first published 1975), p. xiv.

12 Senghor, 'In memoriam', *Chants d'ombre* (Paris, 1945).

13 Léon Laleau, 'Trahison', in L. S. Senghor, ed., *Anthologie de la nouvelle poésie nègre et malgache de langue française* (1948).

14 Tchicaya U Tam'si, Preface to *La Main sèche* (Paris, 1980), quoted by Jouanny, op. cit., p. 339.

15 Ousmane Socé, *Mirages de Paris* (1964), cited by Jouanny, op. cit., p. 334.

16 Aké Loba, *Kocumbo, l'étudiant noir* (1960), cited by Jouanny, op. cit., p. 335.

17 Tzvetan Todorov, 'Bilinguisme, dialogisme et schizophrénie', *Du bilinguisme*, ed. Abdelkebir Khatibi (Paris, 1985) pp. 11–26 (pp. 12–13).

18 Khatibi, *Maghreb pluriel* (Paris, 1983), pp. 14–15.

19 Alain Bounfour, 'La Raison orpheline', *Les Temps Modernes*, 33, no. 375 (October 1977) p. 424.

20 A. Baudot, 'Autonomie et autonymie des littératures francophones?', quoted by E. Sellin, 'Experimentation and poetics in Francophone Literature of the Maghreb', *L'Esprit créateur*, 26 (1986), pp. 31–9.

21 Glissant, *Soleil de la conscience*, p. 11.

22 Ana Paula Coutinho Mendes, 'Soleil de la Conscience: entre le regard du fils et la vision de l'étranger', *Horizons d'Edouard Glissant* (Pau/Porto, 1992), pp. 37–48 (40).

23 Glissant, *Le Discourse Antillais* (Paris, 1981), p. 13.

24 *Yale French Studies*, 81 & 82 (1995).

25 Farès, op. cit., p. 24.

9 *Verena Andermatt Conley: Electronic Paris*

1 The clash of cultural values as a result of time/space compression is the topic of the analyses by David Harvey in *The Condition of Postmodernity* (Oxford, 1988). Harvey, who coined the term, has recourse to Wim Wender's retro film *Wings of Desire* in which Berlin, more than Paris, becomes invested with an 'art of the eco' that is pitted against large-scale American production. Less nostalgically and more cynically, Robert Altman's *Ready to Wear*, in which the international fashion set

converges in Paris and stays in gutted luxury hotels that are of the 'old times' but the facade, shows how people and even products disappear behind the general equivalence of all signs.

2 The expression 'art of the eco' is that of Félix Guattari, who uses it in many of his last texts but especially in *Les Trois Ecologies* (Paris, 1991).

3 Michel de Certeau, *L'Invention du quotidien* (Paris, 1980), trans. by Steven Rendall as *The Practice of Everyday Life* (Berkeley, 1984). For Certeau, the cutting of trees and bushes goes hand in hand with the flattening and elimination of an 'art of the eco' and assigns to a fixed place with its concomitant loss of movement.

4 Certeau does not make gender distinctions here, though in *La Fable mystique*, his analyses of Marguerite Duras, go in that direction. In conversation at the University of California, Berkeley, in 1979, Certeau praised the writings of Luce Irigaray for similar reasons.

5 Certeau is close here to some of the developments of Gilles Deleuze, especially in *Cinema 2: The Time-Image* (Minneapolis, 1988), who, specifically in chapter 5, entitled 'Powers of the False', deals with ungridding through storytelling and speech acts in relation to women's films (Chantal Ackerman, Marguerite Duras, Agnès Varda) and Third World films, such as those by Rouch or Ousmane Sembene.

6 These theses have been adapted and exploited by John Fiske, particularly in his *Popular Culture* (New York and London).

7 See, for example, Kevin Kelly's *Out of Control*, which celebrates the rise of neobiological civilization. For a contrast, see Brzezinski's *Out of Control*, which foretells an era of turmoil and ethnic strife in the twenty-first century. See also Félix Guattari's *Trois Ecologies*, which asks how we are to regain control, and, on the same topic, his essay in *Le Monde diplomatique* (September 1992) that argues for changes in institutions and social practices.

8 F. Druckner, 'The Knowledge Society', *Atlantic Monthly* (September 1995).

9 Rearticulations of movement and stasis are to be found in the work of Hélène Cixous and Marguerite Duras as well as in that by Jean-Luc Godard, Wim Wenders and others. I am pointing to a particular aspect in Certeau's work that is developed differently elsewhere by him. See, for example, 'The Politics of Silence', in *Heterologies*, trans. Brian Massumi (Minneapolis, 1988), where he arrives at a notion of 'federation' that is closer to our concept of 'networking' that is developed later in this essay.

10 In French there is a linguistic proximity between *meute* (pack) and *émeute* (riot).

11 Paul Virilio, *Vitesse et politique* (Paris, 1977), p. 13.

12 This problem is not as much in Certeau's unproductive wanderings or in Virilio's telepresence than it is in Baudrillard's insistence that simulation does away with any kind of physical territory. It is precisely when forgetting the co-existence of physical space with implications of natural and social ecology that massive problems arise. See, for example, Jean Baudrillard's remarks about the benefits of soot to New Yorkers that could be applied to the inhabitants of other cities, such as Paris.

13 This is close to Kevin Kelly's notion of the swarm that moves out of control, decentralized but no longer manipulated by another power. It *is* the power.

14 My view differs here from that of Virilio, for whom the teleterminal citizen has also been 'ejected'.

15 And, of course, the recent hijacking of an Airbus that was perhaps to be blown up over Paris would have been a new stage in development: bodies and luggage would have been the seeds of terrorism dropping, like the plague, onto the city.

16 We can invoke here Benjamin as quoted by Félix Guattari on the art of the storyteller. As with the potter who leaves the marks of his hands on the pot, the storyteller inflects the words with affect that pure information tries to eliminate.

17 See Francisco Varela, who makes the distinction in *Autonomie et connaissance* (Paris, 1988).

18 Virilio links information and biotechnologies to Fascism and Nazi experimentation. It is translated by Julie Rose as *The Art of the Motor* (Minneapolis, 1995).

19 For Virilio, the Nazis urged for recourse to image and voice in order to manipulate and produce affect, not unlike what advertizing does today. A similar hypothesis of the fascism of the film industry – and of which we are a part – is developed by Deleuze in his writings on film.

20 This is what Jacques Derrida, among others, has shown in much of his work. See Anthony Wilden's *System and Structure* (London, 1970 and 1982) and, more recently, Christopher Johnson, *System and Writing in the Philosophy of Jacques Derrida* (Cambridge, 1992). Both justly point to the increased importance of writing and to the massive transformation of our societies from linguistic to scriptural.

21 See Kelly, op. cit.

22 This is where we could insert Certeau's analysis of the Indians in 'Politics of Silence', mentioned above.

23 A good case in point is Derrida. In North America he remains the prosopopœia of Deconstruction, whereas, in the writings from GREPH to *Du droit à la littérature*, including *Spectres de Marx*, the philosophy has a clear political edge and an implicit ecology. A nascent political dimension of the work, latent in *Positions*, seems increasingly resonant and, it might be added, no less pertinent to the issues discussed above.

24 As was manifest in the post-War resistance to the cultural quotas of the Marshall Plan and, more recently, to American film. This resistance underlies much of the New Wave cinema from Godard to Duras and extends to German cinema, such as the work of Wim Wenders.

10 *Marc Augé: Paris and the Ethnography of the Contemporary World*

1 See *La Traversée du Luxembourg: ethno-roman d'une journée française* (Paris, 1985).

2 See *Un Ethnologue dans le métro* (Paris, 1986).

3 See *Paris retrouvé* (Paris, 1992).

4 See *Domaines et Châteaux* (Paris, 1989).

5 'Tableaux parisiens' (Parisian tableaux) in *Les Fleurs du Mal* (1861).

6 *Paris au vingtième siècle* is a novel by Verne that came to light recently and was published for the first time in 1992.

7 See *Non-Places: Introduction to an Anthropology of Supermodernity*, trans. John Howe (London, 1995). For a discussion of my work on the ethnology of the modern world see Michael Sheringham, 'Marc Augé and the Ethno-analysis of Contemporary Life', *Paragraph*, 18, no. 2 (July 1995), pp. 210–22.

Bibliography

Aragon, Louis, *Le Paysan de Paris* Paris [1926] (trans. as *Paris Peasant*, London, 1987).

Augé, Marc, *Un Ethnologue dans le métro*, Paris, 1986.

—, *Non-lieux, introduction à une anthropologie de la surmodernité*, Paris, 1992. (trans. as *Non-Places: Introduction to an Anthropology of Supermodernity*, London, 1995).

—, *La Traversée du Luxembourg*, Paris, 1984.

Bailly, Jean-Christophe, *La Ville à l'œuvre*, Paris, 1992.

Bancquart, Marie-Claire, *Paris des surréalistes*, Paris, 1972. *Images littéraires du Paris 'Fin de Siècle'*, Paris, 1979.

Baudelaire, Charles, 'Tableaux Parisiens', *Les Fleurs du Mal*, [1861] et *Le Spleen de Paris*, [1869] in *Oeuvres complètes*, Paris, 1975–76.

Bauër, Gérard, *Recensement de l'amour à Paris*, Paris, 1992.

Beauvoir, Simone de, *Memoirs of a Dutiful Daughter*, London, 1963.

Benjamin, Walter, *One-Way Street and Other Writings*, London, 1979.

—, *Paris, capitale du XIXème siècle*, 2nd edn, Paris, 1993.

Benstock, Shari, *Women on the Left Bank*, Austin, TX, 1986.

Breton, André, *Nadja*, [1926], Paris, 1964.

—, *Les Vases Communicants* [1932], Paris, 1972.

—, *L'amour fou* [1937], Paris 1976 (trans. as *Mad Love*, Lincoln, NB, 1987).

Buck-Morss, Susan, *The Dialectics of Seeing: Walter Benjamin and the Arcades Project*, Cambridge, MA, and London, 1989.

Burton, Richard E., *Baudelaire in 1859*, Cambridge, 1988.

—, 'The Unseen Seer or Proteus in the City', *French Studies*, XLII, January 1988, pp. 59–61.

Buzard, James, *The Beaten Track*, Oxford, 1993.

Caillois, Roger, 'Paris, mythe moderne', *Nouvelle Revue Française*, XXV, no. 284, May 1973, p. 686.

Camus, Renaud, *Tricks*, (édition définitive), Paris, 1988.

—, *Notes achriennes*, Paris, 1982.

—, *Aguets – Journal 1988*, Paris, 1990.

Carco, Francis, *De Montmartre au Quartier Latin*, Paris, 1927.

Cardinal, Roger, 'Soluble City, the Surrealist Perception of Paris', *Architectural Design*, II–III, 1978, pp. 143–9.

Cauquelin, Anne, *La Ville la Nuit*, Paris, 1977.

Caws, Mary Ann, ed., *City Images: Perspectives from Literature, Philosophy and Film*, New York, 1991.

Chevalier, Louis, *Classes laborieuses, classes dangereuses*, Paris, 1958.

—, *Montmartre du plaisir et du crime*, Paris, 1980.

Chombard de Lauwe, P.-H., *Paris et l'agglomération parisienne*, Paris, 1952.

Citron, Pierre, *La Poésie de Paris de Rousseau à Baudelaire*, 2 vols, Paris, 1964.

Clark, T. J., *The Painting of Modern Life: Paris in the Art of Manet and his Followers*, London, 1985.

Cohen, Margaret, *Profane Illumination: Walter Benjamin and the Paris of Surrealist Revolution*, Berkeley, 1993.

Coquio, Catherine, 'Le Retour éternel du flâneur', *Approches de Jacques Réda*, Pau, 1994.

Culler, Jonathan, 'The Semiotics of Tourism', *Framing the Sign*, Oxford, 1988.

Dadié, Bernard, *Un Nègre à Paris*, Paris, 1959.

Damase, J., *Les Folies du Music-Hall: Histoire du Music-Hall à Paris de 1914 à nos jours*, Paris, 1960.

Debord, Guy, *La Société du spectacle*, Paris, 1967.

De Certeau, Michel, *L'Invention du quotidien*, Paris, 1980 (trans. as *The Practice of Everyday Life*, Berkeley, 1984).

Donald, James, 'Metropolis: the City as Text', in Robert Bocock and Kenneth Thompson, eds, *Social and Cultural Forms of Modernity*, Cambridge, 1992.

Evenson, Norma, *Paris: A Century of Change, 1878–1978*, New Haven, 1979.

Fargue, Léon-Paul, *Le Piéton de Paris*, Paris, 1939.

Ferguson, Priscilla Parkhurst, *Paris as Revolution: Writing the Nineteenth-century City*, Berkeley, 1994.

Flanner, Janet, *Paris was Yesterday: 1925–1939*, New York, 1972.

Frisby, David, *Fragments of Modernity*, Cambridge, 1988.

Gaulmier, Jean, 'Remarques sur le thème de Paris chez André Breton', *Les Critiques de notre temps et André Breton*, Paris, 1974.

Glissant, Edouard, *Soleil de la conscience*, Paris, 1956.

—, *Le Discours antillais*, Paris, 1981.

Haney, L., *Naked at the Feast: A Biography of Josephine Baker*, New York, 1981.

Harvey, David, *The Condition of Postmodernity: An Enquiry into the Origins of Cultural Changes*, Oxford, 1989.

—, *The Urban Experience*, Baltimore, 1989.

Hemingway, Ernest, *A Moveable Feast*, London, 1964.

Hoffet, Frédéric, *Psychanalyse de Paris*, Paris, 1953.

Holland, Clive, *Things seen in Paris*, London, 1926.

Konvitz, Joseph W., *Mapping in France 1660–1848*, Chicago, 1988.

Leduc, Violette, *La Bâtarde*, London, 1965.

Lefebvre, Henri, *Le Droit à la ville*, Paris, 1968.

—, *La Production de l'espace*, Paris, 1974.

—, *Critique de la vie quotidienne*, 3 vols, Paris, 1958–81 (vol. 1 trans. John Moore as *The Critique of Everyday Life*, London, 1991).

Lesourd, Paul, *Montmartre*, Paris, 1973.

Little, Jo, Lida Peak and Pat Richardson, eds, *Women in Cities*, Basingstoke, 1988.

Lottman, Herbert, *The Left Bank: Writers, Artists and Politics from the Popular Front to the Cold War*, Boston, 1982.

Marchand, Bernard, *Paris, histoire d'une ville*, xixe – xxe, Paris, 1993.

O'Connor, P., *Josephine Baker*, London, 1988.

Olsen, Donald J., *The City as a Work of Art*, New Haven and London, 1986.

—, *Paris et le phénomène des capitales littéraires*, 2 vols. Paris, 1984.

Pinkney, David, *Napoleon III and the Rebuilding of Paris*, Princeton, 1958.

Plant, Sadie, *The Most Radical Gesture: the Situationist International in a Postmodern Age*, London, 1992.

Prendergast, Christopher, *Paris and the Nineteenth Century*, Cambridge, MA, and Oxford, 1992.

Preston, Peter and Paul Simpson Housley, eds, *Writing the City*, London and New York, 1994.

Rifkin, Adrian, *Street Noises: Parisian Pleasure, 1900–1940*, Manchester and New York, 1993.

Réda, Jacques, *Les Ruines de Paris*, Paris, 1977.

—, *Châteaux des courants d'air*, Paris, 1986.

—, *Beauté suburbaine*, Périgueux, 1985.

Rose, Gillian, *Feminism and Geography*, Cambridge, 1993.

Ross, Kristin, *The Emergence of Social Space: Rimbaud and the Commune*, Minnesota, 1988.

—, *Fast Cars, Clean Bodies: Decolonization and the Reordering of French Culture*, Cambridge, MA, 1995.

Rouleau, Bernard, 'Mémoires et documents', *La Trace des rues de Paris: Formation, Typologie, Fonction*, Paris, 1967.

Sansot, Pierre, *Poétique de la ville*, Paris, 1988.

Seigel, Jerrold, *Bohemian Paris: Culture, Politics and the Boundaries of Bourgeois Life*, New York, 1986.

Sieburth, Richard, 'Une idéologie du lisible: Le Phénomène des *Physiologies*', *Romantisme*, XLVII, 1985 (for a longer version, see *Notebooks in Cultural Analysis*, I, 1984, pp. 163–99).

Smith, Gary, *Benjamin: Philosophy, Aesthetics, History*, Chicago, 1989.

Soja, Edward W., *Postmodern Geographies: the Reassertion of Space in Critical Social Theory*, London, 1989.

Squier, Susan Merrill, ed., *Women Writers and the City*, Knoxville, 1984.

Terdiman, Richard, *Present Past: Modernity and the Memory Crisis*, Ithaca and London, 1993.

Tester, Keith, ed., *The Flâneur*, London and New York, 1994.

Timms, Edward and David Kelley, eds, *Unreal City*, Manchester, 1985.

Ungar, Steven, 'City and Narrative in Aragon and Breton', in C. W. Thompson, ed., *L'Autre et le sacré: surréalisme, cinema, ethnographie*, Paris, 1995.

Virilio, Paul, *Vitesse et Politique*, Paris, 1981 (trans. as *Speed and Politics*, New York, 1986).

Williams, Raymond, *The Country and the City*, London, 1985.

Wilson, Elizabeth, *The Sphinx in the City: Urban Life, the Control of Disorder and Women*, London, 1991.

Wiser, William, *The Crazy Years: Paris in the Twenties*, Paris and New York, 1983.

Wissman, Heinz, *Walter Benjamin et Paris*, Paris, 1986.

Wolf, Janet, 'The Invisible *Flâneuse*: Women and the Literature of Modernity', *Theory, Culture and Society*, II–III, 1985, pp. 37–46 (reprinted in *Feminine Sentences: Essays on Women and Culture*, Cambridge, 1990).

Wollen, Peter, 'The Situationist International', *New Left Review*, 174, March/April 1989, pp. 67–85.

Index

Albertini, Pepito di 65, 67, 68
Alex, Joe 50, 52
Apollinaire, Guillaume 5, 34, 35, 41, 43,
    44, 76, 85, 87–8
    'Zone' 75, 87
Aragon, Louis 36, 44, 88, 92, 97, 98,
    108, 159, 167
    Le Paysan de Paris (Paris Peasant) 88,
    97, 159
Arnaud, Jaqueline 150–2
Augé, Marc 4, 7, 85, 136, 175–9
    Non-lieux 177
    supermodernity in 7, 177–9

Baedeker, Karl 15, 21–7, 28, 29
Bailly, Jean-Christophe 3, 113
Baker, Josephine 2, 5, 46–70, 47, 52, 55,
    60, 61, 63, 66, 69
    and La Revue nègre 48–57, 51, 52
    and Les Folies-Bergères 57–65, 60, 61,
    63
    and song J'ai deux amours 69
    in banana outfit 60–2, 61, 64
Balzac, Honoré de 8–10, 17, 20, 81, 82,
    98, 168, 170
    Le Père Goriot 8–10, 110
Barthes, Roland 26–7, 134, 146
Baudelaire, Charles 5, 7, 11, 54, 71, 72,
    73, 81, 82, 83, 84, 85–6, 87, 88,
    99, 101, 102, 107, 110, 111, 114,
    177
    'Le Cygne' 71
    epilogue to Fleurs du mal 110
    'Le Peintre de la vie moderne' 85–6
    Le Spleen de Paris 85
    'Tableaux parisiens' 85–7
Beauvoir, Simone de 6, 117, 118–25,
    131, 132, 139
    Mémoires d'une jeune fille rangée
    118–25

Beckett, Samuel 27
Bekri, Tahar 151
Benjamin, Walter 1, 2, 3, 4–5, 7, 72, 73,
    74, 85, 88, 97–102, 107, 108, 109,
    111, 112, 113, 177
    and the dialectical image 1, 5
    and the flâneur 98–101
    and the Passagen-Werk 101–2
    and Surrealism 97
Blanche, Jacques-Emile 52
Blondin, Antoine 36, 44
Bofa, Gus 35
Boilly, Louis-Leopold 10
Bonn, Charles 152
Bonnefoy, Yves 143
Boucher, Alfred 40
Boudjedra, Rachid 150
Braque, Georges 34
Brassens, Georges 13, 44
Breton, André 85, 88–97, 98, 99, 102,
    107, 109, 111, 112, 139
    L'Amour fou 96
    Nadja 92–4, 97, 99
    Poisson soluble 90–2
    'Pont-Neuf' 89
    Les Vases communicants 93–7
Butler, Judith 125, 128

Caillois, Roger 6, 141
Calder, Alexander 65
Camus, Renaud 6, 133–8, 143, 144,
    148, 149
    Aguets 134–5
Carco, Francis 34, 35, 41, 145
Castellane, Jean de 153
Cauquelin, Anne 137–8, 141
Céline, Louis-Ferdinand 35
Cendrars, Blaise 36, 48, 50
Certeau, Michel de 2, 4, 7, 85, 113,
    164–6, 170–3, 176

L'Invention du quotidien 164–6
Chodorow, Nancy 117–8
city, the
  and speed 165–71
  and women 115–17
  future of 112–14
  urban reality 113
  see also Paris
Clair, René 6, 74–6, 83
  Paris qui dort 74, 75, 77
Cocteau, Jean 36, 49, 50, 127, 138
Coleridge, Samuel Taylor 15
Colin, Paul 50, 51, 65, 66
Collard, Cyril 6, 144–5
  Les Nuits fauves 144–5

Dadié, Bernard 151, 157
Daumier, Honoré 17
Daven, André 46, 49
Debord, Guy 142
Delacroix, Eugène 107
Deleuze, Gilles 73, 76
D'Ora, Madame 54, 55
Dorgelès, Roland 35, 41
Drieu La Rochelle, Pierre 36
Duras, Marguerite 44, 117

Ecole Normale Supérieure 30, 120, 121,
  123
Eiffel, Gustave 23, 40 *see also under*
  Paris
Eliot, T.S. 27, 87

Fanon, Frantz 158
Fargue, Léon-Paul 43
Ferré, Léo 44
Feuillade, Louis 74
FHAR (Front homosexuel de l'action
  révolutionnaire) 139, 141, 142
  Rapport contre la normalité 141
flâneur 5, 72, 86, 87, 98–101, 102, 103,
  109, 110, 111, 112, 145, 163, 167,
  178
Flanner, Janet 50
Flaubert, Gustave 12, 72
Flers, Robert de 55
Fort, Paul 41, 43
Foucault, Michel 73, 164

Galignani family 14, 28
Gauguin, Paul 54, 62
Genet, Jean 6, 138–9, 147, 149

Géricault, Théodore 12
Giacometti, Alberto 64, 96
Glissant, Edouard 7, 153, 159, 160
Godard, Jean-Luc 1, 2, 85
  Deux ou trois choses que je sais d'elle
  1, 2
Gramsci, Antonio 142
Gréco, Juliette 44
Green, Julien 6, 139
  Le Malfaiteur 139
Guattari, Félix 7
Guérin, Daniel 146
Guys, Constantin 86

Hardy, Georges 153, 154, 158
Harvey, David 4, 174
Haussmann, Georges, baron 10, 13, 71,
  72, 73, 74, 177
Hazoumé, Paul 153, 158
Hemingway, Ernest 37, 42
Hocquenghem, Guy 146
Hoffet, Fréderic 143

Irigaray, Luce 70, 117–18

Jacob, Max 34
Jouanny, Robert 151, 152, 157
Jouhandeau, Marcel 139

Khatibi, Abdelkebir 157, 158
Klossowski, Pierre 147
Kosma, Joseph 44

Laborde, Chas 35
Laleau, Léon 156, 157
Leduc, Violette 6, 117, 118, 125–31,
  132
  La Bâtarde 125–31
Lefebvre, Henri 4, 85
Léger, Fernand 48, 50, 52
Lévi-Strauss, Claude 173
Levinson, André 53, 56
Lorrain, Jean 143, 149
Lottman, Herbert 30, 43–5

Mac Orlan, Pierre 34, 35, 41, 134
Mallarmé, Stéphane 11
Manet, Edouard 62
Mansfield, Katherine 116
Maré, Rolf de 48, 49
Marchal, Charles 17, *18*
Mascolo, Dionys 44

Maulnier, Thierry 44
Milhaud, Darius 36, 49, 50
Miomandre, Francis de 147
Modigliani, Amedeo 35, 41
Moi, Toril 118, 124
Monnier, Henri 17
Morand, Paul 36
Morin, Edgar 44
Mounicq 175
Murger, Henri 30, 41
Murray, John 15, 21

Nerval, Gérard de 85
New York Times 162
Nimier, Roger 36, 44
Nimmo, John 16
Nouvel Obsevateur 1

Papatakis, Niko 39
*Paris et le phénomène des capitales
    littéraires* 150–2
Paris, topographical and other features
    arcades 88, 109, 107, 177
    barrières 31, 33, 91
    Bastille 165, 175
    Bibliothèque Nationale 109, 121, 122
    Bibliothèque Sainte-Geneviève 121,
        124
    bistros 162, 163, 172, 174
    Bateau-Lavoir 34, 41
    Le Boeuf sur le toit 31, 36, 49
    boulevards 73, 91, 121, 163, 173
    boulevards extérieurs 31–3, 37–9
    Brasserie Lipp 44
    Butte aux Cailles 105
    Buttes Chaumont 88
    cafés 21, 30, 31, 33, 37, 39, 119, 121,
        126, 150
    Café Batifol 94, 95
    Café de Flore 44, 45
    Café des Deux Magots 44, 45
    Canal Saint-Martin 79
    Carrousel, Place du 71, 177
    cemeteries 9, 12, 39, 110
        Montparnasse 39
        Nord 39
        Père-Lachaise 9, 12, 110, 147
    Champs-Elysées 36, 171, 176
    Le Chat Noir 34
    Closerie des Lilas 31, 38, 40
    dance-halls 33–4

    Bal Bullier 31, 38, 40
    Elysées-Montmartre 34
    Moulin de la Galette 34
    Moulin Rouge 34
Eiffel Tower 23, 26, 74–6, 78, 79, 80
fortifications 33, 38
Fontaine, rue 35, 93
guinguettes 34, 38, 39
Halles
    Forum des Halles 165
    halle aux vins 40
    halles centrales 23
Ile de la Cité 81, 89
Ile Saint-Louis 178
Invalides 10, 23
Lapin-Agile 35
Louvre 11–12, 23, 25, 71, 81, 82,
    108, 176, 179
Luxembourg gardens 102, 107, 121,
    124, 134, 163, 175
Marais, le 142, 143
Métro 5, 150, 151, 171, 175
Montmartre 5, 12, 14, 31–45, 165,
    179
Montparnasse 31, 33, 35–45, 119,
    122, 123, 179
Mur de l'Octroi 11, 31, 38
Mur des Fermiers Généraux 31, 37, 45
music-halls 34, 58, 68, 126
    Casino de Paris 34, 68, 69
    Folies-Bergère 34, 57–9, 64, 66
    Moulin Rouge 34, 49
Théâtre des Champs-Elysées 48, 52
Notre-Dame 23, 79, 89, 105, 179
Opéra 134, 175
Palais-Royal 14, 21, 109
Places 33, 37, 38, 41, 43, 89, 142, 179
Pont des Arts 81
Pont Mirabeau 105
Pont-Neuf 89, 102, 107, 108
Quais 81, 83
Quartiers 2, 3, 34, 37–9, 104, 112,
    138, 165
Quartier Latin 8, 14, 30, 34, 36, 37,
    39, 40
railway stations 31, 33, 37, 39, 102,
    107, 109, 150
rive droite (right bank) 127, 131, 134
rive gauche (left bank) 30, 31, 34, 36,
    41, 43, 45, 123, 126, 134
Roissy, aéroport de 170, 178
Sacré-Coeur, church of 96

Saint-Germain-des-Prés 8, 30, 31, 40–5, 179
Saint-Sulpice, church of 102, 107, 124
Seine 78–83, 89, 91, 105, 155, 170
streets 88, 90, 113, 166, 171
Tuileries, Jardin des 71, 72
Paris:
  and autobiography 118–31
  and ethnicity 2, 150–61
  and ethnology 175–9
  and film 6, 71–84
  and Francophone writing 150–61
  and gay experience 133–49
  and gender 2, 3, 6, 115–33, 134–49
  and technology 162–74
  and travel writing 8–29
  as field 3, 95
  as mental space 85–114
  as mirage 160
  as myth 6
  as place of exile 71, 151, 155, 157
  as poetic field 85–114
  as village 176
  guidebooks to 8–29, 147
  in Surrealist writing 90–93
Peyrefitte, Roger 139
Philippe, Charles-Louis 38
Physiologies 3, 17, *18*, 98
Piaf, Edith 48
Picabia, Francis 50
Picasso, Pablo 34, 41, 62, 64
Planta, Edward 14–15, 17–21, 22, 25, 26
Prendergast, Christopher 4, 98
Prévert, Jacques 44
Proust, Marcel 7, 27, 101

Queneau, Raymond 5, 44, 85

Réda, Jacques, 5, 29, 85, 102–13
  Châteaux des courants d'air 102–9
  and arcades 108–9
  and the *flâneur* 102–5
  and Parisian monuments 107–9
Renoir, Jean 6, 76, 81–3
  Boudu sauvé des eaux 81–3
Reverdy, Pierre 35
Rifkin, Adrian 4, 124
Roussel, Raymond 49

Sade, Marquis de 147
Said, Edward 154–6
Saint-Hilaire, Geoffroy 168
Sala, Charles Augustus *18*, 24
Salmon, André 34
Sartre, Jean-Paul 44, 45, 124
Schiaparelli, Elsa 127, 128, 130
Seberg, Jean 163
Senghor, Léopold Sedar 154–7
Situationists 113
Socé, Ousmane 160
Soja, Edward 4
Squier, Susan Merill 116, 131
Stein, Gertrude 131
Sue, Eugène 20
Surrealists 88–100, 111, 113

Téchiné, André 6, 144
  J'embrasse, pas 144
  Les Roseaux sauvages 144
Terdiman, Richard 71
Toulouse-Lautrec, Henride 34
Tristan, Flora 117

U Tam'si, Tchicaya 156–7

Van Dongen, Kies 34, 41, 50
Verne, Jules 22, 177
Vigo, Jean 76, 78–81, 83
  L'Atalante 78–81
Villon, François 88, 166
Virilio, Paul 4, 7, 164–78
  Vitesse et politique 168–70
Vlady, Marina 1
Vlaminck, Maurice 35

Welles, Orson 134
Wharton, Edith 131
Wilson, Edmund 27
Wilson, Elizabeth 115–17, 124, 127, 129
Wiser, William 40

Yale French Studies 160

Zola, Emile 10–11, 12, 22, 166
  L'Assommoir 10–11